Recommended

TOP 500

SHOPS, RESTAURANTS, ARTS & NIGHTLIFE

MANCHESTER

The Ultimate Travel Guide
to Manchester

MANCHESTER GUIDE BOOK 2022
Shops, Restaurants, Arts, Entertainment and Nightlife

© Rebecca R. Queen
© E.G.P. Editorial

ISBN-13: 9798503881349

INDEX

MANCHESTER GUIDE BOOK

Shops, Restaurants, Arts, Entertainment and Nightlife

This directory is dedicated to Manchester Business Owners and Managers
who provide the experience that the locals and tourists enjoy.
Thanks you very much for all that you do and thank for being the "People Choice".

Thanks to everyone that posts their reviews online and
the amazing reviews sites that make our life easier.

The places listed in this book are the most positively reviewed
and recommended by locals and travelers from around the world.

Thank you for your time and enjoy the directory that is
designed with locals and tourist in mind!

TOP 500 SHOPS

The Most Recommended by Locals & Trevelers
(From #1 to #500)

#1
Manchester Craft
Category: Arts & Crafts
Average price: Modest
Area: Northern Quarter
Address: 17 Oak St
Manchester M4 5JD, UK
Phone: 0161 832 4274

#2
Afflecks
Category: Antiques, Vintage, Jewelry
Average price: Modest
Area: Northern Quarter
Address: 52 Church Street
Manchester M4 1PW, UK
Phone: 0161 839 0718

#3
Selfridges & Co
Category: Department Store
Average price: Expensive
Area: City Centre
Address: 1 Exchange Square Central
Manchester M3 1BD, UK
Phone: +44 870 837 7377

#4
Fred Aldous Art, Craft and Hobby Suppliers
Category: Art Supplies, Fabric Store, Cards & Stationery
Average price: Modest
Area: Northern Quarter
Address: 37 Lever Street
Manchester M1 1LW, UK
Phone: 0161 236 4224

#5
Retro Rehab
Category: Used, Vintage, Women's Clothing
Average price: Modest
Area: Northern Quarter
Address: 91 Oldham Street
Manchester M4 1LW, UK
Phone: 0161 839 2050

#6
Museum of Science & Industry
Category: Museum, Art Gallery
Average price: Inexpensive
Area: Castlefield
Address: Liverpool Road
Manchester M3 4FP, UK
Phone: 0161 832 2244

#7
Manchester Arndale
Category: Shopping Center
Average price: Modest
Area: City Centre
Address: Market Street
Manchester M4 3AQ, UK
Phone: 0161 833 9851

#8
Piccadilly Records
Category: Music & DVDs, Vinyl Records
Average price: Modest
Area: Northern Quarter
Address: 53 Oldham Street
Manchester M1 1JR, UK
Phone: 0161 839 8008

#9
Primark
Category: Women's Clothing, Men's Clothing, Baby Gear & Furniture
Average price: Inexpensive
Area: City Centre
Address: 106-122 Market Street
Manchester M1 1WA, UK
Phone: 0161 923 4772

#10
Magma
Category: Bookstore, Comic Books, Cards & Stationery
Average price: Modest
Area: Northern Quarter
Address: 22 Oldham Street
Manchester M1 1JN, UK
Phone: 0161 236 8778

#11
Forbidden Planet
Category: Bookstore
Average price: Modest
Area: Northern Quarter
Address: 65 Oldham Street
Manchester M1 1JR, UK
Phone: 0161 839 4777

#12
Oklahoma
Category: Coffee & Tea, Cards & Stationery, Breakfast & Brunch
Average price: Modest
Area: Northern Quarter
Address: 74-76 High Street
Manchester M4 1ES, UK
Phone: 0161 834 1136

#13
Aldi
Category: Electronics, Grocery
Average price: Inexpensive
Area: Northern Quarter
Address: 67-71 Market Street
Manchester M4 2EA, UK
Phone: +44 844 406 8800

#14
Oi Polloi
Category: Accessories, Sports Wear,
Men's Clothing
Average price: Expensive
Area: Northern Quarter
Address: 63 Thomas Street
Manchester M4 1LQ, UK
Phone: 0161 831 7870

#15
Venus Flowers
Category: Florist
Average price: Expensive
Area: Oxford Road Corridor
Address: 95 Oxford Street
Manchester M1 6ET, UK
Phone: 0161 228 7000

#16
Cow
Category: Women's Clothing,
Used, Vintage
Average price: Modest
Area: Gay Village
Address: Parker Street
Manchester M1 4BD, UK
Phone: +44 844 504 0400

#17
H.Blyth & Co
Category: Art Supplies
Average price: Modest
Area: Northern Quarter
Address: 1 Stevenson Square
Manchester M1 1DN, UK
Phone: 0161 236 1302

#18
Empire Exchange
Category: Bookstore, Antiques
Average price: Modest
Area: Northern Quarter
Address: 1 Newton St
Manchester M1 1HW, UK
Phone: 0161 236 4445

#19
Rockers England
Category: Fashion
Average price: Modest
Area: Northern Quarter
Address: 89 Oldham Street
Manchester M4 1LF, UK
Phone: 0161 839 9202

#20
Paperchase
Category: Cards & Stationery,
Art Supplies
Average price: Expensive
Area: City Centre
Address: 14 Bank House
Manchester M1 1PX, UK
Phone: 0161 835 9935

#21
Manchester Museum
Category: Museum, Art Gallery
Average price: Inexpensive
Area: Oxford Road Corridor
Address: Oxford Road
Manchester M13 9PL, UK
Phone: 0161 275 2634

#22
Forsyth Brothers
Category: Musical Instruments,
Music & DVDs
Average price: Modest
Area: City Centre
Address: 126 Deansgate
Manchester M3 2GR, UK
Phone: 0161 834 3281

#23
Agent Provocateur
Category: Lingerie
Average price: Exclusive
Area: City Centre
Address: 81 King Street
Manchester M2 4AH, UK
Phone: 0161 833 3735

#24
Debenhams
Category: Department Store
Average price: Modest
Area: Northern Quarter
Address: 123 Market Street
Manchester M60 1, UK
Phone: +44 844 561 6161

#25
Blackwell's
Category: Bookstore
Average price: Expensive
Area: Oxford Road Corridor
Address: Precinct Center
Manchester M13 9RN, UK
Phone: 0161 274 3331

#26
Abakhan
Category: Fabric Store
Average price: Modest
Area: Northern Quarter
Address: 111-115 Oldham St
Manchester M4 1LN, UK
Phone: 0161 839 3229

#27
Clarks
Category: Shoe Store
Average price: Modest
Area: City Centre
Address: 47 Market Street
Manchester M1 1WR, UK
Phone: +44 844 499 1789

#28
H&M
Category: Accessories,
Men's Clothing, Women's Clothing
Average price: Inexpensive
Area: City Centre
Address: 58-70 Market Street
Manchester M1 1PN, UK
Phone: 0161 836 2800

#29
Apple
Category: Electronics, Computers
Average price: Expensive
Area: City Centre
Address: Unit 23 New Canon Street Mall
Manchester M4 3AJ, UK
Phone: 0161 216 4570

#30
Thunder Egg
Category: Women's Clothing,
Flowers & Gifts
Average price: Expensive
Area: Piccadilly
Address: 22 Oldham Street
Manchester M1 1JN, UK
Phone: 0161 235 0606

#31
Boots
Category: Pharmacy,
Cosmetics & Beauty Supply
Average price: Modest
Area: City Centre
Address: 32 Market Street
Manchester M2 1PL, UK
Phone: 0161 832 6533

#32
Edinburgh Bicycle Co-operative
Category: Bikes
Average price: Expensive
Area: Oxford Road Corridor, Rusholme
Address: 7 Wilmslow Road
Manchester M14 5FT, UK
Phone: 0161 257 3897

#33
Junk Shop
Category: Used, Vintage
Average price: Modest
Area: West Didsbury
Address: 174 Burton Road
Manchester M20 1LH, UK
Phone: 0161 238 8517

#34
Chorlton Bookshop
Category: Bookstore
Average price: Modest
Area: Chorlton
Address: 506-508 Wilbraham Rd
Manchester M21 9AW, UK
Phone: 0161 881 6374

#35
Quality Save
Category: Discount Store
Average price: Inexpensive
Area: City Centre
Address: Piccadilly Plaza
Manchester M1 4AJ, UK
Phone: 0161 228 3031

#36
Kingbee Records
Category: Music & DVDs
Average price: Modest
Area: Chorlton
Address: 519 Wilbraham Road
Manchester M21 0UF, UK
Phone: 0161 860 4762

#37
Seen Opticians
Category: Optometrists,
Eyewear & Opticians
Area: City Centre
Address: 6 St Anns Arcade
Manchester M2 7HN, UK
Phone: 0161 835 2324

#38
Manchester Buddhist Centre
Category: Buddhist Temple,
Bookstore, Yoga
Area: Northern Quarter
Address: 16-20 Turner St
Manchester M4 1DZ, UK
Phone: 0161 834 9232

#39
Sew In
Category: Arts & Crafts
Average price: Modest
Area: Didsbury Village
Address: 741 Wilmslow Road
Manchester M20 6RN, UK
Phone: 0161 445 5861

#40
Poundland
Category: Department Store
Average price: Inexpensive
Area: City Centre
Address: Lower Floor
Manchester M1 1WR, UK
Phone: 0161 839 9870

#41
Richard Goodall Gallery
Category: Art Gallery
Average price: Expensive
Area: Northern Quarter
Address: 59 Thomas Street
Manchester M4 1NA, UK
Phone: 0161 832 3435

#42
Ken Foster's Cycle Logic
Category: Bikes
Average price: Modest
Area: Chorlton
Address: 374-376 Barlow Moor Rd
Manchester M21 8AZ, UK
Phone: 0161 881 7160

#43
Paramount Books
Category: Bookstore, Comic Books
Average price: Modest
Area: City Centre
Address: 25-27 Shudehill
Manchester M4 2AF, UK
Phone: 0161 834 9509

#44
Belly Button Design
Category: Cards & Stationery, Jewelry
Average price: Modest
Area: West Didsbury
Address: 240 Burton Road
Manchester M20 2LW, UK
Phone: 0161 434 4236

#45
Busy Bee Toy Shop
Category: Toy Store
Average price: Modest
Area: Chorlton
Address: 517 Wilbraham Road
Manchester M21 0UF, UK
Phone: 0161 881 5838

#46
Marks & Spencer
Category: Department Store
Average price: Expensive
Area: City Centre
Address: 7 Market Street
Manchester M1 1WT, UK
Phone: 0161 831 7341

#47
TK Maxx
Category: Fashion
Average price: Modest
Area: City Centre
Address: 106-122 Market Street
Manchester M1 1WA, UK
Phone: 0161 236 1885

#48
Harvey Nichols & Co
Category: Department Store
Average price: Exclusive
Area: City Centre
Address: 21 New Cathedral Street
Manchester M1 1AD, UK
Phone: 0161 828 8888

#49
Harriet & Dee
Category: Flowers & Gifts
Average price: Expensive
Area: Didsbury Village
Address: 8 Warburton Street
Manchester M20 6WA, UK
Phone: 0161 438 2500

#50
Urban Outfitters
Category: Department Store
Average price: Expensive
Area: City Centre
Address: 42-43 Market Street
Manchester M1 1WR, UK
Phone: 0161 817 6640

#51
Monkey Puzzle Toys
Category: Toy Store
Area: Chorlton
Address: 93 Manchester Rd
Manchester M21 9GA, UK
Phone: 0161 862 0100

#52
Centre for Chinese
Contemporary Art
Category: Art Gallery, Arts & Crafts
Average price: Inexpensive
Area: Northern Quarter
Address: 7 Thomas Street
Manchester M4 1EU, UK
Phone: 0161 832 7271

#53
Travelling Man
Category: Toy Store, Hobby Shop,
Comic Books
Average price: Modest
Area: Northern Quarter
Address: 4 Dale Street
Manchester M1 1JW, UK
Phone: 0161 237 1877

#54
Zara
Category: Accessories,
Men's Clothing, Women's Clothing
Average price: Modest
Area: City Centre
Address: New Cathedral St
Manchester M1 4AD, UK
Phone: 0161 831 0940

#55
Northern Flower
Category: Florist
Average price: Expensive
Area: Northern Quarter
Address: 58 Tib St
Manchester M4 1LG, UK
Phone: 0161 832 7731

#56
Schuh
Category: Shoe Store, Leather Goods
Average price: Expensive
Area: City Centre
Address: 31 Market Street
Manchester M1 1WR, UK
Phone: 0161 834 6521

#57
Levenshulme Antiques Village
Category: Antiques, Arts & Crafts
Average price: Modest
Area: Levenshulme
Address: 965 Stockport Road
Manchester M19 3NP, UK
Phone: 0161 225 7025

#58
Junk
Category: Women's Clothing
Average price: Expensive
Area: Northern Quarter
Address: 2 Dale Street
Manchester M1 1JW, UK
Phone: 0161 238 8517

#59
Johnny Roadhouse
Category: Musical Instruments
Average price: Modest
Area: Oxford Road Corridor
Address: 123 Oxford Rd
Manchester M1 7DU, UK
Phone: 0161 273 1000

#60
Argos
Category: Department Store
Average price: Modest
Area: City Centre
Address: R10-R19 Unit
Manchester M4 3AT, UK
Phone: +44 845 165 7661

#61
Beatin' Rhythm Records
Category: Music & DVDs
Average price: Modest
Area: Northern Quarter
Address: 42 Tib Street
Manchester M4 1LA, UK
Phone: 0161 834 7783

#62
Richard Goodall Gallery
Category: Art Gallery, Museum
Average price: Modest
Area: Northern Quarter
Address: 103 High Street
Manchester M4 1HQ, UK
Phone: 0161 834 3330

#63
CUBE
Category: Art Gallery
Area: Oxford Road Corridor
Address: 113-115 Portland Street
Manchester M1 6DW, UK
Phone: 0161 237 5525

#64
Blossom
Category: Florist
Average price: Modest
Area: Chorlton
Address: 97
Manchester Road
Manchester M21 9GA, UK
Phone: 0161 881 4567

#65
**University of Manchester
Student Union Shop**
Category: Office Equipment,
Convenience Store
Average price: Inexpensive
Area: Oxford Road Corridor
Address: Oxford Road
Manchester M13 9PR, UK
Phone: 0161 275 2936

#66
Oxfam
Category: Thrift Store
Average price: Inexpensive
Area: Oxford Road Corridor
Address: 300-302 Oxford Road
Manchester M13 9NS, UK
Phone: 0161 273 2019

#67
Sainsbury's
Category: Grocery, Fashion,
Beer, Wine & Spirits
Average price: Modest
Area: Ordsall
Address: 100 Regent Rd
Manchester M5 4QU, UK
Phone: 0161 839 2441

#68
Richer Sounds
Category: Electronics
Average price: Modest
Area: Castlefield
Address: 268 Deansgate
Manchester M3 4JB, UK
Phone: +44 33 3900 0086

#69
Sainsbury's
Category: Grocery, Fashion,
Beer, Wine & Spirits
Average price: Inexpensive
Area: Fallowfield
Address: 347 Wilmslow Road
Manchester M14 6SS, UK
Phone: 0161 224 4778

#70
Oxfam
Category: Bookstore, Thrift Store
Average price: Modest
Area: Didsbury Village
Address: 778 Wilmslow Road
Manchester M20 2DR, UK
Phone: 0161 434 5380

#71
Didsbury Village Bookshop
Category: Bookstore
Average price: Modest
Area: Didsbury Village
Address: 47 Barlow More Road
Manchester M20 6TW, UK
Phone: 0161 438 0211

#72
**Manchester French
Christmas Market**
Category: Shopping Center
Average price: Inexpensive
Area: City Centre
Address: King St
Manchester M2 4, UK
Phone: 0161 234 7356

#73
Rolex Books & Music Shop
Category: Bookstore, Shopping Center,
Personal Shopping
Average price: Inexpensive
Area: Rusholme
Address: 81-83 Wilmslow Road
Manchester M14 5SU, UK
Phone: 0161 225 4448

#74
Wowie Zowie!
Category: Furniture Store,
Music & DVDs
Average price: Modest
Area: Chorlton
Address: 107
Manchester Road
Manchester M21 9GA, UK
Phone: 0161 860 6470

#75
Size?
Category: Shoe Store
Average price: Expensive
Area: City Centre
Address: 18 Market Street
Manchester M1 1PT, UK
Phone: 0161 839 8086

#76
Attic Fancy Dress
Category: Costumes, Jewelry
Average price: Inexpensive
Area: Northern Quarter
Address: 52 Church Street
Manchester M4 1PW, UK
Phone: 0161 832 3839

#77
Islington Mill
Category: Music Venues, Art Gallery
Average price: Modest
Area: Salford University Campus
Address: James St
Manchester M3 5HW, UK
Phone: +44 7947 649896

#78
Twenty Twenty Two
Category: Bar, Art Gallery, Music Venues
Average price: Modest
Area: Northern Quarter
Address: 20 Dale Street
Manchester M1 1EZ, UK
Phone: 0161 237 9360

#79
Bodycare Health & Beauty
Category: Cosmetics & Beauty Supply
Average price: Inexpensive
Area: City Centre
Address: Arndale Center
Manchester M4 2EA, UK
Phone: 0161 839 3973

#80
Vivienne Westwood
Category: Women's Clothing
Average price: Expensive
Area: City Centre
Address: 47 Spring Garden King Street
Manchester M2 2BG, UK
Phone: 0161 835 2121

#81
Brazilian Waxing Company
Category: Cosmetics & Beauty Supply
Area: City Centre
Address: 7 Cheapside
Manchester M2 4WG, UK
Phone: +44 20 8123 4332

#82
Levi's
Category: Leather Goods,
Men's Clothing, Women's Clothing
Average price: Expensive
Area: City Centre
Address: Arndale Center
Manchester M4 3AQ, UK
Phone: 0161 833 4979

#83
L'Occitane
Category: Cosmetics & Beauty Supply
Average price: Expensive
Area: City Centre
Address: 10 King Street
Manchester M2 6AG, UK
Phone: 0161 839 3216

#84
Sports Direct
Category: Sporting Goods
Average price: Inexpensive
Area: City Centre
Address: Arndale Ctr
Manchester M4 2HU, UK
Phone: +44 870 838 7162

#85
Edwards Of Manchester
Category: Shoe Store
Average price: Expensive
Area: City Centre
Address: 61 Deansgate
Manchester M3 2BW, UK
Phone: 0161 834 1339

#86
Foot Asylum
Category: Shoe Store
Average price: Modest
Area: City Centre
Address: L1/L2 Arndale Centre
Manchester M4 2HU, UK
Phone: 0161 839 5407

#87
French Connection
Category: Accessories,
Women's Clothing
Average price: Expensive
Area: City Centre
Address: 2-4 Exchange Square
Manchester M2 7HA, UK
Phone: 0161 835 1727

#88
Oasis
Category: Women's Clothing
Average price: Expensive
Area: City Centre
Address: Upper Level
Manchester M1, UK
Phone: 0161 831 9967

#89
Original Levi Store
Category: Fashion
Area: Altrincham
Address: 156 Regent Cresent
Manchester M17 8AP, UK
Phone: 0161 746 8800

#90
Loop!
Category: Cards & Stationery
Average price: Expensive
Area: Chorlton
Address: 66 Beech Road
Manchester M21 9EG, UK
Phone: 0161 882 0801

#91
Mango
Category: Women's Clothing
Average price: Expensive
Area: City Centre
Address: 48-50 Market Street
Manchester M1 1PW, UK
Phone: 0161 835 9100

#92
Foot Locker
Category: Shoe Store
Average price: Modest
Area: Northern Quarter
Address: 49 Market Street
Manchester M1 1WR, UK
Phone: 0161 819 5990

#93
PAD
Category: Flowers & Gifts, Home Decor
Average price: Modest
Area: Chorlton
Address: 105 Manchester Road
Manchester M21 9GA, UK
Phone: 0161 881 0088

#94
Levenshulme Market
Category: Shopping Center
Average price: Inexpensive
Area: Levenshulme
Address: Stockport Road
Manchester M19 3AB, UK
Phone: +44 7853 266598

#95
Pound Empire
Category: Discount Store
Average price: Inexpensive
Area: Piccadilly
Address: 12 Piccadilly
Manchester M1 3AN, UK
Phone: 0161 923 4609

#96
Me & Yu
Category: Accessories
Average price: Modest
Area: Northern Quarter
Address: 52 Church Street
Manchester M4 1PW, UK
Phone: 0161 839 0399

#97
RIBA Bookshop
Category: Bookstore
Average price: Modest
Area: Oxford Road Corridor
Address: 113-115 Portland Street
Manchester M1 6DW, UK
Phone: 0161 236 7691

#98
Longsight Market
Category: Shopping Center
Average price: Inexpensive
Area: Longsight
Address: Dickenson Road
Manchester M13 0WG, UK
Phone: 0161 225 9859

#99
The Disney Store
Category: Toy Store
Average price: Expensive
Area: City Centre
Address: Unit 22
Manchester M4 3AJ, UK
Phone: 0161 832 2492

#100
The Cook Shop
Category: Kitchen & Bath
Average price: Modest
Address: Arndale Centre
Manchester M1 1XY, UK
Phone: +44 7814 796228

#101
Easytel UK
Category: Mobile Phones, Computers
Average price: Inexpensive
Area: Rusholme
Address: 8 Wilmslow Road
Manchester M14 5TP, UK
Phone: 0161 224 8600

#102
Clas Ohlson
Category: Hardware Store, Appliances
Average price: Modest
Area: City Centre
Address: Manchester Arndale
Manchester M4 3AQ, UK
Phone: 0161 832 7375

#103
Pop Boutique
Category: Antiques, Jewelry,
Used, Vintage
Average price: Modest
Area: Northern Quarter
Address: 34-36 Oldham Street
Manchester M1 1JN, UK
Phone: 0161 236 5797

#104
Build-A-Bear Workshop
Category: Toy Store
Average price: Expensive
Area: City Centre
Address: Unit 36, Halle Square
Manchester M4 3AQ, UK
Phone: 0161 839 4308

#105
East
Category: Women's Clothing,
Jewelry, Accessories
Average price: Expensive
Area: City Centre
Address: 18a The Triangle
Manchester M4 3TR, UK
Phone: 0161 839 5102

#106
Kiku Boutique
Category: Lingerie, Bridal
Average price: Modest
Area: Northern Quarter
Address: 100 Tib Street
Manchester M4 1LR, UK
Phone: 0161 819 5031

#107
Tutzy News
Category: Newspapers & Magazines
Average price: Inexpensive
Area: City Centre
Address: Piccadilly Plaza
Manchester M1 4AJ, UK
Phone: 0161 236 9763

#108
The Gap
Category: Men's Clothing, Women's
Clothing, Children's Clothing
Average price: Expensive
Area: City Centre
Address: 30 St Ann Street
Manchester M2 7LF, UK
Phone: 0161 835 4110

#109
The Works
Category: Arts & Crafts, Books,
Mags, Music & Video
Average price: Inexpensive
Area: City Centre
Address: Arndale Center
Manchester M4 3AQ, UK
Phone: 0161 835 2297

#110
Den Furniture
Category: Furniture Store
Average price: Exclusive
Area: Northern Quarter
Address: 42-44 Oldham Street
Manchester M4 1LE, UK
Phone: 0161 236 1112

#111
The Black Sheep Store
Category: Shoe Store, Sports Wear,
Outdoor Gear
Average price: Modest
Area: Northern Quarter
Address: 59 Church Street
Manchester M4 1PD, UK
Phone: 0161 839 9313

#112
Waterstones
Category: Coffee & Tea, Bookstore,
Newspapers & Magazines
Average price: Modest
Area: City Centre
Address: Arndale Center
Manchester M4 3AQ, UK
Phone: 0161 832 8563

#113
Timberland
Category: Shoe Store, Men's Clothing
Average price: Exclusive
Area: City Centre
Address: 40-42 King Street
Manchester M2 6BA, UK
Phone: 0161 834 6643

#114
Swatch
Category: Watches
Average price: Modest
Area: City Centre
Address: Market Street
Manchester M2 1NP, UK
Phone: 0161 832 0755

#115
Elm Interiors
Category: Home & Garden,
Cards & Stationery
Average price: Expensive
Area: Didsbury Village
Address: 766 Wilmslow Road
Manchester M20 2DR, UK
Phone: 0161 448 8551

#116
Steranko Fashion Shop
Category: Fashion
Average price: Modest
Area: West Didsbury
Address: 172 Burton Road
Manchester M20 1LH, UK
Phone: 0161 448 0108

#117
Castlefield Artisan Market
Category: Farmers Market,
Used, Vintage
Average price: Modest
Area: Castlefield
Address: Duke Street
Manchester M3 4NF, UK
Phone: +44 7826 465673

#118
W H Lung Cash & Carry
Category: Wholesale Store,
Specialty Food, Chinese
Average price: Modest
Area: Oxford Road Corridor
Address: 97 Upper Brook Street
Manchester M13 9TX, UK
Phone: 0161 274 3177

#119
Vintage Vogue
Category: Jewelry, Used, Vintage
Average price: Expensive
Area: Chorlton
Address: 390 Barlow Moor Road
Manchester M21 8BH, UK
Phone: 0161 881 7150

#120
Diesel
Category: Men's Clothing,
Women's Clothing, Swimwear
Average price: Expensive
Area: City Centre
Address: 74 King Street
Manchester M2 4NJ, UK
Phone: 0161 839 8868

#121
Joy
Category: Fashion, Flowers & Gifts
Average price: Exclusive
Area: City Centre
Address: 37 Hanging Ditch
Manchester M4 3TR, UK
Phone: 0161 832 9823

#122
Schuh
Category: Shoe Store
Average price: Modest
Area: Rusholme
Address: 138 Regent Cresent
Manchester M17 8AA, UK
Phone: 0161 202 9044

#123
The Perfume Shop
Category: Cosmetics & Beauty Supply
Average price: Modest
Area: City Centre
Address: 9a Arndale Ctr
Manchester M4 2EA, UK
Phone: 0161 819 1700

#124
Esprit
Category: Fashion
Average price: Modest
Area: City Centre
Address: 33 Market Street
Manchester M1 1WR, UK
Phone: 0161 214 5170

#125
**New Cross Army
SurplusMilitary Kit**
Category: Sporting Goods,
Men's Clothing, Women's Clothing
Average price: Modest
Area: Northern Quarter
Address: 25-27 Tib Street
Manchester M4 1LX, UK
Phone: 0161 832 9683

#126
Lipsy
Category: Women's Clothing
Average price: Modest
Area: City Centre
Address: Arndale Ctr
Manchester M4 3AB, UK
Phone: 0161 837 7021

#127
The Co-operative Food
Category: Grocery, Tobacco Shop, Beer,
Wine & Spirits
Average price: Expensive
Area: Chorlton
Address: 599-601 Wilbraham Road
Manchester M21 9AN, UK
Phone: 0161 881 8211

#128
Wanderland Boutique
Category: Women's Clothing
Average price: Expensive
Area: Salford University Campus
Address: 52 Church Street
Manchester M4 1, UK
Phone: 0161 236 2379

#129
Sally Hair & Beauty Supplies
Category: Cosmetics & Beauty Supply
Area: City Centre
Address: 16 The Mall Arndale Centre
Manchester M4 3AD, UK
Phone: 0161 865 2252

#130
Ran
Category: Shoe Store, Men's Clothing
Average price: Modest
Area: City Centre
Address: 8 St Anns Arcade
Manchester M2 7HW, UK
Phone: 0161 832 9650

#131
The Bead Shop
Category: Jewelry, Arts & Crafts
Average price: Inexpensive
Area: Northern Quarter
Address: 52 Church Street
Manchester M4 1PW, UK
Phone: 0161 833 9950

#132
Elysia
Category: Men's Clothing,
Women's Clothing
Area: Salford University Campus
Address: 52 Church Street
Manchester M4 1, UK
Phone: 0161 839 7820

#133
Cotswold Outdoor
Category: Outdoor Gear,
Men's Clothing, Accessories
Area: Oxford Road Corridor
Address: 6a Oxford Road
Manchester M1 5QA, UK
Phone: 0161 236 4123

#134
Ryman Stationery
Category: Office Equipment
Average price: Modest
Area: City Centre
Address: 85 Halle Mall
Manchester M4 2HU, UK
Phone: 0161 834 6566

#135
Aldo
Category: Shoe Store
Average price: Expensive
Area: City Centre
Address: Arndale Ctr
Manchester M4 3AQ, UK
Phone: 0161 832 3754

#136
Pottery Corner
Category: Arts & Crafts
Average price: Modest
Area: Chorlton
Address: 34 Beech Road
Manchester M21 9EL, UK
Phone: 0161 882 0010

#137
Castle Gallery
Category: Art Gallery
Average price: Exclusive
Area: City Centre
Address: 75 Deansgate
Manchester M2 7, UK
Phone: 0161 839 3800

#138
Fossil
Category: Watches
Average price: Expensive
Area: City Centre
Address: Arndale Centre
Manchester M4 3AQ, UK
Phone: 0161 838 9010

#139
Mashed
Category: Men's Clothing, Outdoor Gear
Area: Northern Quarter
Address: 52 Church Street
Manchester M4 1PW, UK
Phone: 0161 839 4692

#140
Sweatshop
Category: Sporting Goods
Average price: Expensive
Area: City Centre
Address: Manchester Arndale Center
Manchester M4 3AQ, UK
Phone: +44 845 217 7587

#141
Ark
Category: Accessories, Men's Clothing,
Women's Clothing
Average price: Modest
Area: City Centre
Address: Unit L36
Manchester M4 3AQ, UK
Phone: 0161 832 2774

#142
House of Fraser
Category: Department Store,
Men's Clothing, Women's Clothing
Average price: Expensive
Area: City Centre
Address: 92-96 Deansgate
Manchester M3 2QG, UK
Phone: 0161 832 3414

#143
Alankar
Category: Women's Clothing, Bridal
Average price: Expensive
Area: Rusholme
Address: 46 - 48 Wilmslow Road
Manchester M14 5TQ, UK
Phone: 0161 256 3780

#144
All In One Garden Centre
Category: Nurseries & Gardening
Average price: Exclusive
Area: Oldham
Address: Rochdale Road
Manchester M24 2RB, UK
Phone: +44 1706 711711

#145
Monsoon
Category: Fashion
Average price: Modest
Area: Altrincham
Address: 72a Regent CR
Manchester M17 8AR, UK
Phone: 0161 747 8954

#146
Next
Category: Women's Clothing,
Men's Clothing, Furniture Store
Average price: Expensive
Area: City Centre
Address: 100 Corporation Street
Manchester M4 3AJ, UK
Phone: +44 844 844 5523

#147
All Saints
Category: Men's Clothing,
Women's Clothing
Average price: Expensive
Area: City Centre
Address: 45 Market Street
Manchester M1 1WR, UK
Phone: 0161 817 4820

#148
Gamestation
Category: Books, Mags, Music & Video
Average price: Inexpensive
Area: City Centre
Address: 180a Arndale Centre
Manchester M4 2HU, UK
Phone: 0161 833 1982

#149
WH Smith
Category: Bookstore, Cards & Stationery,
Newspapers & Magazines
Average price: Modest
Area: Piccadilly
Address: Piccadilly Station
Manchester M1 2PB, UK
Phone: 0161 236 5919

#150
Jilanis Newsagents
Category: Newspapers & Magazines
Average price: Inexpensive
Area: Rusholme
Address: 173 Wilmslow Road
Manchester M14 5AP, UK
Phone: 0161 256 4490

#151
Novus Contemporary Art
Category: Art Gallery
Average price: Modest
Area: West Didsbury
Address: Burton Road
Manchester M20 2LW, UK
Phone: 0161 438 3888

#152
Dr Hermans
Category: Tobacco Shop
Average price: Modest
Area: Northern Quarter
Address: 57 Church Street
Manchester M4 1PD, UK
Phone: 0161 834 1130

#153
The Deli on Burton Road
Category: Department Store, Sandwiches
Average price: Expensive
Area: West Didsbury
Address: BUrton Road
Manchester M20 1LH, UK
Phone: 0161 445 2912

#154
Staples
Category: Electronics, Office Equipment
Area: City Centre
Address: 118-124 Deansgate
Manchester M3 2GB, UK
Phone: 0161 827 3490

#155
Burton
Category: Men's Clothing,
Leather Goods, Accessories
Average price: Modest
Area: City Centre
Address: 99-101 Arndale Center
Manchester M4 3AB, UK
Phone: 0161 839 3201

#156
Grosvenor Supermarket
Category: Grocery, Tobacco Shop
Average price: Inexpensive
Area: Oxford Road Corridor
Address: 133a Grosvenor Street
Manchester M1 7HE, UK
Phone: 0161 273 8050

#157
Evans
Category: Women's Clothing
Average price: Modest
Area: City Centre
Address: 99-101 Arndale Centre
Manchester M4 3AB, UK
Phone: +44 845 121 4516

#158
Muse
Category: Jewelry
Average price: Inexpensive
Area: City Centre
Address: Lower Level
Manchester M1, UK
Phone: 0161 833 4183

#159
Lookey Newsagents
Category: Newspapers & Magazines
Average price: Modest
Area: Gay Village
Address: 76 Sackville Street
Manchester M1 3NJ, UK
Phone: 0161 273 4655

#160
Hugo Boss
Category: Men's Clothing
Average price: Exclusive
Area: City Centre
Address: 16-18 King Street
Manchester M2 6AG, UK
Phone: 0161 831 9548

#161
Dunnes
Category: Home & Garden, Fashion
Area: Ordsall
Address: Regent Retail Park
Manchester M5 4DE, UK
Phone: 0161 831 7444

#162
Millets
Category: Outdoor Gear, Sports Wear
Average price: Modest
Area: City Centre
Address: 49 Arndale Ctr
Manchester M4 2HU, UK
Phone: 0161 832 7547

#163
Carhartt
Category: Women's Clothing,
Men's Clothing
Average price: Modest
Area: Northern Quarter
Address: 59-61 Oldham Street
Manchester M1 1JR, UK
Phone: 0161 831 9488

#164
B & Q
Category: Hardware Store
Average price: Modest
Area: East Didsbury
Address: Kingsway
Manchester M19 1BB, UK
Phone: 0161 257 2839

#165
Mothercare
Category: Children's Clothing,
Baby Gear & Furniture, Toy Store
Average price: Modest
Area: Ancoats, Petersfield
Address: Great Ancoats Street
Manchester M4 6DL, UK
Phone: 0161 274 3818

#166
World Of Islam
Category: Bookstore
Area: Rusholme
Address: 211 Wilmslow Road
Manchester M14 5AG, UK
Phone: 0161 256 3232

#167
Long Tall Sally
Category: Fashion
Average price: Modest
Area: City Centre
Address: 16 South King Street
Manchester M2 6DW, UK
Phone: 0161 839 0425

#168
Pop-up
Category: Fashion
Area: Salford University Campus
Address: 52 Church Street
Manchester M4 1, UK
Phone: 0161 839 0718

#169
Hmv Manchester
Category: Books, Mags, Music & Video
Average price: Modest
Area: Northern Quarter
Address: 90 - 100 Market Street
Manchester M1 1PD, UK
Phone: 0161 834 8550

#170
Manchester Book Market
Category: Bookstore
Area: City Centre
Address: St Ann's Square
Manchester M2 7, UK
Phone: 0161 234735

#171
NOTE Skateboard Shop
Category: Sporting Goods
Average price: Modest
Area: Northern Quarter
Address: 34 Tib Street
Manchester M4 1LA, UK
Phone: 0161 839 7077

#172
Incognito Gallery
Category: Art Gallery
Average price: Modest
Area: Northern Quarter
Address: 5 Stevenson Square
Manchester M1 1DN, UK
Phone: 0161 228 7999

#173
Nokia Retail
Category: Mobile Phones
Average price: Inexpensive
Area: City Centre
Address: 35 Market St
Manchester M1 1WR, UK
Phone: 0161 834 7107

#174
Ali's DIY
Category: Hardware Store
Average price: Inexpensive
Area: Longsight
Address: 167 Dickenson Road
Manchester M13 0YN, UK
Phone: 0161 256 4500

#175
Nevisport
Category: Outdoor Gear
Average price: Expensive
Area: Spinningfields
Address: 188 - 192 Deansgate
Manchester M3 3ND, UK
Phone: 0161 839 9880

#176
Knock - Ireland
Category: Bookstore,
Religious Organization
Average price: Modest
Area: City Centre
Address: 101 Deansgate
Manchester M60 8, UK
Phone: 0161 819 2558

#177
Pen Shop
Category: Jewelry, Office Equipment
Average price: Expensive
Area: City Centre
Address: 54 King Street
Manchester M2 4LY, UK
Phone: 0161 839 3966

#178
Bang & Olufsen
Category: Electronics, Music & DVDs
Average price: Exclusive
Area: City Centre
Address: Unit 4 55 King Street
Manchester M2 4LQ, UK
Phone: 0161 832 6159

#179
Whistles
Category: Women's Clothing
Average price: Expensive
Area: City Centre
Address: 55 King Street
Manchester M2 4LQ, UK
Phone: 0161 839 5399

#180
Aston's Of Manchester
Category: Tobacco Shop
Average price: Modest
Area: City Centre
Address: 12 Royal Exchange Arcade
Manchester M2 7EA, UK
Phone: 0161 832 7895

#181
Adidas
Category: Sports Wear, Men's Clothing
Average price: Expensive
Area: City Centre
Address: 52-56 Market Street
Manchester M1 1PW, UK
Phone: 0161 832 6745

#182
Ridelow
Category: Bikes, Fashion
Area: Northern Quarter
Address: 27-29 Church Street
Manchester M4 1PE, UK
Phone: 0161 834 5788

#183
Milner & Webb
Category: Antiques
Area: Northern Quarter
Address: 52 Church Street
Manchester M4 1PW, UK
Phone: 0161 839 0718

#184
Lomography Store
Category: Photographers,
Photography Store& Services
Average price: Expensive
Area: Northern Quarter
Address: 20 Oldham Street
Manchester M1 1JN, UK
Phone: 0161 228 2360

#185
Vox Pop Music
Category: Music & DVDs
Average price: Modest
Area: Northern Quarter
Address: 53-55 Thomas Street
Manchester M4 1NA, UK
Phone: 0161 832 3233

#186
Aspecto
Category: Women's Clothing,
Men's Clothing, Shoe Store
Average price: Expensive
Area: City Centre
Address: The Triangle Exchange Square
Manchester M4 3TR, UK
Phone: 0161 839 1196

#187
Russell & Bromley
Category: Shoe Store
Average price: Expensive
Address: St Anns Place
Manchester M2 7LP, UK
Phone: 0161 834 3131

#188
Grin
Category: Flowers & Gifts
Average price: Inexpensive
Area: Northern Quarter
Address: 52 Church Street
Manchester M4 1PW, UK
Phone: 0161 839 6392

#189
The Gallery Café
Category: Coffee & Tea, Art Gallery
Average price: Modest
Area: Chinatown
Address: Mosley Street
Manchester M2 3JL, UK
Phone: 0161 235 8888

#190
GNC
Category: Sporting Goods
Area: City Centre
Address: 174 Arndale Centre
Manchester M4 2HU, UK
Phone: 0161 819 2201

#191
Dune Footwear
Category: Shoe Store
Average price: Expensive
Area: City Centre
Address: Arndale House
Manchester M4 3AQ, UK
Phone: 0161 832 4021

#192
Waterside Arts Centre
Category: Art Gallery, Performing Arts
Average price: Modest
Area: Sale
Address: 1 Waterside Plaza
Manchester M33 7ZF, UK
Phone: 0161 912 5616

#193
British Red Cross
Category: Thrift Store
Average price: Inexpensive
Area: Chorlton
Address: 21 Chorlton Place
Manchester M21 9AQ, UK
Phone: 0161 881 5249

#194
Didsbury Eyecare
Category: Eyewear & Opticians
Area: Didsbury Village
Address: 717 Wilmslow Rd
Manchester M20 6WF, UK
Phone: 0161 445 7668

#195
Modern Army Store
Category: Outdoor Gear, Active Life
Average price: Inexpensive
Area: Chorlton
Address: 488 Wilbraham Rd
Manchester M21 9AS, UK
Phone: 0161 881 6858

#196
Manchester Superstore
Category: Wholesale Store,
Grocery, Meat Shop
Area: Longsight
Address: 536-538 Stockport Road
Manchester M12 4JJ, UK
Phone: 0161 224 3441

#197
Lloyds News
Category: Convenience Store,
Tobacco Shop
Average price: Inexpensive
Area: Didsbury Village
Address: 232 Wilmslow Rd
Manchester M20 2, UK
Phone: 0161 224 2174

#198
Miss Selfridge
Category: Women's Clothing, Accessories
Average price: Expensive
Area: City Centre
Address: 74 Market St
Manchester M1 1PN, UK
Phone: 0161 834 3924

#199
Boots
Category: Pharmacy,
Cosmetics & Beauty Supply
Average price: Expensive
Area: Northern Quarter
Address: 11-13 Piccadilly
Manchester M1 1LY, UK
Phone: 0161 834 8244

#200
**Wesley Community
Furniture Project**
Category: Furniture Store
Average price: Inexpensive
Area: Rusholme
Address: 56-58 Lloyd St S
Manchester M14 7HT, UK
Phone: 0161 226 9051

#201
Euronews
Category: Tobacco Shop, Convenience
Store, Newspapers & Magazines
Average price: Inexpensive
Area: City Centre
Address: Piccadilly Garden
Manchester M2 3BA, UK
Phone: 0161 236 0319

#202
Lush
Category: Cosmetics & Beauty Supply
Average price: Modest
Area: Ancoats, Petersfield
Address: Arndale Ctr
Manchester M4 3QA, UK
Phone: 0161 832 3294

#203
Moda In Pelle
Category: Shoe Store, Leather Goods
Average price: Modest
Area: City Centre
Address: 4 Market St
Manchester M1 1PT, UK
Phone: 0161 839 5072

#204
Cafe Society Clothing
Category: Fashion
Average price: Modest
Area: Northern Quarter
Address: 35-39 Oldham Street
Manchester M1 1JG, UK
Phone: 0161 839 1195

#205
Inman's
Category: Newspapers & Magazines
Average price: Modest
Area: Didsbury Village
Address: 105-107 Lapwing Lane
Manchester M20 6UR, UK
Phone: 0161 446 2464

#206
Currys
Category: Electronics, Appliances
Average price: Modest
Area: Ancoats, Petersfield
Address: Great Ancoats Street
Manchester M4 6DL, UK
Phone: +44 870 609 7494

#207
Bismi Jewellers
Category: Jewelry
Average price: Exclusive
Area: Rusholme
Address: 99 Wilmslow Road
Manchester M14 5SU, UK
Phone: 0161 256 3599

#208
Clone Zone
Category: Fashion, Adult
Average price: Expensive
Area: Gay Village
Address: 36-38 Sackville St
Manchester M1 3WA, UK
Phone: 0161 236 1398

#209
Blacks
Category: Outdoor Gear, Sports Wear
Average price: Expensive
Area: Spinningfields
Address: 200 Deansgate
Manchester M3 3NN, UK
Phone: 0161 833 0349

#210
Lakeland
Category: Leather Goods,
Men's Clothing, Women's Clothing
Average price: Modest
Area: City Centre
Address: 14 St Ann's Square
Manchester M2 7HQ, UK
Phone: 0161 831 7103

#211
Blue Inc
Category: Men's Clothing
Average price: Inexpensive
Area: City Centre
Address: 31 Market Street
Manchester M1 1WR, UK
Phone: 0161 832 3866

#212
Panic Posters
Category: Hobby Shop, Home & Garden
Area: Salford University Campus
Address: 52 Church Street
Manchester M4 1, UK
Phone: 0161 833 0667

#213
Topman
Category: Men's Clothing, Shoe Store
Average price: Modest
Area: City Centre
Address: 19 Market St
Manchester M1 1WR, UK
Phone: 0161 839 6940

#214
Cyberdog Fashion Shop
Category: Fashion
Average price: Inexpensive
Area: Northern Quarter
Address: Afflecks Arcade
Manchester M1 1JG, UK
Phone: 0161 833 2177

#215
Metro Convenience Store
Category: Tobacco Shop, Wine & Spirits
Average price: Inexpensive
Area: Oxford Road Corridor
Address: 131 Oxford Rd
Manchester M1 7DY, UK
Phone: 0161 273 8777

#216
MenKind
Category: Gifts & Gadgets
Average price: Modest
Area: City Centre
Address: The Arndale
Manchester M4 3AQ, UK
Phone: +44 1384 7796

#217
Superdrug
Category: Cosmetics & Beauty Supply
Average price: Modest
Area: City Centre
Address: Arndale Ctr
Manchester M4 3AQ, UK
Phone: 0161 839 0581

#218
Finlays
Category: Newspapers & Magazines,
Tobacco Shop
Area: Oxford Road Corridor
Address: 26 Precinct Centre
Manchester M13 9RN, UK
Phone: 0161 273 6133

#219
Nood
Category: Women's Clothing
Average price: Modest
Area: Chorlton
Address: 36 Beech Road
Manchester M21 9EL, UK
Phone: 0161 860 0461

#220
T La Art and Gallery Shop
Category: Arts & Crafts, Gift Shop
Average price: Inexpensive
Area: Chinatown
Address: 16 Nicholas St
Manchester M1 4, UK
Phone: 0161 236 2333

#221
Monsoon
Category: Fashion
Average price: Expensive
Area: City Centre
Address: King St
Manchester M2 6AW, UK
Phone: 0161 834 3236

#222
Jake Shoes
Category: Shoe Store
Average price: Modest
Area: City Centre
Address: Arndale Centre
Manchester M4 3AQ, UK
Phone: 0161 833 9799

#223
Model Zone
Category: Hobby Shop, Toy Store
Average price: Modest
Area: Spinningfields
Address: 209 Deansgate
Manchester M3 3NW, UK
Phone: 0161 834 3972

#224
North Face Ellis Brigham
Category: Climbing, Outdoor Gear
Average price: Expensive
Area: Spinningfields
Address: 211 Deansgate
Manchester M3 3NW, UK
Phone: 0161 834 7278

#225
Cotswold
Category: Outdoor Gear, Sports Wear
Average price: Modest
Area: City Centre
Address: Unit 2 118 - 124 Deansgate
Manchester M3 2GQ, UK
Phone: 0161 839 9255

#226
Nike
Category: Sports Wear
Average price: Expensive
Area: City Centre
Address: 39 Market Street
Manchester M1 1WR, UK
Phone: 0161 819 2333

#227
Ernest Jones
Category: Jewelry
Average price: Expensive
Area: City Centre
Address: 97 Arndale Centre
Manchester M4 3AB, UK
Phone: 0161 839 7040

#228
Goldsmiths Jewellers
Category: Jewelry, Flowers & Gifts
Average price: Exclusive
Area: City Centre
Address: 87 Arndale Centre
Manchester M4 2HU, UK
Phone: 0161 839 1584

#229
The Carphone Warehouse
Category: Mobile Phones
Average price: Modest
Area: City Centre
Address: 181 Arndale Centre
Manchester M4 2HU, UK
Phone: +44 870 168 2532

#230
Nicholas
Category: Tobacco Shop,
Beer, Wine & Spirits
Area: Spinningfields
Address: 8 Barton Arcade
Manchester M3 2BW, UK
Phone: 0161 834 7328

#231
Generation Pop
Category: Art Gallery
Area: City Centre
Address: E3 New York Street
Manchester M1 4BD, UK
Phone: 0161 848 0880

#232
Bank Fashion
Category: Women's Clothing,
Men's Clothing
Average price: Modest
Area: City Centre
Address: Unit L38
Manchester M4 3AQ, UK
Phone: 0161 831 7500

#233
Clampdown Records
Category: Music & DVDs
Average price: Modest
Area: Northern Quarter
Address: 9-11 Paton St
Manchester M1 2BA, UK
Phone: 0161 237 5932

#234
Manchester Framing Co
Category: Framing
Average price: Modest
Area: Northern Quarter
Address: 68 Tib Street
Manchester M4 1LG, UK
Phone: 0161 835 2600

#235
Soundbase Megastore
Category: Electronics, Vinyl Records
Average price: Modest
Area: Northern Quarter
Address: 64 Oldham Street
Manchester M4 1LE, UK
Phone: 0161 238 8727

#236
Renegade Marmalade
Category: Women's Clothing,
Men's Clothing
Average price: Expensive
Area: City Centre
Address: 7 St James Square
Manchester M2 6XX, UK
Phone: 0161 834 5733

#237
G T Blagg
Category: Hardware Store
Area: West Didsbury
Address: 146 Burton Rd
Manchester M20 1LH, UK
Phone: 0161 445 4113

#238
Longboon Pharmacy
Category: Pharmacy
Average price: Modest
Area: Rusholme
Address: 181 Wilmslow Road
Manchester M14 5AP, UK
Phone: 0161 224 5510

#239
Oxfam
Category: Thrift Store
Area: Chorlton
Address: 494 Wilbraham Road
Manchester M21 9AS, UK
Phone: 0161 861 0108

#240
Mcqueen Fashion Shop
Category: Fashion
Average price: Expensive
Area: Chorlton
Address: 54 Beech Road
Manchester M21 9EG, UK
Phone: 0161 881 4718

#241
Hurricane Gift Shop
Category: Flowers & Gifts
Average price: Modest
Area: Chorlton
Address: 115 Beech Road
Manchester M21 9EQ, UK
Phone: 0161 881 8813

#242
Red 5
Category: Flowers & Gifts,
Hobby Shop, Toy Store
Area: City Centre
Address: 48 Barbirolli Mall
Manchester M4 3AQ, UK
Phone: 0161 835 1300

#243
Frog Furniture
Category: Furniture Store
Average price: Modest
Area: West Didsbury
Address: 168 Burton Road
Manchester M20 1LH, UK
Phone: 0161 448 9566

#244
The Bike Room
Category: Bikes
Area: Castlefield
Address: 274 Deansgate
Manchester M3 4JB, UK
Phone: 0161 870 8195

#245
Espionage Manchester
Category: Performing Arts, Florist
Area: Spinningfields
Address: Quay Street
Manchester M3, UK
Phone: +44 7502 000072

#246
Elite Dress Agency
Category: Accessories,
Women's Clothing, Used, Vintage
Area: City Centre
Address: 35 King St W
Manchester M3 2PW, UK
Phone: 0161 832 3670

#247
Planet Shop The
Category: Women's Clothing
Average price: Modest
Area: City Centre
Address: 34-36 King Street
Manchester M2 6AZ, UK
Phone: 0161 839 6225

#248
Charles Tyrwhitt
Category: Men's Clothing
Average price: Modest
Area: City Centre
Address: 30 King St
Manchester M2 6AZ, UK
Phone: 0161 833 0504

#249
Vivienne Westwood Anglomania
Category: Women's Clothing, Accessories
Average price: Expensive
Area: City Centre
Address: 47 Spring Garden
Manchester M3 3BN, UK
Phone: 0161 835 2228

#250
Calvin Klein
Category: Fashion
Average price: Expensive
Area: City Centre
Address: 37 Hanging Ditch
Manchester M4 4BG, UK
Phone: 0161 839 7910

#251
Manchester Spring Market
Category: Local Flavor, Shopping
Area: City Centre
Address: St Ann's Square
Manchester M2 7DH, UK
Phone: 0161 234 7356

#252
Stephens Photo Centre
Category: Photography Store& Services
Average price: Expensive
Area: City Centre
Address: Unit 19a Barton Arcade
Manchester M3 2BJ, UK
Phone: 0161 834 7754

#253
Porcelanosa
Category: Kitchen & Bath
Area: Castlefield
Address: Water Street
Manchester M3 4JU, UK
Phone: 0161 817 3300

#254
Alfred E Mutter
Category: Jewelry
Area: Northern Quarter
Address: 33 Thomas Street
Manchester M4 1NA, UK
Phone: 0161 832 7147

#255
Tiny's Tipple
Category: Home Decor
Average price: Expensive
Area: Northern Quarter
Address: 12 Hilton Street
Manchester M1 1JF, UK
Phone: 0161 236 1412

#256
The Mustard Tree
Category: Thrift Store
Average price: Inexpensive
Area: Ancoats, Petersfield
Address: 110 Oldham Rd
Manchester M4 5AG, UK
Phone: 0161 228 7331

#257
Fat Face
Category: Fashion
Average price: Expensive
Area: City Centre
Address: 8-10 Exchange St
Manchester M2 7HA, UK
Phone: 0161 833 1544

#258
The Carphone Warehouse
Category: Mobile Phones
Area: City Centre
Address: 26 Market Street
Manchester M1 1PW, UK
Phone: +44 870 168 2393

#259
Topshop
Category: Fashion
Average price: Expensive
Area: City Centre
Address: 74 Market Street
Manchester M1 1, UK
Phone: 0161 834 3924

#260
G-Star Raw Store
Category: Men's Clothing,
Women's Clothing
Average price: Expensive
Area: City Centre
Address: Unit U1 Arndale Centre
Manchester M4 3QA, UK
Phone: 0161 839 2299

#261
The Brass Teacher
Category: Musical Instruments
Average price: Inexpensive
Area: Levenshulme
Address: 77 Osborne Road
Manchester M19 2DZ, UK
Phone: +44 7930 517864

#262
Conrad Office & Art
Category: Art Supplies
Average price: Modest
Area: Chorlton
Address: 567 Wilbraham Rd
Manchester M21 0AE, UK
Phone: 0161 881 4076

#263
**Michele Jones Wedding
Photography**
Category: Wedding Planning,
Photography Store& Services
Area: Didsbury Village
Address: 11 The Beeches Mews
Manchester M20 2PF, UK
Phone: 0161 448 1080

#264
The Flower Lounge
Category: Florist
Average price: Modest
Area: West Didsbury
Address: 98 Barlow Moor Road
Manchester M20 2PN, UK
Phone: 0161 446 2556

#265
Build A Bear Workshop
Category: Toy Store
Average price: Modest
Area: Rusholme
Address: 26 Regent Crescent
Manchester M14 7, UK
Phone: 0161 749 4791

#266
Giddy Goat Toys
Category: Toy Store
Area: Didsbury Village
Address: 2 Albert Hill Street
Manchester M20 6RF, UK
Phone: 0161 445 1097

#267
Living Flowers
Category: Florist
Average price: Exclusive
Area: West Didsbury
Address: 232 Burton Rd
Manchester M20 2LW, UK
Phone: +44 7970 448675

#268
BHS
Category: Department Store
Average price: Inexpensive
Area: City Centre
Address: 57 Market St
Manchester M1 1WN, UK
Phone: 0161 834 1151

#269
Cornerhouse Bookshop
Category: Bookstore
Average price: Modest
Area: Oxford Road Corridor
Address: 70 Oxford Street
Manchester M1 5NH, UK
Phone: 0161 200 1500

#270
Maliks
Category: Tobacco Shop,
Convenience Store
Average price: Inexpensive
Area: Oxford Road Corridor
Address: 66 Hathersage Road
Manchester M13 0FN, UK
Phone: 0161 224 2005

#271
Phillip Stoner the Jeweller
Category: Jewelry
Average price: Exclusive
Area: Oldham
Address: Unit G20 The Avenue
Manchester M3 3HF, UK
Phone: 0161 833 1751

#272
Star News Office Licence
Category: Newspapers & Magazines
Average price: Inexpensive
Area: Rusholme
Address: 165 Wilmslow Road
Manchester M14 5AP, UK
Phone: 0161 249 0188

#273
Hidden Corner
Category: Women's Clothing,
Costumes, Adult
Average price: Modest
Area: City Centre
Address: Arndale Centre
Manchester M4 3AQ, UK
Phone: 0161 839 2118

#274
Accessorize
Category: Accessories,
Women's Clothing
Average price: Modest
Area: Piccadilly
Address: Unit 10 Piccadilly Station
Manchester M1 2BN, UK
Phone: 0161 236 0199

#275
Jack & Jones, Vero Moda
Category: Fashion
Area: City Centre
Address: 93 Halle Mall
Manchester M4 3AQ, UK
Phone: 0161 828 3000

#276
Superdrug
Category: Pharmacy, Cosmetics
Average price: Modest
Area: Northern Quarter
Address: 7-9 Piccadilly
Manchester M1 1LZ, UK
Phone: 0161 834 6091

#277
Oxfam Originals
Category: Used, Vintage
Average price: Modest
Area: Northern Quarter
Address: 51 Oldham Street
Manchester M1 1JR, UK
Phone: 0161 839 3160

#278
Diamond Telecom
Category: Computers, Mobile Phones
Area: Rusholme
Address: 53 Wilmslow Road
Manchester M14 5TB, UK
Phone: 0161 257 2450

#279
Superstar Extra
Category: Videos & Video Game Rental,
Beer, Wine & Spirits
Average price: Modest
Area: Rusholme
Address: 57-59 Wilmslow Road
Manchester M14 5TB, UK
Phone: 0161 225 9729

#280
Aftabs Convenience Store
Category: Tobacco Shop, Grocery,
Convenience Store
Area: Oxford Road Corridor
Address: 1 Bonsall St
Manchester M15 6DR, UK
Phone: 0161 868 0614

#281
Marks & Spencer
Category: Department Store
Area: Ancoats, Petersfield
Address: Great Ancoats Street
Manchester M4 6DE, UK
Phone: 0161 236 7672

#282
Slaters
Category: Men's Clothing
Area: City Centre
Address: 1 Brown Street
Manchester M2 1DA, UK
Phone: 0161 819 6680

#283
Abacus
Category: Jewelry
Area: Salford University Campus
Address: 52 Church St
Manchester M4 1, UK
Phone: 0161 832 9300

#284
Specsavers
Category: Eyewear & Opticians
Area: City Centre
Address: 84 Arndale Ctr
Manchester M4 2HU, UK
Phone: 0161 834 6665

#285
Church Street Market
Category: Grocery, Fashion
Average price: Modest
Area: Northern Quarter
Address: Church St
Manchester M4 1, UK
Phone: 0161 832 3552

#286
Kraak
Category: Art Gallery, Music Venues
Average price: Modest
Area: Northern Quarter
Address: 11 Stevenson Square
Manchester M1 1DB, UK
Phone: +44 7855 939129

#287
Berwick Electronics
Category: Appliances
Average price: Modest
Area: Northern Quarter
Address: 53 Tib Street
Manchester M4 1LS, UK
Phone: 0161 834 4416

#288
Boardmans Teleflora
Category: Florist
Area: Oxford Road Corridor
Address: 296 Oxford Road
Manchester M13 9NS, UK
Phone: 0161 273 4582

#289
Argos
Category: Department Store
Average price: Modest
Area: Rusholme
Address: Arndale Centre
Manchester M32 9BA, UK
Phone: +44 845 165 7215

#290
Up & Running
Category: Sporting Goods, Shoe Store
Address: 32 Hanging Ditch
Manchester M4 3TR, UK
Phone: 0161 832 8338

#291
Beaverbrooks
Category: Jewelry, Flowers & Gifts
Average price: Modest
Area: City Centre
Address: 86 Arndale Centre
Manchester M4 2HU, UK
Phone: 0161 834 4904

#292
Adidas
Category: Sports Wear, Shoe Store
Average price: Expensive
Area: City Centre
Address: Unit 24 Arndale Ctr
Manchester M4 3AJ, UK
Phone: 0161 833 0902

#293
Orange
Category: Mobile Phones
Average price: Expensive
Area: City Centre
Address: Arndale Ctr
Manchester M4 3AQ, UK
Phone: +44 870 376 3385

#294
The Hilton Aqua Emporium
Category: Appliances, Pet Store
Average price: Modest
Area: Northern Quarter
Address: 5a Hilton Street
Manchester M4 1LP, UK
Phone: 0161 839 5757

#295
Fanboy 3
Category: Hobby Shop
Average price: Modest
Area: Northern Quarter
Address: 17 Newton Street
Manchester M1 1FZ, UK
Phone: 0161 247 7735

#296
Topshop
Category: Shoe Store, Accessories
Average price: Expensive
Area: City Centre
Address: Arndale Ctr
Manchester M4 3AQ, UK
Phone: 0161 615 8660

#297
Pastiche
Category: Women's Clothing
Average price: Expensive
Area: Oxford Road Corridor
Address: 34 Halle Square
Manchester M4 2HU, UK
Phone: 0161 834 3146

#298
GameXchange
Category: Computers
Area: Rusholme
Address: Arndale Ctr
Manchester M32 9BB, UK
Phone: 0161 864 3444

#299
General Store
Category: Women's Clothing,
Accessories, Men's Clothing
Average price: Expensive
Area: City Centre
Address: 7 Barton Arcade
Manchester M3 2BW, UK
Phone: 0161 839 3864

#300
3 Store
Category: Mobile Phones
Average price: Expensive
Area: City Centre
Address: 27 Market St
Manchester M2 7, UK
Phone: 0161 832 8489

#301
Sole Trader
Category: Shoe Store
Average price: Modest
Area: City Centre
Address: Unit 21
Manchester M4 3AQ, UK
Phone: 0161 839 2442

#302
Miss Selfridge
Category: Women's Clothing
Average price: Modest
Area: City Centre
Address: Market Street
Manchester M1 1PN, UK
Phone: 0161 834 3924

#303
New Look
Category: Fashion
Average price: Inexpensive
Area: City Centre
Address: Arndale Ctr
Manchester M4 2HU, UK
Phone: 0161 214 0880

#304
Jeffery-West
Category: Shoe Store
Area: Spinningfields
Address: 1 Barton Arcade
Manchester M3 2BB, UK
Phone: 0161 835 9284

#305
Boots
Category: Pharmacy,
Cosmetics & Beauty Supply
Average price: Modest
Area: Piccadilly
Address: Unit 5 Manchester 2BN, UK
Phone: 0161 228 2059

#306
Fopp
Category: Music & DVDs,
Vinyl Records, Bookstore
Average price: Inexpensive
Area: City Centre
Address: 19 Brown Street
Manchester M2 1DA, UK
Phone: 0161 830 7630

#307
Lahore Store
Category: Convenience Store
Average price: Inexpensive
Area: Longsight
Address: 32 Laindon Road
Manchester M14 5DP, UK
Phone: 0161 224 4208

#308
PDSA
Category: Thrift Store
Area: Chorlton
Address: 460 Wilbraham Road
Manchester M21 0AG, UK
Phone: 0161 860 4004

#309
Lloyds Pharmacy
Category: Pharmacy
Average price: Inexpensive
Area: Fallowfield
Address: 228 Wilmslow Road
Manchester M14 6LE, UK
Phone: 0161 224 7782

#310
IKEA
Category: Furniture Store
Average price: Modest
Area: Ashton Under Lyne
Address: Wellington Road
Manchester OL6 7TE, UK
Phone: +44 845 355 2186

#311
Poshu
Category: Shoe Store, Accessories
Area: City Centre
Address: 5 Police Street
Manchester M2 6, UK
Phone: 0161 819 2444

#312
Shuropody
Category: Shoe Store
Average price: Modest
Area: City Centre
Address: 49 Deansgate
Manchester M3 2, UK
Phone: 0161 834 8570

#313
Office Sale Shop
Category: Shoe Store
Area: City Centre
Address: 3 St Anne's Square
Manchester M2 7LP, UK
Phone: 0161 832 7337

#314
Molton Brown
Category: Cosmetics & Beauty Supply
Average price: Expensive
Area: City Centre
Address: 7 St Ann's Square
Manchester M2 7EF, UK
Phone: 0161 873 8018

#315
Games Workshop
Category: Hobby Shop, Toy Store
Area: City Centre
Address: Unit R35 Arndale Center
Manchester M4 3AT, UK
Phone: 0161 834 6871

#316
Invicta Studio
Category: Photographers,
Electronics, Personal Shopping
Area: Oxford Road Corridor
Address: 83 Oxford Street
Manchester M1 6EG, UK
Phone: 0161 236 4644

#317
Vom Fass
Category: Flowers & Gifts
Average price: Expensive
Area: City Centre
Address: Exchange Square
Manchester M3 1BD, UK
Phone: +44 800 123400

#318
Knickerbox
Category: Lingerie
Average price: Modest
Area: City Centre
Address: Arndale Centre
Manchester M4 2HU, UK
Phone: 0161 831 9797

#319
Coast
Category: Accessories,
Women's Clothing
Average price: Expensive
Area: City Centre
Address:
Manchester Arndale
Manchester M60 1TA, UK
Phone: 0161 832 6341

#320
Chase Music
Category: Musical Instruments
Area: Northern Quarter
Address: 58 Oldham Street
Manchester M4 1LE, UK
Phone: 0161 236 6794

#321
Extreme Largeness
Category: Jewelry, Accessories,
Women's Clothing
Area: City Centre
Address: 52 Church Street
Manchester M4 1PW, UK
Phone: 0161 839 0595

#322
Baylis & Knight
Category: Women's Clothing
Area: Northern Quarter
Address: 301 Aflex Palace
Manchester M4 1PW, UK
Phone: 0161 881 8002

#323
WH Smith
Category: Books, Mags, Music & Video
Average price: Modest
Area: City Centre
Address: Store 5
Manchester M4 2HU, UK
Phone: 0161 834 8300

#324
Lacoste
Category: Men's Clothing,
Women's Clothing
Average price: Modest
Area: Ancoats, Petersfield
Address: 4 New Cathedral Street
Manchester M4 1AD, UK
Phone: 0161 834 9559

#325
Morrison's Local
Category: Shopping, Food
Area: Oxford Road Corridor
Address: 60 Grafton Street
Manchester M13 9NU, UK
Phone: 0161 274 4095

#326
B&M Bargains
Category: Outlet Store
Area: Chorlton
Address: 595-597 Wilbraham Road
Manchester M21 9AJ, UK
Phone: 0161 881 6860

#327
Maplin Electronics
Category: Electronics, Computers
Average price: Expensive
Area: Oxford Road Corridor
Address: 8 Oxford Road
Manchester M1 5QA, UK
Phone: 0161 236 0281

#328
Ellis Brigham Mountain Equipment
Category: Outdoor Gear
Average price: Expensive
Area: Spinningfields
Address: 211 Deansgate
Manchester M3 3NW, UK
Phone: 0161 839 8468

#329
Mulberry
Category: Women's Clothing
Average price: Exclusive
Area: City Centre
Address: 62 King Street
Manchester M2 4ND, UK
Phone: 0161 839 3333

#330
Tommy Hilfiger
Category: Men's Clothing
Average price: Expensive
Area: City Centre
Address: 51 King St
Manchester M2 7AZ, UK
Phone: 0161 831 7364

#331
Phones 4U
Category: Mobile Phones
Average price: Modest
Area: City Centre
Address: 72 Market St
Manchester M1 1PN, UK
Phone: 0161 831 9103

#332
The Fragrance Shop
Category: Cosmetics & Beauty Supply
Average price: Modest
Area: City Centre
Address: 60D Cromford Ct
Manchester M4 2HU, UK
Phone: 0161 833 1723

#333
The Card Factory
Category: Cards & Stationery
Average price: Modest
Area: City Centre
Address: 58 Arndale Centre
Manchester M4 3AB, UK
Phone: 0161 834 1080

#334
United Footwear
Category: Shoe Store
Average price: Inexpensive
Area: Northern Quarter
Address: 68-70 Oldham Street
Manchester M4 1LE, UK
Phone: 0161 228 1706

#335
Walia News
Category: Newspapers & Magazines
Average price: Inexpensive
Area: Northern Quarter
Address: Church Street
Manchester M4 1PW, UK
Phone: 0161 839 6450

#336
Superdry
Category: Men's Clothing,
Women's Clothing
Average price: Expensive
Area: City Centre
Address: Arndale Centre
Manchester M4 3AQ, UK
Phone: 0161 832 2774

#337
Currys Digital
Category: Electronics, Computers,
Office Equipment
Average price: Modest
Area: City Centre
Address: 165 Halle Mall
Manchester M4 3AB, UK
Phone: +44 844 561 6263

#338
A & A Pharmacy
Category: Pharmacy
Average price: Modest
Area: Rusholme
Address: 58 Wilmslow Road
Manchester M14 5AL, UK
Phone: 0161 224 8501

#339
Crocs
Category: Shoe Store
Average price: Modest
Area: City Centre
Address: Arndale Centre
Manchester M4 3AJ, UK
Phone: 0161 832 8178

#340
Cushion Couture
Category: Home Decor
Average price: Modest
Address: Unit 94-96 Halle Mall
Manchester M4 3AB, UK
Phone: 0161 839 7934

#341
BodyActive
Category: Sporting Goods
Area: Fallowfield
Address: 74 Mosley St
Manchester M2 3LW, UK
Phone: 0161 228 0898

#342
French Connection
Category: Accessories,
Women's Clothing
Average price: Modest
Area: Altrincham
Address: 125 Regent Crescent
Manchester M17 8AR, UK
Phone: 0161 746 8396

#343
Anand Fashions
Category: Shoe Store,
Women's Clothing
Area: Fallowfield
Address: 219 Wilmslow Road
Manchester M14 5AG, UK
Phone: 0161 256 0026

#344
Medlock
Category: Convenience Store
Average price: Inexpensive
Area: Oxford Road Corridor
Address: 74 Hathersage Road
Manchester M13 0FN, UK
Phone: 0161 224 1909

#345
The International 3
Category: Art Gallery
Area: Piccadilly
Address: 8 Fairfield St
Manchester M1 2, UK
Phone: 0161 237 3336

#346
Chaal Shoes 4 You
Category: Shoe Store
Average price: Modest
Area: Rusholme
Address: 126 Wilmslow Road
Manchester M14 5AH, UK
Phone: 0161 225 4411

#347
Pound Choice Plus
Category: Hardware Store, Discount Store
Average price: Inexpensive
Area: Levenshulme
Address: Stockport Road
Manchester M19 3AW, UK
Phone: 0161 224 7666

#348
Legends
Category: Framing
Average price: Modest
Area: Rochdale
Address: 4 Royal Exchange Arcade
Manchester M1, UK
Phone: +44 7754 812290

#349
Simon Green at Rankin Styles Interiors
Category: Furniture Store
Average price: Modest
Area: Spinningfields, City Centre
Address: 64 Bridge Street
Manchester M3 3BN, UK
Phone: 0161 839 6662

#350
Nomad Travel & Outdoor
Category: Outdoor Gear
Area: Spinningfields, City Centre
Address: 66-68 Bridge St
Manchester M3 3RJ, UK
Phone: 0161 832 2134

#351
Audio T
Category: Electronics
Average price: Expensive
Area: City Centre
Address: 63 Bridge Street
Manchester M3 3BQ, UK
Phone: 0161 839 8869

#352
T M Lewin
Category: Fashion
Average price: Modest
Area: City Centre
Address: 44 King Street
Manchester M2 6BA, UK
Phone: 0161 835 1330

#353
Fred Perry
Category: Fashion
Average price: Modest
Area: City Centre
Address: 11 Police Street
Manchester M2 7LQ, UK
Phone: 0161 832 9874

#354
Jones Bootmaker
Category: Shoe Store
Average price: Modest
Area: City Centre
Address: 47 King Street
Manchester M2 7AY, UK
Phone: +44 845 602 8168

#355
Jack Wills
Category: Men's Clothing,
Women's Clothing
Area: City Centre
Address: 35 King Street
Manchester M2 7AT, UK
Phone: 0161 831 9508

#356
The Crombie Store
Category: Women's Clothing,
Men's Clothing
Average price: Modest
Area: City Centre
Address: 33 King St
Manchester M2 6AA, UK
Phone: 0161 832 8977

#357
Dkny
Category: Fashion
Average price: Expensive
Area: City Centre
Address: 76-80 King Street
Manchester M2 4NH, UK
Phone: 0161 819 1048

#358
Nicholas Jones Bespoke
Category: Women's Clothing,
Men's Clothing, Sewing & Alterations
Average price: Exclusive
Area: City Centre
Address: 10 St Anns Arcade
Manchester M2 7HW, UK
Phone: +44 845 459 0161

#359
Oilily
Category: Children's Clothing
Area: City Centre
Address: Barton Arcade
Manchester M3 2BB, UK
Phone: 0161 839 2832

#360
Wildings Photo & Video Centre
Category: Photography Store& Services
Area: City Centre
Address: 47 Deansgate
Manchester M3 2AY, UK
Phone: 0161 832 2656

#361
Hervia Bazaar
Category: Women's Clothing,
Accessories, Men's Clothing
Area: City Centre
Address: 40 Spring Garden
Manchester M2 1EN, UK
Phone: 0161 835 2777

#362
Huk
Category: Fashion
Area: Salford University Campus
Address: 52 Church Street
Manchester M4 1, UK
Phone: 0161 834 1340

#363
Dorothy Perkins
Category: Women's Clothing
Area: City Centre
Address: 99-101 Arndale Centre
Manchester M4 3AB, UK
Phone: 0161 839 0426

#364
Chisholm Hunter
Category: Jewelry
Area: City Centre
Address: 60 Arndale Center
Manchester M4 3AB, UK
Phone: 0161 833 3859

#365
Top Shop / Top Man
Category: Men's Clothing
Area: City Centre
Address: 23-31 Market Street
Manchester M1 1WR, UK
Phone: 0161 834 5793

#366
D&A
Category: Eyewear & Opticians
Average price: Expensive
Area: City Centre
Address: Unit 55 Arndale Centre
Manchester M4 2HU, UK
Phone: 0161 865 1306

#367
Flower Style Manchester
Category: Florist
Average price: Modest
Area: Spinningfields
Address: Quay Street
Manchester M3 3JZ, UK
Phone: 0161 834 4044

#368
Eduardo Pelle
Category: Accessories
Area: City Centre
Address: The Triangle
Manchester M4 3TR, UK
Phone: 0161 832 8908

#369
Manchester French Market
Category: Local Flavor
Average price: Modest
Area: City Centre
Address: St Ann's Square
Manchester M2 7DH, UK
Phone: 0161 234 7356

#370
Entertainment Trader
Category: Pawn Shop
Area: Northern Quarter
Address: 50-56 High Street
Manchester M4 1ED, UK
Phone: 0161 831 9697

#371
Ellis Brigham
Category: Sporting Goods
Average price: Exclusive
Area: Castlefield
Address: Duke Street
Manchester M3 4NF, UK
Phone: 0161 833 0746

#372
Capes Dunn & Co
Category: Antiques
Average price: Exclusive
Area: Oxford Road Corridor
Address: 38 Charles Street
Manchester M1 7DB, UK
Phone: 0161 273 1911

#373
Scarce Clothing
Category: Men's Clothing
Area: Northern Quarter
Address: 16 Oldham Street
Manchester M1 1JQ, UK
Phone: 0161 236 2659

#374
Clark Brothers
Category: Office Equipment,
Arts & Crafts
Average price: Modest
Area: Northern Quarter
Address: 34-36 Thomas Street
Manchester M4 1ER, UK
Phone: 0161 834 5880

#375
G W Lofthouse
Category: Engraver,
Trophies and Medals
Average price: Modest
Area: Northern Quarter, City Centre
Address: 44 Shudehill
Manchester M4 4AA, UK
Phone: 0161 834 4562

#376
Beauty With In
Category: Gift Shop,
Cosmetics & Beauty Supply
Area: Northern Quarter
Address: Manchester M1 1HW, UK
Phone: +44 843 289 2941

#377
Bags Of Flavor
Category: Shoe Store,
Men's Clothing, Used, Vintage
Average price: Expensive
Area: Northern Quarter
Address: 55 Oldham St
Manchester M1 1JR, UK
Phone: 0161 834 6166

#378
Nell
Category: Women's Clothing
Area: Northern Quarter
Address: 17 Oak Street
Manchester M4 5JD, UK
Phone: +44 7855 752088

#379
T Shirt Xpress
Category: Fashion
Area: Northern Quarter
Address: 93 Oldham Street
Manchester M4 1LW, UK
Phone: 0161 839 5668

#380
Big In Amsterdam
Category: Music & DVDs, Adult
Area: Northern Quarter
Address: 78 Tib Street
Manchester M4 1LG, UK
Phone: 0161 833 4135

#381
Flannels Clearance
Category: Accessories,
Men's Clothing, Women's Clothing
Area: Spinningfields
Address: The Avenue
Manchester M3 3FL, UK
Phone: 0161 837 6292

#382
Urban Suite
Category: Furniture Store
Average price: Expensive
Area: Northern Quarter
Address: 2 New George Street
Manchester M4 4AE, UK
Phone: 0161 831 9966

#383
Nua
Category: Adult
Average price: Modest
Area: Northern Quarter
Address: 49 Tib Street
Manchester M4 1LS, UK
Phone: 0161 839 5580

#384
Strawberri Peach
Category: Fashion
Average price: Modest
Area: Northern Quarter
Address: 52 Church Street
Manchester M4 1PW, UK
Phone: 0161 839 1110

#385
Cherry Cherry Clothing
Category: Women's Clothing
Area: Northern Quarter
Address: 52 Church Street
Manchester M4 1PW, UK
Phone: 0161 839 0718

#386
Purl City Yarns
Category: Knitting Supplies
Area: Northern Quarter
Address: 62 Port Street
Manchester M1 2EQ, UK
Phone: 0161 425 3864

#387
The Black Sheep Store
Category: Sporting Goods,
Men's Clothing
Area: Ancoats, Petersfield
Address: 28 Mason Street
Manchester M4 5EY, UK
Phone: 0161 834 7974

#388
Celebrate!
Category: Cards & Stationery
Area: City Centre
Address: Manchester Arndale
Manchester M4 3AQ, UK
Phone: 0161 833 9851

#389
RcMods
Category: Hobby Shop
Area: City Centre
Address: The Triangle
Manchester M4 3TR, UK
Phone: 0161 839 6090

#390
Vanisha's Design Boutique
Category: Women's Clothing, Accessories
Area: City Centre
Address: 52 Church Street
Manchester M4 1, UK
Phone: +44 7864 094466

#391
Bicycle Boutique
Category: Bike Rental, Bikes
Area: Oxford Road Corridor
Address: Hillcourt St
Manchester M1 7HU, UK
Phone: 0161 273 7801

#392
The Carphone Warehouse
Category: Mobile Phones, Electronics
Area: Oxford Road Corridor
Address: 99 Oxford Road
Manchester M1 7EL, UK
Phone: +44 870 168 2851

#393
Reiss Menswear
Category: Men's Clothing,
Women's Clothing
Average price: Expensive
Area: Rusholme
Address: 159 Regent Crescent
Manchester M17 8AR, UK
Phone: 0161 746 8700

#394
Scope
Category: Thrift Store
Area: Levenshulme
Address: 386 Dickenson Road
Manchester M13 0WQ, UK
Phone: 0161 224 2062

#395
British Red Cross
Category: Thrift Store
Area: Chorlton
Address: 611 Wilbraham Road
Manchester M21 9AN, UK
Phone: 0161 860 6965

#396
Franny & Filer
Category: Jewelry
Area: Chorlton
Address: 70 Beech Road
Manchester M21 9EG, UK
Phone: 0161 881 4912

#397
C & W Etchells
Category: Newspapers & Magazines
Area: Chorlton
Address: 44 Beech Road
Manchester M21 9EL, UK
Phone: 0161 881 1764

#398
Creative Recycling
Category: Art Gallery
Area: Chorlton
Address: 40 Beech Road
Manchester M21 9EL, UK
Phone: 0161 881 4422

#399
Kiss My Feet
Category: Shoe Store
Area: Chorlton
Address: 93 Beech Road
Manchester M21 9EQ, UK
Phone: 0161 860 4800

#400
Joypad Video Games
Category: Computers,
Videos & Video Game Rental
Area: Chorlton
Address: 444 Barlow Moor Road
Manchester M21 0BQ, UK
Phone: 0161 861 0909

#401
Manchester Car Audio
Category: Automotive, Electronics
Average price: Expensive
Area: Levenshulme
Address: 850 Stockport Road
Manchester M19 3AH, UK
Phone: 0161 225 2222

#402
Everest DIY Store
Category: Hardware Store
Average price: Inexpensive
Area: Levenshulme
Address: 854-856 Stockport Road
Manchester M19 3AH, UK
Phone: 0161 249 0999

#403
Carpeteria
Category: Home Decor
Area: Levenshulme
Address: 787 Stockport Road
Manchester M19 3DL, UK
Phone: 0161 224 1628

#404
Ladybarn News
Category: Newspapers & Magazines
Area: Ladybarn
Address: 106 Mauldeth Road
Manchester M14 6SQ, UK
Phone: 0161 445 4039

#405
St. Ann's Hospice
Category: Thrift Store
Area: Ladybarn
Address: 124 Mauldeth Rd W
Manchester M14 6, UK
Phone: 0161 448 9977

#406
St. Ann's Hospice
Category: Furniture Store
Area: Ladybarn
Address: 128 Mauldeth Road
Manchester M14 6SQ, UK
Phone: 0161 445 7990

#407
Sue Ryder Care
Category: Thrift Store
Area: Ladybarn
Address: 103 Mauldeth Road
Manchester M14 6SR, UK
Phone: 0161 248 0522

#408
Stella's Wedding Dresses
Category: Bridal, Flowers & Gifts
Area: West Didsbury
Address: 116 Burton Road
Manchester M20 1LP, UK
Phone: 0161 445 4646

#409
Frames
Category: Framing
Area: West Didsbury
Address: 33 Lawping Ln
Manchester M20 2NT, UK
Phone: 0161 445 2354

#410
The White Closet
Category: Women's Clothing
Area: West Didsbury
Address: 204 Burton Rd
Manchester M20 2LW, UK
Phone: 0161 445 5678

#411
Sterling Pharmacy
Category: Pharmacy
Area: Didsbury Village
Address: 103 Lapwing Lane
Manchester M20 6UR, UK
Phone: 0161 445 3753

#412
Wendy J Levy Contemporary Art
Category: Art Gallery
Area: Didsbury Village
Address: 17 Warburton Street
Manchester M20 6WA, UK
Phone: 0161 446 4880

#413
Dunelm
Category: Furniture Store
Area: Bolton
Address: Green Street
Manchester M26 3ED, UK
Phone: 0161 724 1004

#414
Radley & Co
Category: Accessories, Leather Goods
Average price: Exclusive
Area: City Centre
Address: 8 New Cathedral St
Manchester M1 1AD, UK
Phone: 0161 834 0531

#415
River Island
Category: Fashion, Jewelry
Average price: Modest
Area: City Centre
Address: 92 Arndale Ctr
Manchester M4 3AB, UK
Phone: 0161 834 2268

#416
Swagger Menswear
Category: Men's Clothing
Average price: Expensive
Area: Northern Quarter
Address: 93 Piccadilly
Manchester M1 2DA, UK
Phone: 0161 236 0388

#417
JD Sports
Category: Sporting Goods,
Shoe Store, Men's Clothing
Average price: Expensive
Area: City Centre
Address: 16-18 Barbirolli Mall
Manchester M4 3AB, UK
Phone: 0161 819 5221

#418
H Samuel
Category: Jewelry
Area: City Centre
Address: 7-7A Upper Level
Manchester M4 2EA, UK
Phone: 0161 835 1317

#419
Delia's Florist
Category: Florist
Average price: Modest
Area: Chorlton
Address: 289 Barlow Moor Road
Manchester M21 7GH, UK
Phone: 0161 445 1279

#420
Boots
Category: Pharmacy,
Cosmetics & Beauty Supply
Average price: Modest
Address: 39-43 King St
Manchester M2 7AT, UK
Phone: 0161 834 8315

#421
THREE Mobile
Category: Mobile Phones
Area: City Centre
Address: 24 St Ann's Square
Manchester M2 7JB, UK
Phone: 0161 839 1744

#422
Twilight Salons
Category: Hair Salons,
Cosmetics & Beauty Supply
Average price: Modest
Area: Northern Quarter
Address: 5 Kelvin Street
Manchester M4 1ET, UK
Phone: 0161 833 0249

#423
No Angel
Category: Women's Clothing
Area: Northern Quarter
Address: 20 Oldham St
Manchester M1 1JN, UK
Phone: 0161 236 8982

#424
Aleef
Category: Newspapers & Magazines,
Convenience Store
Average price: Inexpensive
Area: Northern Quarter
Address: 1a High Street
Manchester M4 1QB, UK
Phone: 0161 832 9739

#425
JD Sports
Category: Sporting Goods
Average price: Modest
Area: Piccadilly
Address: Great Ancoats Street
Manchester M4 6DJ, UK
Phone: 0161 273 5637

#426
Ryman Stationery
Category: Office Equipment
Area: Oxford Road Corridor
Address: Oxford Road
Manchester M13 9RN, UK
Phone: 0161 272 7060

#427
Get Connected
Category: Mobile Phones
Area: Oxford Road Corridor
Address: 342 Oxford Road
Manchester M13 9NG, UK
Phone: 0161 273 5000

#428
Bond
Category: Women's Clothing
Average price: Modest
Area: West Didsbury
Address: 130 Burton Rd
Manchester M20 1JQ, UK
Phone: 0161 434 5434

#429
The Picture House
Category: Framing
Area: Didsbury Village
Address: 47 Barlow Moor Road
Manchester M20 6TW, UK
Phone: +44 7738 068030

#430
Jenny Jones
Category: Jewelry
Average price: Modest
Area: Rochdale
Address: 9 Royal Exchange Arcade
Manchester M2 7EA, UK
Phone: 0161 839 0102

#431
**Erica and Edwards
Diamond Specialist**
Category: Jewelry
Average price: Expensive
Area: Rochdale
Address: Royal Exchange Arcade
Manchester M2 7EA, UK
Phone: 0161 831 9937

#432
Photo Studio
Category: Photography Store& Services
Average price: Inexpensive
Area: Rusholme
Address: 69 Wilmslow Road
Manchester M14 5TB, UK
Phone: 0161 257 0010

#433
Fancy Jewellers
Category: Jewelry
Average price: Expensive
Area: Rusholme
Address: 85 Wilmslow Road
Manchester M14 5SU, UK
Phone: 0161 224 0589

#434
Bravissimo
Category: Lingerie
Average price: Expensive
Area: City Centre
Address: Exchange Square
Manchester M3 1BD, UK
Phone: 0161 839 7050

#435
H&M
Category: Fashion, Jewelry
Average price: Modest
Area: City Centre
Address: 90 Halle Mall
Manchester M4 2HU, UK
Phone: 0161 214 1130

#436
Waterstones
Category: Bookstore, Coffee & Tea
Average price: Modest
Area: City Centre
Address: 91 Deansgate
Manchester M3 2BW, UK
Phone: 0161 837 3000

#437
All Saints
Category: Department Store
Average price: Exclusive
Area: City Centre
Address: Exchange Square
Manchester M3 1BD, UK
Phone: 0161 838 0566

#438
Berketex Brides
Category: Bridal, Flowers & Gifts
Average price: Modest
Area: City Centre
Address: Marsden Way Arndale Centre
Manchester M4 3AQ, UK
Phone: 0161 839 6781

#439
Cameolord
Category: Pharmacy
Average price: Modest
Area: Chinatown
Address: 7 Oxford Street
Manchester M1 4PB, UK
Phone: 0161 236 1445

#440
Toys 'R' Us
Category: Toy Store, Electronics, Furniture
Average price: Expensive
Area: Piccadilly
Address: Great Ancoats Street
Manchester M4 6DJ, UK
Phone: 0161 272 6515

#441
Office
Category: Shoe Store, Leather Goods
Average price: Modest
Area: City Centre
Address: 3 St Ann's Place
Manchester M2 7LP, UK
Phone: 0161 834 3804

#442
Wave Contemporary Jewellery
Category: Jewelry, Watches
Average price: Modest
Area: City Centre
Address: 16-18 Royal Exchange
Manchester M2 7EA, UK
Phone: 0161 832 9868

#443
Deichman Shoes UK
Category: Shoe Store
Average price: Modest
Area: City Centre
Address: 37 Arndale Centre
Manchester M4 2HU, UK
Phone: 0161 834 5752

#444
UGG Australia
Category: Shoe Store
Average price: Expensive
Area: City Centre
Address: 3 New Cathedral Street
Manchester M1 1AD, UK
Phone: 0161 839 7956

#445
WH Smith
Category: Bookstore
Average price: Modest
Area: City Centre
Address: 2 Victoria Station Approach
Manchester M3 1NY, UK
Phone: 0161 834 5591

#446
Aleef Newsagents
Category: Newspapers & Magazines
Average price: Modest
Area: City Centre
Address: Unit K9 Arndale Centre
Manchester M4 3AT, UK
Phone: 0161 834 7400

#447
No Angel
Category: Women's Clothing
Average price: Modest
Area: Northern Quarter
Address: 52 Church St
Manchester M4 1PW, UK
Phone: 0161 834 7379

#448
Gold Centre
Category: Jewelry, Flowers & Gifts
Average price: Inexpensive
Area: City Centre
Address: Arndale Centre
Manchester M4 3AD, UK
Phone: 0161 835 3933

#449
Dr & Herbs
Category: Pharmacy
Area: Gay Village
Address: Arndale Centre
Manchester M1, UK
Phone: 0161 831 7688

#450
O2
Category: Mobile Phones
Average price: Modest
Area: City Centre
Address: Upper Level
Manchester M1, UK
Phone: 0161 834 3681

#451
The Vestry
Category: Women's Clothing
Average price: Modest
Area: Longsight
Address: Manchester Arndale Centre
Manchester M1, UK
Phone: 0161 819 2492

#452
Chorlton Family Photography
Category: Photographers,
Photography Store& Services
Area: Chorlton
Address: Chorlton
Manchester M21 9NW, UK
Phone: +44 7735 479490

#453
Tesco
Category: Department Store
Area: Levenshulme
Address: 998-990 Stockport Road
Manchester M19 3NN, UK
Phone: +44 845 671 9386

#454
Aleef Newsagents
Category: Newspapers & Magazines
Average price: Inexpensive
Area: Spinningfields, City Centre
Address: 76 Bridge Street
Manchester M3 2RJ, UK
Phone: 0161 236 5049

#455
Advanced Photo
Category: Photography Store& Services
Average price: Modest
Area: City Centre
Address: 25 John Dalton Street
Manchester M2 6FW, UK
Phone: 0161 839 8838

#456
Wrapped In Leather
Category: Leather Goods
Average price: Expensive
Area: City Centre
Address: 43 King St W
Manchester M3 2PW, UK
Phone: 0161 834 9629

#457
Boodles
Category: Jewelry
Average price: Exclusive
Area: City Centre
Address: 1 King Street
Manchester M2 6AW, UK
Phone: 0161 833 9000

#458
Oasis
Category: Women's Clothing
Area: City Centre
Address: 50 King Street
Manchester M2 4LY, UK
Phone: 0161 839 4735

#459
Christopher James
Category: Jewelry
Area: City Centre
Address: 7 - 9 St Ann Street
Manchester M2 7LG, UK
Phone: 0161 819 1213

#460
3 Store
Category: Mobile Phones
Area: City Centre
Address: 24 St Ann's Square
Manchester M2 7JB, UK
Phone: 0161 839 1744

#461
High & Mighty
Category: Men's Clothing,
Personal Shopping
Area: City Centre
Address: 55 King Street
Manchester M1 1PX, UK
Phone: 0161 834 7367

#462
Crumpler
Category: Luggage, Accessories
Area: City Centre
Address: 18 Cross Street
Manchester M2 7AE, UK
Phone: 0161 832 9997

#463
Jacobs
Category: Photography Store& Services
Average price: Expensive
Area: City Centre
Address: 16 Cross Street
Manchester M2 7AE, UK
Phone: 0161 834 7500

#464
The Whisky Shop
Category: Whisky Specialist
Average price: Exclusive
Area: City Centre
Address: 3 Exchange Street
Manchester M2 7EE, UK
Phone: 0161 832 6110

#465
Aleef
Category: Newspapers & Magazines,
Convenience Store
Area: Oxford Road Corridor
Address: 91-93 Oxford Street
Manchester M1 6ET, UK
Phone: 0161 228 7420

#466
O2
Category: Mobile Phones
Area: City Centre
Address: Unit 168
Manchester M4 2HU, UK
Phone: 0161 834 3681

#467
Tokyo Royale
Category: Fashion
Area: Salford University Campus
Address: 52 Church Street
Manchester M4 1, UK
Phone: 0161 834 3661

#468
Wilkinson
Category: Department Store
Average price: Inexpensive
Area: City Centre
Address: 65-66 The Mall
Manchester M24 4EL, UK
Phone: 0161 655 3814

#469
Withy Grove Store
Category: Office Equipment
Area: City Centre
Address: 35-39 Withy Grove
Manchester M4 2BJ, UK
Phone: 0161 834 0044

#470
Ted Baker
Category: Accessories,
Men's Clothing, Women's Clothing
Average price: Modest
Area: City Centre
Address: 6 New Cathedral Street
Manchester M1 1AD, UK
Phone: 0161 834 8332

#471
Louis Vuitton
Category: Luggage, Italian,
Leather Goods
Average price: Modest
Address: Exchange Sq
Manchester M3 1BD, UK
Phone: 0161 828 0400

#472
Shudehill Book Centre
Category: Bookstore, Adult
Average price: Modest
Area: Northern Quarter
Address: 34 Shudehill
Manchester M4 1EZ, UK
Phone: 0161 839 0376

#473
Central Radio
Category: Electronics
Average price: Expensive
Area: Northern Quarter
Address: 30-32 Shudehill
Manchester M4 1EZ, UK
Phone: 0161 834 6700

#474
Vision Express
Category: Eyewear & Opticians
Average price: Modest
Area: City Centre
Address: 52 Arndale Centre
Manchester M4 2HU, UK
Phone: 0161 832 8855

#475
Marhaba Newsagents
Category: Newspapers & Magazines,
Convenience Store
Average price: Inexpensive
Area: Northern Quarter
Address: 47 Piccadilly
Manchester M1 2AP, UK
Phone: 0161 236 7526

#476
Fanboy Three
Category: Computers, Toy Store
Average price: Modest
Area: Northern Quarter
Address: 17 Newton Street
Manchester M1 1FZ, UK
Phone: 0161 247 7735

#477
A.L.M Traders
Category: Newspapers & Magazines
Average price: Inexpensive
Area: Northern Quarter
Address: 62 Oldham Street
Manchester M4 1LE, UK
Phone: 0161 236 9590

#478
Scarce Clothing
Category: Men's Clothing
Area: Northern Quarter
Address: 4 Afflecks Arcade
Manchester M1 1JG, UK
Phone: 0161 819 1114

#479
Rohan
Category: Outdoor Gear
Area: City Centre
Address: 8-10 Acresfield
Manchester M2 7HA, UK
Phone: 0161 832 6272

#480
Sports Direct
Category: Sporting Goods
Area: Salford University Campus
Address: Old Field Rd
Manchester M5 4BT, UK
Phone: +44 870 333 9544

#481
Dojo Ecoshop
Category: Home Decor
Average price: Modest
Area: Ancoats, Petersfield
Address: 38 Mason St
Manchester M4 5EZ, UK
Phone: 0161 834 5432

#482
Cards Galore
Category: Cards & Stationery
Average price: Modest
Area: Piccadilly
Address: Unit 12
Manchester M1 2BN, UK
Phone: 0161 236 0337

#483
Rowfers
Category: Fashion
Average price: Modest
Area: Northern Quarter
Address: 52 Church St
Manchester M4 1PW, UK
Phone: 0161 833 4640

#484
Faith Pharmacy
Category: Pharmacy
Area: Oxford Road Corridor
Address: 59 Booth St West
Manchester M15 6PQ, UK
Phone: 0161 232 8044

#485
Kurt Geiger
Category: Shoe Store
Area: Ancoats, Petersfield
Address: Kendals
Manchester M60 3AU, UK
Phone: +44 844 800 3744

#486
Superdrug
Category: Cosmetics & Beauty
Supply, Pharmacy
Area: Oxford Road Corridor
Address: Oxford Road
Manchester M13 9RN, UK
Phone: 0161 249 3816

#487
Unicorn Home Furnishings
Category: Furniture Store
Average price: Modest
Area: Longsight
Address: 525 Stockport Road
Manchester M12 4JH, UK
Phone: 0161 248 9595

#488
Uptown Girl
Category: Fashion
Area: Longsight
Address: 555 Stockport Road
Manchester M12 4JH, UK
Phone: 0161 256 2400

#489
Boots
Category: Pharmacy,
Cosmetics & Beauty Supply
Area: Chorlton
Address: 20-22 Chorlton Place
Manchester M21 9AQ, UK
Phone: 0161 881 1121

#490
Max Spielmann
Category: Photography Store& Services
Area: Chorlton
Address: 436 Barlow Moor Road
Manchester M21 0AB, UK
Phone: +44 870 750 5626

#491
Joseph Gleave & Son
Category: Hardware Store
Area: Chorlton
Address: 995 Chester Road
Manchester M32 0NB, UK
Phone: 0161 865 6025

#492
Lighthouse Charity Shop
Category: Thrift Store
Area: Chorlton
Address: 364 Barlow Moor Rd
Manchester M21 8AZ, UK
Phone: 0161 786 1440

#493
Jean Genie
Category: Children's Clothing,
Men's Clothing, Women's Clothing
Average price: Modest
Area: Chorlton
Address: 97 Beech Rd
Manchester M21 9, UK
Phone: 0161 860 4976

#494
Sound Studio
Category: Automotive, Electronics
Average price: Expensive
Area: Levenshulme
Address: 848 Stockport Road
Manchester M19 3AW, UK
Phone: 0161 256 1939

#495
Photo Express
Category: Photography Store& Services,
Video/Film Production
Area: Levenshulme
Address: 900 Stockport Road
Manchester M19 3AD, UK
Phone: 0161 257 0500

#496
B Kemp
Category: Newspapers & Magazines
Area: West Didsbury
Address: 542 Wilmslow Road
Manchester M20 4BY, UK
Phone: 0161 445 4346

#497
Sifters Records
Category: Music & DVDs
Average price: Modest
Area: East Didsbury
Address: 177 Fog Ln
Manchester M20 6FJ, UK
Phone: 0161 445 8697

#498
Andrew Graham Shoes
Category: Shoe Store
Average price: Modest
Area: Didsbury Village
Address: 673 Wilmslow Rd
Manchester M20 6RA, UK
Phone: 0161 445 8243

#499
Cancer Research UK
Category: Thrift Store
Area: Didsbury Village
Address: 800 Wilmslow Road
Manchester M20 6UH, UK
Phone: 0161 445 1182

#500
Fonda
Category: Women's Clothing,
Men's Clothing
Average price: Expensive
Area: Didsbury Village
Address: 677 Wilmslow Road
Manchester M20 6RA, UK
Phone: 0161 446 1177

#1
Barbakan Delicatessen
Cuisines: Bakery, Desserts, Deli
Average price: £11-25
Area: Chorlton
Address: 67-71 Manchester Road
Manchester M21 9PW
Phone: 0161 881 7053

#2
The Marble Arch
Cuisines: Pub, Gastropub
Average price: £11-25
Area: Ancoats, Petersfield
Address: 73 Rochdale Road
Manchester M4 4HY
Phone: 0161 832 5914

#3
Cornerhouse
Cuisines: Cinema, Bar, Cafe
Average price: £11-25
Area: Oxford Road Corridor
Address: 70 Oxford Street
Manchester M1 5NH
Phone: 0161 200 1500

#4
Mughli
Cuisines: Indian, Pakistani
Average price: £11-25
Area: Rusholme
Address: 30 Wilmslow Road
Manchester M14 5TQ
Phone: 0161 248 0900

#5
Gaucho Grill
Cuisines: Argentine
Average price: £26-45
Address: 2a St Marys Street
Manchester M3 2LB
Phone: 0161 833 4333

#6
Katsouris Deli
Cuisines: Deli, Sandwiches
Average price: Under £10
Area: City Centre
Address: 113 Deansgate
Manchester M3 2BQ
Phone: 0161 937 0010

#7
Home Sweet Home
Cuisines: American, Coffee & Tea,
Breakfast & Brunch
Average price: £11-25
Area: Northern Quarter
Address: 49-51 Edge Street
Manchester M4 1HE
Phone: 0161 244 9424

#8
Akbar's
Cuisines: Indian
Average price: £11-25
Area: Castlefield
Address: 73-83 Liverpool Road
Manchester M3 4NQ
Phone: 0161 834 8444

#9
Sinclair's Oyster Bar
Cuisines: Pub, British
Average price: Under £10
Area: City Centre
Address: 2 Cathedral Gates
Manchester M3 1SW
Phone: 0161 834 0430

#10
Croma
Cuisines: Pizza, Italian
Average price: £11-25
Area: City Centre
Address: 1 Clarence Street
Manchester M2 4DE
Phone: 0161 237 9799

#11
Pi
Cuisines: British, Pub
Average price: £11-25
Area: Chorlton
Address: 99 Manchester Road
Manchester M21 9GA
Phone: 0161 882 0000

#12
Try Thai
Cuisines: Thai
Average price: £11-25
Area: Chinatown
Address: 52 Faulkner Street
Manchester M1 4FH
Phone: 0161 228 1822

#13
Grill On The Alley
Cuisines: Lounge, British, Gastropub
Average price: £26-45
Address: 5 Ridgefield
Manchester M2 6EG
Phone: 0161 833 3465

#14
Yuzu
Cuisines: Japanese
Average price: £11-25
Area: Chinatown
Address: 39 Faulkner Street
Manchester M1 4EE
Phone: 0161 236 4159

#15
Teacup
Cuisines: Coffee & Tea, Tea Room, Breakfast & Brunch
Average price: £11-25
Area: Northern Quarter
Address: 53-55 Thomas Street
Manchester M4 1NA
Phone: 0161 832 3233

#16
The Deaf Institute
Cuisines: Burgers, Lounge
Average price: £11-25
Area: Oxford Road Corridor
Address: 135 Grosvenor Street
Manchester M1 7HE
Phone: 0161 276 9350

#17
Fuzion
Cuisines: Japanese, Asian Fusion, Thai
Average price: £11-25
Area: Fallowfield
Address: 264 Wilmslow Road
Manchester M14 6JR
Phone: 0161 248 6688

#18
Seoul Kimchi
Cuisines: Korean, Japanese
Average price: £11-25
Area: Oxford Road Corridor
Address: 275 Upper Brook Street
Manchester M13 0HR
Phone: 0161 273 5556

#19
Chaophraya
Cuisines: Thai, Bar
Average price: £26-45
Address: Chapel Walks Manchester
Manchester M2 1HN
Phone: 0161 832 8342

#20
Knott Bar
Cuisines: Pub, British, Burgers
Average price: £11-25
Area: Castlefield
Address: 374 Deansgate
Manchester M3 4LY
Phone: 0161 839 9229

#21
Trof
Cuisines: Bar, British
Average price: £11-25
Area: City Centre
Address: 6-8 Thomas Street
Manchester M4 1EU
Phone: 0161 833 3197

#22
SoLIta
Cuisines: Barbeque, Burgers, American
Average price: £11-25
Area: Northern Quarter
Address: 37 Turner Street
Manchester M4 1DW
Phone: 0161 839 2200

#23
The Didsbury
Cuisines: Bar, Gastropub
Average price: £11-25
Address: 852 Wilmslow Road
Manchester M20 2SG
Phone: 0161 445 5389

#24
Sam's Chop House
Cuisines: British, Pub
Average price: £11-25
Area: City Centre
Address: Blackpool Hold
Manchester M2 1HN
Phone: 0161 834 3210

#25
Greens
Cuisines: Vegetarian
Average price: £11-25
Area: West Didsbury
Address: 43 Lapwing Lane
Manchester M20 2NT
Phone: 0161 434 4259

#26
Caspian
Cuisines: Fast Food, Takeaway, Middle Eastern
Average price: Under £10
Area: Rusholme
Address: 61-63 Wilmslow Road
Manchester M14 5TB
Phone: 0161 225 1057

#27
Dough
Cuisines: Pizza, Italian
Average price: £11-25
Area: Northern Quarter
Address: 75-77 High Street
Manchester M4 1FS
Phone: 0161 834 9411

#28
Thyme Out Delicatessen
Cuisines: Deli, Breakfast & Brunch
Average price: Under £10
Area: West Didsbury
Address: 147 Nell Lane
Manchester M20 2LG
Phone: 0161 434 8686

#29
Soup Kitchen
Cuisines: Bar, Cafe, Sandwiches
Average price: £11-25
Area: Northern Quarter
Address: 31-33 Spear Street
Manchester M1 1DF
Phone: 0161 236 5100

#30
Tampopo
Cuisines: Asian Fusion,
Vietnamese, Thai
Average price: £11-25
Area: City Centre
Address: 38 Exchange Sq Unit 2
Manchester M4 3TR
Phone: 0161 839 6484

#31
Sweet Mandarin
Cuisines: Chinese, Specialty Food
Average price: £26-45
Area: Northern Quarter
Address: 19 Copperas Street
Manchester M4 1HS
Phone: 0161 832 8848

#32
Mr Thomas's Chop House
Cuisines: British, Pub
Average price: £26-45
Area: City Centre
Address: 52 Cross Street
Manchester M2 7AR
Phone: 0161 832 2245

#33
El Rincon de Rafa
Cuisines: Spanish, Basque
Average price: £11-25
Area: Castlefield
Address: 244 Deansgate
Manchester M3 4BQ
Phone: 0161 839 8819

#34
BrewDog Manchester
Cuisines: Pub, Burgers, Barbeque
Average price: £11-25
Address: 35 Peter Street
Manchester M2 5BG
Phone: 0161 832 9038

#35
Don Giovanni's
Cuisines: Italian, Bar, Pizza
Average price: £11-25
Address: 11 Oxford Street
Manchester M1 5AN
Phone: 0161 228 2482

#36
The Ox
Cuisines: Hotel, Gastropub, Bar
Average price: £26-45
Area: Castlefield
Address: Liverpool Road
Manchester M3 4NQ
Phone: 0161 839 7740

#37
Ning
Cuisines: Thai, Malaysian, Asian Fusion
Average price: £11-25
Area: Ancoats, Petersfield
Address: 92 Oldham Street
Manchester M4 1LJ
Phone: 0844 414 5484

#38
Phetpailin
Cuisines: Thai
Average price: £11-25
Area: Chinatown
Address: 46 George Street
Manchester M1 4HF
Phone: 0161 228 6500

#39
Wings
Cuisines: Chinese, Bar
Average price: £26-45
Address: 1 Lincoln Square
Manchester M2 5LN
Phone: 0161 834 9000

#40
Falafel
Cuisines: Falafel
Average price: Under £10
Area: Rusholme
Address: Wilmslow Road
Manchester M14 5TG
Phone: 0161 256 1372

#41
San Carlo Cicchetti
Cuisines: Tapas, Italian,
Breakfast & Brunch
Average price: £26-45
Area: City Centre
Address: 40-42 King Street W
Manchester M3 2QG
Phone: 0161 839 2233

#42
The Old Wellington
Cuisines: Gastropub, Pub, British
Average price: £11-25
Area: City Centre
Address: 4 Cathedral Gates
Manchester M3 1SW
Phone: 0161 839 5179

#43
Nawaab
Cuisines: Indian, Pakistani
Average price: £11-25
Area: Levenshulme
Address: 1008 Stockport Road
Manchester M19 3WN
Phone: 0161 224 6969

#44
Kro Bar
Cuisines: Pub, European
Average price: £11-25
Area: Oxford Road Corridor
Address: 325 Oxford Road
Manchester M13 9PG
Phone: 0161 274 3100

#45
Gorilla
Cuisines: Cafe, Breakfast & Brunch
Average price: £11-25
Address: 54-56 Whitworth Street West
Manchester M1 5WW
Phone: 0161 407 0301

#46
This & That
Cuisines: Indian
Average price: Under £10
Area: Northern Quarter
Address: 3 Soap Street
Manchester M4 1EW
Phone: 0161 832 4971

#47
The Northern Quarter
Cuisines: British
Average price: £11-25
Area: Northern Quarter
Address: 108 High Street
Manchester M4 1HT
Phone: 0161 832 7115

#48
Dukes 92
Cuisines: Pub, British
Average price: £11-25
Area: Castlefield
Address: 18 Castle Street
Manchester M3 4LZ
Phone: 0161 839 3522

#49
Wagamama
Cuisines: Chinese, Japanese, Soup
Average price: £11-25
Area: City Centre
Address: 1 Print Works
Manchester M4 2BS
Phone: 0161 839 5916

#50
The Rice Bowl
Cuisines: Chinese
Average price: £11-25
Area: City Centre
Address: 33a Cross Street
Manchester M2 1NL
Phone: 0161 832 9033

#51
Room
Cuisines: Bar, European
Average price: £26-45
Area: City Centre
Address: 81 King Street
Manchester M2 4AH
Phone: 0161 839 2005

#52
Herbi Vores
Cuisines: Vegetarian, Coffee & Tea
Average price: Under £10
Area: Oxford Road Corridor
Address: Burlington Street
Manchester M13 9PL
Phone: 0161 275 2408

#53
Michael Caines Restaurant
Cuisines: British, Champagne Bar
Average price: £26-45
Area: Piccadilly
Address: 107 Piccadilly
Manchester M1 2DB
Phone: 0161 200 5678

#54
Trove
Cuisines: Bakery, Breakfast & Brunch
Average price: Under £10
Area: Levenshulme
Address: 1032 Stockport Road
Manchester M19 3EX
Phone: 0161 224 8588

#55
Vermilion
Cuisines: Thai, Lounge
Average price: £26-45
Address: Hulme Hall Lane
Manchester M40 8AD
Phone: 0161 202 0055

#56
Oklahoma
Cuisines: Coffee & Tea,
Breakfast & Brunch
Average price: £11-25
Area: Northern Quarter
Address: 74-76 High Street
Manchester M4 1ES
Phone: 0161 834 1136

#57
English Lounge
Cuisines: Pub, British, Burgers
Average price: £11-25
Area: Northern Quarter
Address: 64-66 High Street
Manchester M4 1EA
Phone: 0161 832 4824

#58
Red Chilli
Cuisines: Chinese
Average price: £11-25
Area: Chinatown
Address: 70 Portland Street
Manchester M1 4GU
Phone: 0161 236 2888

#59
Kosmos Taverna
Cuisines: Greek
Average price: £11-25
Area: Fallowfield
Address: 248 Wilmslow Road
Manchester M14 6LD
Phone: 0161 225 9106

#60
Yakisoba
Cuisines: Asian Fusion, Japanese, Thai
Average price: £11-25
Area: Chorlton
Address: 360 Barlow Moor Road
Manchester M21 8AZ
Phone: 0161 862 0888

#61
The Alchemist
Cuisines: British, European, Cocktail Bar
Average price: £26-45
Area: Spinningfields
Address: 3 Hardman Street
Manchester M3 3HF
Phone: 0161 817 2950

#62
Battered Cod
Cuisines: Fish & Chips
Average price: Under £10
Area: Fallowfield
Address: 1 Ladybarn Lane
Manchester M14 6NQ
Phone: 0161 224 2379

#63
Saints & Scholars
Cuisines: British
Average price: £11-25
Area: Didsbury Village
Address: 694 Wilmslow Road
Manchester M20 2DN
Phone: 0161 448 2457

#64
Odder Bar
Cuisines: Bar, Breakfast & Brunch
Average price: £11-25
Area: Oxford Road Corridor
Address: 14 Oxford Road
Manchester M1 5QA
Phone: 0161 238 9132

#65
Dimitri's
Cuisines: Greek, Tapas Bar
Average price: £11-25
Area: Castlefield
Address: Campfield Arcade
Manchester M3 4FN
Phone: 0161 839 3319

#66
I Am Pho
Cuisines: Vietnamese
Average price: Under £10
Area: Chinatown
Address: 44 George Street
Manchester M1 4HF
Phone: 0161 236 1230

#67
Luck Lust Liquor & Burn
Cuisines: Mexican
Average price: £11-25
Area: Northern Quarter
Address: 100-102 High Street
Manchester M4 1HP
Phone: 0161 244 9425

#68
Lime Tree
Cuisines: British
Average price: Above £46
Area: West Didsbury
Address: 8 Lapwing Lane
Manchester M20 2WS
Phone: 0161 445 1217

#69
The Woodstock
Cuisines: Pub, Gastropub
Average price: £11-25
Area: Didsbury Village
Address: 139 Barlow Moor Road
Manchester M20 2DY
Phone: 0161 448 7951

#70
La Viña
Cuisines: Spanish, Tapas
Average price: £11-25
Area: City Centre
Address: 105-107 Deansgate
Manchester M3 2BQ
Phone: 0161 835 3144

#71
Red's True Barbecue
Cuisines: Barbeque, Burgers, American
Average price: £11-25
Address: 22 Lloyd Street
Manchester M2 5WA
Phone: 0161 820 9140

#72
Retro Bar
Cuisines: Breakfast & Brunch, Dive Bar
Average price: Under £10
Area: Gay Village
Address: 78 Sackville Street
Manchester M1 3NJ
Phone: 0161 274 4892

#73
Sapporo Teppanyaki
Cuisines: Japanese, Sushi Bar
Average price: £26-45
Area: Castlefield
Address: 91-93 Liverpool Road
Manchester M3 4JN

#74
Panama Hatty's
Cuisines: European, Mexican
Average price: £11-25
Area: City Centre
Address: 43a Brown Street
Manchester M2 2JJ
Phone: 0161 832 8688

#75
Cachumba
Cuisines: Cafe
Average price: £11-25
Area: West Didsbury
Address: 220 Burton Road
Manchester M20 2LW
Phone: 0161 445 2479

#76
Gemini Café
Cuisines: Breakfast & Brunch, Pizza
Average price: Under £10
Area: Oxford Road Corridor
Address: 328-330 Oxford Road
Manchester M13 9NG
Phone: 0161 272 7723

#77
Isinglass English Dining Room
Cuisines: European, British
Average price: £26-45
Address: 46 Flixton Road
Manchester M41 5AB
Phone: 0161 749 8400

#78
Tokyo Season
Cuisines: Japanese, Sushi Bar,
Asian Fusion
Average price: £11-25
Area: Chinatown
Address: 52 Portland Street
Manchester M1 4QU
Phone: 0161 236 7898

#79
Simple
Cuisines: British, American
Average price: £11-25
Area: Northern Quarter
Address: 44 Tib Street
Manchester M4 1LA
Phone: 0161 832 8764

#80
Habesha
Cuisines: Ethiopian, Halal, African
Average price: £11-25
Area: Gay Village
Address: 29-31 Sackville Street
Manchester M1 3LZ
Phone: 0161 228 7396

#81
The Gallery Café
Cuisines: Breakfast & Brunch
Average price: Under £10
Area: Oxford Road Corridor
Address: Oxford Road
Manchester M15 6ER
Phone: 0161 275 7497

#82
Dogs 'n' Dough
Cuisines: Hot Dogs, Pizza, American
Average price: £11-25
Area: City Centre
Address: 55 Cross Street
Manchester M2 4JN
Phone: 0161 834 3996

#83
Piccolino
Cuisines: Italian
Average price: £11-25
Address: 8 Clarence Street
Manchester M2 4DW
Phone: 0161 835 9860

#84
Bistro West 156
Cuisines: British
Average price: £26-45
Area: West Didsbury
Address: 156 Burton Rd
Manchester M20 1LH
Phone: 0161 445 1921

#85
Folk Café Bar
Cuisines: Bar, Cafe, Sandwiches
Average price: £11-25
Area: West Didsbury
Address: 169-171 Burton Road
Manchester M20 2LN
Phone: 0161 445 2912

#86
Little Yang Sing
Cuisines: Chinese
Average price: £26-45
Area: Chinatown
Address: 17 George Street
Manchester M1 4HE
Phone: 0161 228 7722

#87
The French By Simon Rogan
Cuisines: British
Average price: Above £46
Address: Peter Street
Manchester M60 2DS
Phone: 0161 236 3333

#88
Efes Taverna
Cuisines: Turkish, Bar
Average price: Under £10
Area: Oxford Road Corridor
Address: 46 Princess Street
Manchester M1 6HR
Phone: 0161 236 1824

#89
Tampopo
Cuisines: Asian Fusion, Japanese
Average price: £11-25
Address: 16 Albert Square
Manchester M2 5PF
Phone: 0161 819 1966

#90
Umami
Cuisines: Japanese, Sushi Bar
Average price: Under £10
Area: Oxford Road Corridor
Address: 149/153 Oxford Road
Manchester M1 1EE
Phone: 0161 273 2300

#91
The Friendship Inn
Cuisines: Pub, Coffee & Tea, British
Average price: £11-25
Area: Fallowfield
Address: 351-353 Wilmslow Road
Manchester M14 6XS
Phone: 0161 224 5758

#92
Turkish Delight
Cuisines: Turkish, Ethnic Food
Average price: £11-25
Area: Chorlton
Address: 573 Barlow Moor Road
Manchester M21 8AE
Phone: 0161 881 0503

#93
Slice Pizza & Bread Bar
Cuisines: Pizza, Fast Food, Takeaway
Average price: Under £10
Area: Northern Quarter
Address: Stevenson Square
Manchester M1 1JJ
Phone: 0161 236 9032

#94
Rice
Cuisines: Asian Fusion, Chinese,
Fast Food, Takeaway
Average price: Under £10
Area: Northern Quarter
Address: 1 Piccadilly Garden
Manchester M1 1RG
Phone: 0161 244 5540

#95
Rustica
Cuisines: Sandwiches, Cafe
Average price: Under £10
Area: Northern Quarter
Address: 7 Hilton Street
Manchester M1 2
Phone: 0161 835 3850

#96
Armenian Taverna
Cuisines: Middle Eastern
Average price: £11-25
Address: 3 Princess Street
Manchester M2 4DF
Phone: 0161 834 9025

#97
Punjab Tandoori
Cuisines: Indian, Fast Food, Takeaway
Average price: £11-25
Area: Rusholme
Address: 177 Wilmslow Road
Manchester M14 5AP
Phone: 0161 225 2960

#98
Christie's Bistro
Cuisines: French, Coffee & Tea
Average price: £11-25
Area: Oxford Road Corridor
Address: Oxford Road
Manchester M13 9PL
Phone: 0161 275 7702

#99
Blue Ginger
Cuisines: Chinese, Fast Food, Takeaway
Average price: Above £46
Area: Fallowfield
Address: 5a Wilbraham Road
Manchester M14 6JS
Phone: 0161 257 3184

#100
Piccolino
Cuisines: Italian
Average price: £26-45
Area: West Didsbury
Address: 6 Lapwing Lane
Manchester M20 2WS
Phone: 0161 434 7524

#101
Kro Piccadilly
Cuisines: Bar, European, British
Average price: £11-25
Area: Piccadilly
Address: 1 Piccadilly Garden
Manchester M1 1RG
Phone: 0161 244 5765

#102
Nandos Fallowfield
Cuisines: Portuguese
Average price: Above £46
Area: Fallowfield
Address: 351 Wilmslow Rd
Manchester M14 6SS
Phone: 0161 249 3972

#103
Fish Hut
Cuisines: Fish & Chips, Takeaway
Average price: Under £10
Area: Castlefield
Address: 27 Liverpool Road
Manchester M3 4NW
Phone: 0161 839 0957

#104
EastZEast
Cuisines: Indian
Average price: £11-25
Area: Oxford Road Corridor
Address: Princess Street
Manchester M1 7DG
Phone: 0161 244 5353

#105
EastZEast
Cuisines: Indian
Average price: £26-45
Area: City Centre
Address: Blackfriars Street
Manchester M3 5BQ
Phone: 0161 834 3500

#106
Kebabish
Cuisines: Fast Food, Takeaway
Average price: £11-25
Area: Rusholme
Address: 109 Wilmslow Road
Manchester M14 5AN
Phone: 0161 224 4994

#107
Southern 11
Cuisines: American, Barbeque, Burgers
Average price: £11-25
Area: Spinningfields
Address: Unit 26 3 Hardman Street
Manchester M3 3EB
Phone: 0161 832 0482

#108
Don Marco
Cuisines: Italian, Pizza
Average price: £11-25
Area: Castlefield
Address: 1 Campfield Avenue Arcade
Manchester M3 4FN
Phone: 0161 831 9130

#109
The Blue Pig
Cuisines: Bar, Persian/Iranian
Average price: £11-25
Area: Northern Quarter
Address: 69 High St Manchester
Manchester M4 1FS
Phone: 0161 832 0630

#110
Topkapi Palace
Cuisines: Turkish
Average price: £11-25
Address: 205 Deansgate
Manchester M3 3NW
Phone: 0161 832 9803

#111
Frankie & Benny's
Cuisines: American, Italian
Average price: £11-25
Area: City Centre
Address: 36 St Ann's Street
Manchester M2 7LE
Phone: 0161 835 2479

#112
Walrus
Cuisines: Lounge, Tapas
Average price: £11-25
Area: Northern Quarter
Address: 78-88 High Street
Manchester M4 1ES
Phone: 0161 828 8700

#113
Olive Delicatessen
Cuisines: Deli, Coffee & Tea
Average price: £11-25
Area: Gay Village
Address: 36-38 Whitworth Street
Manchester M1 3NR
Phone: 0161 236 2360

#114
Solomon Grundy
Cuisines: Bar, Breakfast & Brunch
Average price: £11-25
Address: 447 Wilmslow Rd
Manchester M20 4AN
Phone: 0161 7466 592069

#115
Caffeine & Co
Cuisines: Cafe, Coffee & Tea
Average price: Under £10
Area: City Centre
Address: 11 St James Square
Manchester M2 6WH
Phone: 07789 113334

#116
Bonbon Chocolate Boutique
Cuisines: Cafe, Chocolatiers
Average price: £11-25
Area: Northern Quarter
Address: 9 John Street
Manchester M4 1EQ
Phone: 0161 839 4416

#117
Pancho's Burritos
Cuisines: Mexican, Street Vendors
Average price: Under £10
Area: Northern Quarter, City Centre
Address: 49 High St
Manchester M4 3AH
Phone: 07947 976346

#118
On the Corner
Cuisines: Sandwiches, Cafe, Desserts
Average price: £11-25
Area: Chorlton
Address: 93 Beech Road
Manchester M21 9EQ
Phone: 0161 881 4841

#119
Moose Coffee
Cuisines: American, Coffee & Tea,
Breakfast & Brunch
Average price: £11-25
Area: City Centre
Address: 20 York Street
Manchester M2 3BB
Phone: 0161 228 7994

#120
Laughing Buddha
Cuisines: Chinese, Fast Food, Takeaway
Average price: £11-25
Area: Didsbury Village
Address: 782 Wilmslow Rd
Manchester M20 2DJ
Phone: 0871 963 2865

#121
Red Chilli Chinese Restaurant
Cuisines: Chinese
Average price: £11-25
Area: Oxford Road Corridor
Address: 403-419 Oxford Road
Manchester M13 9WL
Phone: 0161 273 1288

#122
Japan Deli/Little Samsi
Cuisines: Japanese, Sushi Bar,
Delicatessen
Average price: £11-25
Area: West Didsbury
Address: 521 Wilmslow Road
Manchester M20 4BA
Phone: 0161 445 9205

#123
Buzzrocks Caribbean Caterers
Cuisines: Caribbean
Average price: Under £10
Address: 166 Stretford Road
Manchester M15 5TL
Phone: 0161 227 7770

#124
Vnam
Cuisines: Vietnamese, Chinese, Thai
Average price: £11-25
Area: Ancoats, Petersfield
Address: 140 Oldham Road
Manchester M4 6BG
Phone: 0161 205 2700

#125
**Great Kathmandu Tandoori
Restaurant**
Cuisines: Indian, Pakistani
Average price: £11-25
Area: West Didsbury
Address: 140 Burton Road
Manchester M20 1JQ
Phone: 0161 445 2145

#126
Yang Sing
Cuisines: Chinese
Average price: £26-45
Address: 34 Princess Street
Manchester M1 4JY
Phone: 0161 236 2200

#127
La Tasca Restaurant
Cuisines: Spanish, Tapas
Average price: £11-25
Area: City Centre
Address: 76 Deansgate
Manchester M3 2FW
Phone: 0161 834 8234

#128
Albert's Shed
Cuisines: Italian, British, Gastropub
Average price: £26-45
Area: Castlefield
Address: 20 Castle Street
Manchester M3 4LZ
Phone: 0161 839 9818

#129
St. Petersburg
Cuisines: Russian, Greek
Average price: £11-25
Area: Gay Village
Address: 68 Sackville Street
Manchester M1 3NJ
Phone: 0161 236 6333

#130
The Albert Square Chop House
Cuisines: British, Pub
Average price: £26-45
Address: Albert Square
Manchester M2 5PF
Phone: 0161 834 1866

#131
Gordon's Kitchen
Cuisines: Chinese, Fast Food, Takeaway
Average price: Under £10
Address: 293 Chester Rd
Manchester M15 4EY
Phone: 0161 839 3836

#132
Rice
Cuisines: Fast Food, Takeaway, Asian
Fusion, Indonesian
Average price: £11-25
Area: Oxford Road Corridor
Address: Oxford Road
Manchester M1 5QS
Phone: 0161 237 1570

#133
Zinc Bar and Grill
Cuisines: British, Bar, American
Average price: £26-45
Area: City Centre
Address: The Triangle
Manchester M4 3TR
Phone: 0161 827 4200

#134
Lal Qila
Cuisines: Indian, Pakistani
Average price: £11-25
Area: Rusholme
Address: 123-127 Wilmslow Road
Manchester M14 5
Phone: 0161 224 9999

#135
The Rose Garden
Cuisines: British
Average price: Above £46
Area: West Didsbury
Address: 218 Burton Road
Manchester M20 2LW
Phone: 0161 478 0747

#136
The Grill on New York Street
Cuisines: Steakhouse, British
Average price: £26-45
Area: Chinatown, City Centre
Address: New York St
Manchester M1 4BD
Phone: 0161 238 9790

#137
Albert's
Cuisines: British
Average price: Above £46
Area: West Didsbury
Address: 120-122 Barlow Moor Road
Manchester M20 2PU
Phone: 0161 434 8289

#138
On The 8th Day
Cuisines: Health Food, Cafe
Average price: £11-25
Area: Oxford Road Corridor
Address: 111 Oxford Road
Manchester M1 7DU
Phone: 0161 273 4878

#139
Felicini
Cuisines: Italian, Wine Bar, Pizza
Average price: £11-25
Address: 60 Oxford Street
Manchester M1 5EE
Phone: 0161 228 6633

#140
Beautiful British Butty
and Portland Plaice
Cuisines: Takeaway, Fish & Chips
Average price: Under £10
Area: Chinatown
Address: 88 Portland Street
Manchester M1 4GX
Phone: 0161 237 1002

#141
Yadgar Cafe
Cuisines: Indian, Pakistani
Average price: Under £10
Area: Northern Quarter
Address: 71 Thomas Street
Manchester M4 1ES
Phone: 0161 831 7753

#142
Eastern Bloc Records
Cuisines: Music Venues, Cafe
Average price: £11-25
Area: Northern Quarter
Address: 5A Stevenson Square
Manchester M1 1DN
Phone: 0161 228 6555

#143
Hard Rock Cafe
Cuisines: American, Bar
Average price: £11-25
Area: City Centre
Address: 27 Withy Grove
Manchester M4 2BS
Phone: 0161 831 6700

#144
Nando's
Cuisines: Portuguese, Chicken Wings
Average price: £11-25
Area: Oxford Road Corridor
Address: 3 Chester Street
Manchester M1 5QS
Phone: 0161 236 5600

#145
Moonlight
Cuisines: Takeaway, Sweet Shop
Average price: Under £10
Area: Rusholme
Address: 75 Wilmslow Road
Manchester M14 5TB
Phone: 0161 248 9327

#146
Blue Ginger
Cuisines: Chinese, Fast Food, Takeaway
Average price: £11-25
Area: Oxford Road Corridor
Address: Chester Street
Manchester M1 5QS
Phone: 0161 235 0700

#147
Choice
Cuisines: British
Average price: £26-45
Area: Castlefield
Address: Castle Quay
Manchester M15 4NT
Phone: 0161 833 3400

#148
Revolucion De Cuba
Cuisines: Club, Cuban, Cocktail Bar
Average price: £26-45
Address: 11 Peter Street
Manchester M2 5QR
Phone: 0161 826 8266

#149
Velvet Bar & Restaurant
Cuisines: British, Lounge, Hotel
Average price: £11-25
Area: Gay Village
Address: 2 Canal Street
Manchester M1 3HE
Phone: 0161 236 9003

#150
Tai Wu
Cuisines: Chinese, Buffet
Average price: £11-25
Address: 44 Oxford Street
Manchester M1 5EJ
Phone: 0161 937 2853

#151
Eden Bar
Cuisines: British, Italian, Gastropub
Average price: £11-25
Area: Gay Village
Address: 3 Brazil Street
Manchester M1 3PJ
Phone: 0161 237 9852

#152
Sangam
Cuisines: Indian
Average price: £11-25
Area: Rusholme
Address: 9 Wilmslow Road
Manchester M14 5TB
Phone: 0161 225 9248

#153
Bluu
Cuisines: Lounge, British
Average price: £11-25
Area: Northern Quarter
Address: 85 High Street
Manchester M4 1BD
Phone: 0161 839 7195

#154
Black Dog Ballroom
Cuisines: Lounge, Snooker & Pool Hall
Average price: £11-25
Area: Northern Quarter
Address: 43 Oldham Street
Manchester M1 1JG
Phone: 0161 839 0664

#155
Kabana
Cuisines: Indian, Pakistani, Takeaway
Average price: Under £10
Area: Northern Quarter
Address: 52 Back Turner Street
Manchester M4 1FP
Phone: 0161 835 2447

#156
Pie and Ale
Cuisines: Specialty Food, British
Average price: £11-25
Area: Northern Quarter
Address: Lever Street
Manchester M1 1FN
Phone: 0161 228 1610

#157
Gusto
Cuisines: Italian, Bar
Average price: £11-25
Area: Didsbury Village
Address: 756 Wilmslow Road
Manchester M20 2DW
Phone: 0161 445 8209

#158
Australasia
Cuisines: Asian Fusion
Average price: £26-45
Area: Spinningfields
Address: 1 The Avenue
Manchester M3 3AP
Phone: 0161 831 0288

#159
The Bank
Cuisines: Pub, British
Average price: £11-25
Area: Chinatown, City Centre
Address: 57 Mosley Street
Manchester M2 3FF
Phone: 0872 107 7077

#160
Bem Brasil
Cuisines: Brazilian, Wine Bar
Average price: £26-45
Area: Northern Quarter
Address: 58 Lever Street
Manchester M1 1FJ
Phone: 0161 923 6888

#161
Wing's Dai Pai Dong
Cuisines: Asian Fusion, Takeaway
Average price: Under £10
Area: City Centre
Address: 49 High Street
Manchester M4 3AH
Phone: 0161 832 0088

#162
Lammars
Cuisines: Lounge, Tapas Bar
Average price: £11-25
Area: Northern Quarter
Address: 57 Hilton Street
Manchester M1 2EJ
Phone: 0161 237 9058

#163
Pizza Express
Cuisines: Pizza, Italian
Average price: £11-25
Area: City Centre
Address: 37 Hanging Ditch
Manchester M4 3TR
Phone: 0161 834 6130

#164
TGI Fridays
Cuisines: American
Average price: £26-45
Address: Cross Street
Manchester M33 7JR
Phone: 0161 962 2962

#165
The Footage
Cuisines: Pub, Burgers, Club
Average price: Under £10
Area: Oxford Road Corridor
Address: 137 Grosvenor Street
Manchester M1 7DZ
Phone: 0161 275 9164

#166
Barburrito
Cuisines: Mexican, Fast Food,
Takeaway, Food
Average price: Under £10
Area: City Centre
Address: 68 Deansgate
Manchester M3 2BW
Phone: 0161 839 1311

#167
Black Dog Ballroom NWS
Cuisines: Barbeque, Lounge,
Snooker & Pool Hall
Average price: £11-25
Area: Oxford Road Corridor
Address: 11-13 New Wakefield Street
Manchester M1 5NP
Phone: 0161 236 4899

#168
Barburrito
Cuisines: Mexican, Tex-Mex
Average price: Under £10
Address: 134 The Orient
Manchester M17 8EH
Phone: 0161 747 6165

#169
Koffee Pot
Cuisines: Cafe
Average price: £11-25
Area: Northern Quarter
Address: 21 Hilton Street
Manchester M1 1JJ

#170
The Waterhouse
Cuisines: Pub, British, Burgers
Average price: Under £10
Area: City Centre
Address: 67-71 Princess Street
Manchester M2 4EG
Phone: 0161 200 5380

#171
Persia Grill House
Cuisines: Persian/Iranian
Average price: £11-25
Area: Chorlton
Address: 255 Barlow Moor Road
Manchester M21 7GJ
Phone: 0161 860 6864

#172
Volta Eaterie & Bar
Cuisines: Gastropub, Pub
Average price: £26-45
Area: West Didsbury
Address: 167 Burton Rd
Manchester M20 2LN
Phone: 0161 448 8887

#173
Kingfisher Fish & Chips
Cuisines: Fish & Chips
Average price: Under £10
Area: Northern Quarter
Address: 43 Tib Street
Manchester M4 1LX
Phone: 0161 270 5806

#174
Moon
Cuisines: Indian
Average price: £11-25
Area: Didsbury Village
Address: 452 Wilmslow Road
Manchester M20 3BW
Phone: 0161 448 8700

#175
47 King Street West
Cuisines: Coffee & Tea, Sandwiches
Average price: £11-25
Area: City Centre
Address: 47 King Street West
Manchester M3 2PW
Phone: 0161 839 1929

#176
New Bilash Balti House
Cuisines: Indian, Pakistani
Average price: £11-25
Address: 555 Bolton Road
Manchester M27 8QT
Phone: 0161 728 5333

#177
Pacific
Cuisines: Chinese
Average price: £11-25
Area: Chinatown
Address: 58-60 George Street
Manchester M1 4HF
Phone: 0161 228 6668

#178
Lucha Libre
Cuisines: Mexican
Average price: £11-25
Address: Unit 4
Manchester M3 3HN
Phone: 0161 850 0629

#179
Carluccio's
Cuisines: Italian
Average price: £11-25
Area: Spinningfields
Address: 3 Hardman Square
Manchester M3 3EB
Phone: 0161 839 0623

#180
The Alchemist
Cuisines: American
Average price: £11-25
Area: Chinatown
Address: 1 New York Street
Manchester M1 4HD
Phone: 0161 228 3856

#181
Buffet City
Cuisines: Chinese, Buffet
Average price: Under £10
Area: Oxford Road Corridor
Address: 111 Portland Street
Manchester M1 6DN
Phone: 0161 228 3388

#182
Neighbourhood
Cuisines: American
Average price: £11-25
Area: Spinningfields
Address: Avenue North Manchester
Phone: 0161 832 6334

#183
Kim By The Sea
Cuisines: European,
Breakfast & Brunch, Bar
Average price: £11-25
Address: 49 Old Birley Street
Manchester M15 5RF
Phone: 0161 232 7667

#184
Fu's Chinese Restaurant Café
Cuisines: Chinese
Average price: £11-25
Area: Chinatown
Address: 56 Faulkner Street
Manchester M1 4FH
Phone: 0161 237 1444

#185
Thai Spice
Cuisines: Thai
Average price: £11-25
Area: Chorlton
Address: 66a Beech Road
Manchester M21 9EG
Phone: 0161 881 0400

#186
Nando's
Cuisines: Portuguese, Chicken Wings
Average price: £11-25
Area: Didsbury Village
Address: Wilmslow Road
Manchester M20 5PG
Phone: 0161 438 0054

#187
Giraffe
Cuisines: American
Average price: £11-25
Address: 136-138 The Orient
Manchester M17 8EQ
Phone: 0161 747 2100

#188
Restaurant Bar & Grill
Cuisines: British, European
Average price: £26-45
Area: City Centre
Address: 14 John Dalton Street
Manchester M2 6JP
Phone: 0161 839 1999

#189
Koh Samui
Cuisines: Thai
Average price: £11-25
Area: Chinatown
Address: 16 Princess St
Manchester M1 4NB
Phone: 0161 237 9511

#190
Tops
Cuisines: Buffet
Average price: £11-25
Area: Oxford Road Corridor
Address: 106 Portland Street
Manchester M1 4RJ
Phone: 0161 237 1000

#191
Puccini Pizzeria
Cuisines: Italian
Average price: £11-25
Address: 173 Chorley Road
Manchester M27 4AE
Phone: 0161 794 1847

#192
The Market Restaurant
Cuisines: British
Average price: £26-45
Area: Northern Quarter
Address: 104 High Street
Manchester M4 1HQ
Phone: 0161 834 3743

#193
Abdul's
Cuisines: Fast Food, Takeaway
Average price: £11-25
Area: Rusholme
Address: 121 Wilmslow Road
Manchester M14 5AN
Phone: 0161 256 2627

#194
The Rising Sun
Cuisines: Pub, British
Average price: Under £10
Address: 22 Queen Street
Manchester M2 5HX
Phone: 0161 834 1193

#195
Manchester 235
Cuisines: Gambling, Chinese, Bar
Average price: £26-45
Address: 2 Watson Street
Manchester M3 4LP
Phone: 0161 828 0300

#196
Bakery
Cuisines: Bakery, Wine Bar
Average price: £11-25
Area: Northern Quarter
Address: 43-45 Lever Street
Manchester M1 1FN
Phone: 0161 236 9014

#197
Babylon
Cuisines: Fast Food, Takeaway
Average price: Under £10
Area: Oxford Road Corridor
Address: 125 Oxford Road
Manchester M1 7DU
Phone: 0161 273 5680

#198
Umezushi
Cuisines: Japanese, Sushi Bar
Average price: £26-45
Area: City Centre
Address: Mirabel Street
Manchester M3 1PJ
Phone: 0161 832 1852

#199
Coriander
Cuisines: Indian
Average price: £11-25
Area: Chorlton
Address: 279 Barlow Moor Road
Manchester M21 7GH
Phone: 0161 881 7750

#200
Dosa Xpress
Cuisines: Indian
Average price: Under £10
Address: 19 Copson Street
Manchester M20 3HE
Phone: 0161 434 4494

#201
Frankie & Benny's UK
Cuisines: Italian
Average price: £11-25
Address: Wilmslow Road
Manchester M20 5PG
Phone: 0161 446 4140

#202
Corbieres
Cuisines: Wine Bar, Pizza, Dive Bar
Average price: Under £10
Area: City Centre
Address: 2 Half Moon Street
Manchester M2 7PB
Phone: 0161 834 3381

#203
Popolino
Cuisines: Pizza, Fast Food, Takeaway
Average price: Under £10
Area: Oxford Road Corridor
Address: 119 Oxford Road
Manchester M1 7DU
Phone: 0161 273 3335

#204
Rosso Restaurant
Cuisines: Italian, Cocktail Bar
Average price: £26-45
Area: City Centre
Address: 43 Spring Garden
Manchester M2 2BG
Phone: 0161 832 1400

#205
Tai Pan Restaurant
Cuisines: Chinese
Average price: £11-25
Area: Oxford Road Corridor
Address: 81-97 Upper Brook Street
Manchester M13 9TX
Phone: 0161 273 2798

#206
Rozafa
Cuisines: Greek, Mediterranean
Average price: £11-25
Area: City Centre
Address: 63 Princess Street
Manchester M2 4EQ
Phone: 0161 236 6389

#207
Al Faisal Tandoori
Cuisines: Indian, Pakistani, Takeaway
Average price: Under £10
Area: Northern Quarter
Address: 58 Thomas Street
Manchester M4 1EG
Phone: 0161 834 3266

#208
Café Istanbul
Cuisines: Turkish
Average price: £11-25
Area: Spinningfields, City Centre
Address: 79 Bridge Street
Manchester M3 2RH
Phone: 0161 833 9942

#209
North Star Piccadilly
Cuisines: Deli
Average price: Under £10
Area: Piccadilly
Address: 77 Dale Street
Manchester M1 2HG
Phone: 0161 237 9619

#210
Nando's
Cuisines: Portuguese, Chicken Wings
Average price: £26-45
Area: City Centre
Address: 27 Withy Grove
Manchester M4 2BS
Phone: 0161 832 0884

#211
Musicana Cafe
Cuisines: Cafe
Average price: £11-25
Area: Rusholme
Address: 10A Wilmslow Road
Manchester M14 5TP
Phone: 0161 225 1930

#212
Jamie's Italian
Cuisines: Italian
Average price: £26-45
Area: City Centre
Address: 100 King Street
Manchester M2 4WU
Phone: 0161 241 3901

#213
Nasi Lemak
Cuisines: Fast Food, Takeaway,
Malaysian, Chinese
Average price: £11-25
Area: Fallowfield
Address: 353 Wilmslow Road
Manchester M14 6XS
Phone: 0161 637 2752

#214
Azad Manzil
Cuisines: Indian, Pakistani
Average price: £11-25
Area: Chorlton
Address: 495 Barlow Moor Rd
Manchester M21 8AG
Phone: 0161 881 1021

#215
Rajdoot Restaurant
Cuisines: Indian, Pakistani
Average price: £11-25
Address: 18 Albert Square
Manchester M2 5PE
Phone: 0161 834 2176

#216
Pinchjo's
Cuisines: Spanish
Average price: £11-25
Area: West Didsbury
Address: 192 Burton Road
Manchester M20 1LH
Phone: 0161 434 2020

#217
Sanam Sweets Centre
Cuisines: Indian, Pakistani, Sweet Shop
Average price: £11-25
Area: Rusholme
Address: 169 Wilmslow Road
Manchester M14 5AP
Phone: 0161 224 3852

#218
W H Lung Cash & Carry
Cuisines: Chinese, Wholesalers
Average price: £11-25
Area: Oxford Road Corridor
Address: 97 Upper Brook Street
Manchester M13 9TX
Phone: 0161 274 3177

#219
Ithaca Manchester
Cuisines: Japanese
Average price: £26-45
Area: City Centre
Address: 36 John Dalton Street
Manchester M2 6LE
Phone: 0161 831 7409

#220
Janam Take Away Food Shop
Cuisines: Fast Food, Takeaway
Average price: Under £10
Area: Chinatown
Address: 78 Portland Street
Manchester M1 4QX
Phone: 0161 228 2485

#221
Pin-Up Bowling
Cuisines: Bowling Alley,
Desserts, Burgers
Average price: £11-25
Area: Spinningfields
Address: 1 Hardman Square
Manchester M3 3EB
Phone: 07585 890023

#222
Salvi's Mozzarella Bar
Cuisines: Delicatessen, Italian
Average price: £11-25
Area: City Centre
Address: Unit 22b
Manchester M4 3TR
Phone: 0161 222 8021

#223
Fresh Loaf
Cuisines: Fast Food, Takeaway,
Coffee & Tea
Average price: Under £10
Area: Northern Quarter
Address: 2 Central Buildings
Manchester M1 1JQ
Phone: 0161 228 7899

#224
Nafees Take Away Food Shop
Cuisines: Fast Food, Takeaway, Indian
Average price: Under £10
Area: Levenshulme
Address: 616 Stockport Road
Manchester M13 0RQ
Phone: 0161 225 6652

#225
Wok & Flame
Cuisines: Chinese, Fast Food, Takeaway
Average price: £11-25
Area: West Didsbury
Address: 206 Burton Road
Manchester M20 2LW
Phone: 0161 434 6318

#226
Dilshad Tandoori Restaurant
Cuisines: Ethiopian, Indian, Pakistani
Average price: £11-25
Address: 385 Hollinwood Avenue
Manchester M40 0JQ
Phone: 0161 681 2204

#227
Rosylee Tearoom
Cuisines: British, Coffee & Tea,
Breakfast & Brunch, Tea Room
Average price: £11-25
Area: Northern Quarter
Address: 11 Stevenson Square
Manchester M1 1DB
Phone: 0161 228 6629

#228
Moon Under Water
Cuisines: Pub, British
Average price: Under £10
Area: City Centre
Address: 68-74 Deansgate
Manchester M3 2FN
Phone: 0161 834 5882

#229
The Font
Cuisines: Lounge, Burgers
Average price: Under £10
Area: Fallowfield
Address: 236 Wilmslow Road
Manchester M14 6LE
Phone: 0161 248 4820

#230
Pizza Express
Cuisines: Pizza, Italian
Average price: £11-25
Address: 56 Peter Street
Manchester M2 3NQ
Phone: 0161 839 9300

#231
Sandinista
Cuisines: Tapas Bar, Lounge
Average price: £11-25
Area: City Centre
Address: 2 Old Bank Street
Manchester M2 7PF
Phone: 0161 832 9955

#232
Atlas Bar
Cuisines: Wine Bar, British,
Breakfast & Brunch
Average price: £11-25
Address: 376 Deansgate
Manchester M3 4LY
Phone: 0161 834 2124

#233
Saajan
Cuisines: Indian
Average price: Under £10
Area: Fallowfield
Address: 316 Wilmslow Road
Manchester M14 6XQ
Phone: 0161 248 4944

#234
Taco Bell
Cuisines: Mexican, Food Court,
Fast Food, Takeaway
Average price: Under £10
Area: City Centre
Address: Manchester Arndale Food Court
Manchester M4 3AQ

#235
Mary & Archie
Cuisines: British, Pub, Gastropub
Average price: £11-25
Area: West Didsbury
Address: 200 Burton Rd
Manchester M20 2LW
Phone: 0161 445 3130

#236
Paan House
Cuisines: Indian, Pakistani
Average price: £11-25
Address: 29 Ayres Road
Manchester M16 9WA
Phone: 0161 226 0518

#237
The Village Restaurant
Cuisines: Indian, Pakistani
Average price: £11-25
Area: Rusholme
Address: 97 Wilmslow Road
Manchester M14 5SU
Phone: 0161 225 2614

#238
Anand's Vegetarian Deli
Cuisines: Deli, Indian, Fast Food, Takeaway
Average price: Under £10
Area: Rusholme
Address: 217 Wilmslow Road
Manchester M14 5AG
Phone: 0161 225 6742

#239
Hickson & Black's
Cuisines: Cheese Shop, Butcher, Sandwiches
Average price: £26-45
Area: Chorlton
Address: 559 Barlow Moor Road
Manchester M21 8AN
Phone: 0161 881 2001

#240
The Whim Wham Cafe
Cuisines: Jazz & Blues, Bar, British
Average price: £11-25
Address: Arch 64 Whitworth Street West
Manchester M1 5WQ
Phone: 0161 236 0930

#241
Loco Express
Cuisines: Indian, Fast Food, Takeaway
Average price: £11-25
Area: Oxford Road Corridor
Address: 65 Arches Manchester M1 5WQ
Phone: 0161 237 3949

#242
Chunky Chicken
Cuisines: Fast Food, Takeaway
Average price: Under £10
Area: Rusholme
Address: 106 Wilmslow Road
Manchester M14 5AJ
Phone: 0161 248 9709

#243
Aladdin Restaurant
Cuisines: Middle Eastern
Average price: £11-25
Area: West Didsbury
Address: 529 Wilmslow Road
Manchester M20 4BA
Phone: 0161 434 8558

#244
Giovanni's Deli
Cuisines: Tea Room, Sandwiches
Average price: Under £10
Area: Gay Village
Address: 1 Pine Street
Manchester M1 4DY
Phone: 0161 228 7400

#245
International Society
Cuisines: University, Diner
Average price: Under £10
Area: Oxford Road Corridor
Address: 327 Oxford Road
Manchester M13 9PG
Phone: 0161 275 4959

#246
San Rocco
Cuisines: Italian, Mediterranean
Average price: £11-25
Address: 96 Bury Old Road
Manchester M8 5BW
Phone: 0161 795 5300

#247
Artisan
Cuisines: British
Average price: £11-25
Area: Spinningfields
Address: 22-28 Bridge Street
Manchester M3 3AB

#248
Dixy Chicken
Cuisines: Fast Food, Takeaway, Chicken Wings
Average price: Under £10
Area: Fallowfield
Address: Wilbraham Road
Manchester M14 6JS
Phone: 0161 224 5577

#249
Paradise Take Away
Cuisines: Fast Food, Takeaway
Average price: Under £10
Area: Levenshulme
Address: 600 Stockport Road
Manchester M13 0RQ
Phone: 0161 225 1931

#250
Kukoos Street Food
Cuisines: Halal, Moroccan
Average price: Under £10
Area: Oxford Road Corridor
Address: 12A Oxford Road
Manchester M1 5QA
Phone: 0161 235 8536

#251
Chicken King
Cuisines: Fast Food, Takeaway, Chicken Wings
Average price: Under £10
Area: Fallowfield
Address: 316 Wilmslow Road
Manchester M14 6
Phone: 0161 248 8989

#252
Panacea
Cuisines: Champagne Bar, British
Average price: Above £46
Area: City Centre
Address: 14 John Dalton St
Manchester M2 6JP
Phone: 0161 833 1111

#253
Continental
Cuisines: Fast Food, Takeaway
Average price: Under £10
Area: West Didsbury
Address: 127 Burton Road
Manchester M20 1JP
Phone: 0161 445 0560

#254
The Living Room
Cuisines: Wine Bar, British, Club
Average price: £26-45
Area: City Centre
Address: 80 Deansgate
Manchester M3 2ER
Phone: 0161 832 0083

#255
Grand Pacific
Cuisines: Asian Fusion, Bar
Average price: Above £46
Area: Oldham
Address: 1 The Avenue
Manchester M3 3AP
Phone: 0161 831 0288

#256
Harvey Nichols
Cuisines: British, Bar, Brasserie
Average price: Above £46
Area: City Centre
Address: 21 New Cathedral Street
Manchester M1 1AD
Phone: 0161 828 8898

#257
Zizzi's
Cuisines: Italian
Average price: £11-25
Area: Spinningfields
Address: Left Bank Spinningfields
Manchester M3 3AN
Phone: 0161 839 7984

#258
Patisserie Valerie
Cuisines: Bakery, French, Desserts
Average price: £26-45
Area: City Centre
Address: 2-4 St Ann Street
Manchester M2 7
Phone: 0161 839 9116

#259
The Bay Horse
Cuisines: Pub, Salad, Hot Dogs
Average price: £11-25
Area: Northern Quarter
Address: 35-37 Thomas Street
Manchester M4 1NA
Phone: 0161 661 1041

#260
Tampopo
Cuisines: Vietnamese, Thai
Average price: £11-25
Address: 135 The Orient
Manchester M17 8EH
Phone: 0161 747 8878

#261
Prohibition
Cuisines: Lounge, British
Average price: £11-25
Area: City Centre
Address: 2-10 St Mary's St
Manchester M3 2LB
Phone: 0161 831 9326

#262
Red Hot World Buffet
Cuisines: Buffet, Chinese, Indian
Average price: £11-25
Area: City Centre
Address: 48 Deansgate
Manchester M3 2EG
Phone: 0161 819 1240

#263
Hunters BBQ & Asian Take Away
Cuisines: American, Asian Fusion,
Fast Food, Takeaway
Average price: Under £10
Area: Northern Quarter
Address: 94 High Street
Manchester M4 1EF
Phone: 0161 839 5060

#264
Petra
Cuisines: Greek, Indian, Mediterranean
Average price: £11-25
Area: Oxford Road Corridor
Address: 267 Upper Brook Street
Manchester M13 0HR
Phone: 0161 274 4441

#265
Philpotts
Cuisines: Fast Food, Takeaway
Average price: £26-45
Area: Oxford Road Corridor
Address: 131 Portland Street
Manchester M1 4PY
Phone: 0161 923 6969

#266
Wetherspoons
Cuisines: Pub, British
Average price: £11-25
Area: Northern Quarter
Address: 49 Piccadilly
Manchester M1 2AP
Phone: 0161 236 9206

#267
The Piccadilly
Cuisines: British, Breakfast & Brunch
Average price: £11-25
Area: Northern Quarter
Address: 60 - 75 Piccadilly
Manchester M1 2BS
Phone: 0872 107 7077

#268
Frankie & Benny's
Cuisines: Italian
Average price: Above £46
Address: Trafford Centre
Manchester M17 8WW
Phone: 0161 747 1600

#269
Cafe Rouge
Cuisines: Cafe
Average price: £11-25
Address: 137 The Orient
Manchester M7 4TB
Phone: 0161 747 1927

#270
Woo Sang
Cuisines: Supermarket, Chinese
Average price: £11-25
Area: Chinatown
Address: 19-21 George Street
Manchester M1 4HE
Phone: 0161 236 4353

#271
Viet Shack
Cuisines: Vietnamese
Average price: Under £10
Area: Northern Quarter
Address: 49-61 High Street
Manchester M4

#272
Sweet Box
Cuisines: Sweet Shop, Juice Bar,
Ice Cream, Fast Food, Takeaway
Average price: £11-25
Area: Rusholme
Address: 155 - 157 Wilmslow Road
Manchester M14 5A
Phone: 0161 248 9760

#273
Sindhoor
Cuisines: Indian
Average price: £11-25
Address: 198-200 Mauldeth Rd
Manchester M19 1AJ
Phone: 0161 432 5246

#274
Cafe Rouge
Cuisines: Coffee & Tea, French
Average price: £26-45
Area: Didsbury Village
Address: 651 - 653 Unit D 651-653
Wilmslow Road
Manchester M20 6QZ
Phone: 0161 438 0444

#275
La Tasca
Cuisines: Spanish, Basque, Tapas
Average price: £11-25
Area: Didsbury Village
Address: Warburton Street
Manchester M20 6WA
Phone: 0161 438 0044

#276
Abergeldie Cafe
Cuisines: Coffee & Tea,
Fish & Chips, Pizza
Average price: £11-25
Area: Northern Quarter
Address: 40 Shudehill
Manchester M4 1EZ
Phone: 0161 834 5548

#277
Cuba Cafe
Cuisines: Cuban
Average price: £11-25
Area: Northern Quarter
Address: 43 Port St
Manchester M1 2EQ
Phone: 0161 236 3630

#278
Chilli Peri Chicken
Cuisines: Fast Food, Takeaway
Average price: Under £10
Area: Rusholme
Address: 120 Wilmslow Road
Manchester M14 5AH

#279
Sadaf Halaal
Cuisines: Fast Food, Takeaway
Average price: Under £10
Area: Rusholme
Address: 167 Wilmslow Road
Manchester M14 5AP
Phone: 0161 257 3557

#280
The Baths Supper Bar
Cuisines: Fish & Chips
Average price: £11-25
Area: Chorlton
Address: 113 Manchester Rd
Manchester M21 9PG
Phone: 0161 881 5104

#281
Treasure Pot
Cuisines: Chinese, Fast Food, Takeaway
Average price: £11-25
Area: Chorlton
Address: 101 Manchester Road
Manchester M21 9GA
Phone: 0161 881 3609

#282
Namaste Nepal
Cuisines: Himalayan/Nepalese, Indian
Average price: £26-45
Area: West Didsbury
Address: 164-166 Burton Road
Manchester M20 1LH
Phone: 0161 445 9060

#283
Persian Tasty Grill
Cuisines: Persian/Iranian
Average price: Under £10
Area: Levenshulme
Address: Stockport Road
Manchester M19 2

#284
Loaf
Cuisines: Wine Bar, British
Average price: Above £46
Address: Deansgate Locks
Manchester M1 5LH
Phone: 0161 819 5858

#285
Williams Sandwich Bar
Cuisines: Fast Food, Takeaway,
Coffee & Tea, Deli
Average price: Under £10
Area: Northern Quarter
Address: 45 Hilton Street
Manchester M1 2EF
Phone: 0161 236 1833

#286
Cedar Tree
Cuisines: British
Average price: £11-25
Area: Stockport
Address: 64 Middle Hillgate
Manchester SK1 3EH
Phone: 0161 480 0028

#287
Hadramout
Cuisines: Takeaway, Middle Eastern
Average price: £11-25
Area: Rusholme
Address: 1 Walmar Street East
Manchester M14 5SS
Phone: 0161 248 8843

#288
Thaikhun
Cuisines: Thai
Average price: £11-25
Area: Spinningfields
Address: 3 Hardman Street The Avenue
Manchester M3 3EB
Phone: 0161 819 2065

#289
Genting Club
Cuisines: Lounge, Sandwiches
Average price: £26-45
Area: Oxford Road Corridor
Address: 110 Portland Street
Manchester M1 4RL
Phone: 0161 228 0077

#290
Turtle Bay
Cuisines: Caribbean
Average price: £11-25
Area: Chinatown
Address: 33-35 Oxford St
Manchester M1 4BH

#291
Vivid Lounge
Cuisines: Coffee & Tea,
Sandwiches, Thai
Average price: £11-25
Area: Ancoats, Petersfield
Address: 149A Great Ancoats Street
Manchester M4 6DH
Phone: 0161 272 8474

#292
Bar San Juan
Cuisines: Spanish
Average price: £11-25
Area: Chorlton
Address: 56 Beech Road
Manchester M21 9EG
Phone: 0161 881 9259

#293
Jazera Charcoal Cuisine
Cuisines: Middle Eastern
Average price: Under £10
Area: Rusholme
Address: 22 Wilmslow Rd
Manchester M14 5TQ
Phone: 0161 257 3337

#294
Shahi Masala
Cuisines: Indian
Average price: £26-45
Area: Rusholme
Address: 16-18 Wilmslow Road
Manchester M14 5TQ
Phone: 0161 248 8344

#295
Zam Zam Tandoori
Cuisines: Indian, Fast Food, Takeaway
Average price: Under £10
Area: Chorlton
Address: 452 Wilborougham Road
Manchester M21 0AG
Phone: 0161 862 0999

#296
Canada Grill
Cuisines: Fast Food, Takeaway
Average price: Under £10
Area: Chorlton
Address: 613A Wilbraham Road
Manchester M21 9AN
Phone: 0161 881 1205

#297
Pinto's
Cuisines: Cafe, British
Average price: £11-25
Address: 3 Fairfax Road
Manchester M25
Phone: 0161 773 4774

#298
Armstrongs
Cuisines: Fish & Chips,
Fast Food, Takeaway
Average price: £11-25
Address: 486 Bury Old Road
Manchester M25 1NL
Phone: 0161 773 6023

#299
Ambiente
Cuisines: Spanish, Tapas Bar
Average price: £26-45
Address: 4b Worsley Road
Manchester M28 2NL
Phone: 0161 793 6003

#300
The Bar
Cuisines: Bar, British
Average price: £11-25
Area: Chorlton
Address: 533 Wilbraham Rd
Manchester M21 0UE
Phone: 0161 861 7576

#301
La Roma Restaurant
Cuisines: Italian
Average price: £11-25
Area: Bolton
Address: Ringley Road
Manchester M26 1GT
Phone: 01204 707932

#302
Tandle Hill Tavern
Cuisines: Pub, British
Average price: Under £10
Area: Oldham
Address: 14 Thornham Lane
Manchester M24 2SD
Phone: 01706 345297

#303
Chiquito
Cuisines: Mexican, Spanish
Average price: £11-25
Area: City Centre
Address: The Printworks
Manchester M4 2BS
Phone: 0161 830 1560

#304
The Slug & Lettuce
Cuisines: Wine Bar, Lounge, European
Average price: £11-25
Area: Spinningfields
Address: Left Bank Irwell Square
Manchester M3 3AN
Phone: 0845 126 2915

#305
By The Slice
Cuisines: Fast Food, Takeaway, Pizza
Average price: Under £10
Area: City Centre
Address: 2 Chapel Street
Manchester M3 7WJ
Phone: 0161 832 5553

#306
Bouzouki Restaurant
Cuisines: Greek, Mediterranean
Average price: £11-25
Area: Oxford Road Corridor
Address: 88 Princess Street
Manchester M1 6NG
Phone: 0161 236 9282

#307
Smoak Bar & Grill
Cuisines: Steakhouse
Average price: Above £46
Area: Piccadilly
Address: Smoak Bar & Grill at Malmaison
Manchester M1 1LZ
Phone: 0161 278 1000

#308
Baekdu
Cuisines: Korean
Average price: £11-25
Area: City Centre
Address: 77 Shudehill
Manchester M4 4AN
Phone: 0161 834 2227

#309
Subway
Cuisines: Sandwiches
Average price: Under £10
Area: Oxford Road Corridor
Address: 149 Oxford Road
Manchester M13 9DJ
Phone: 0161 273 8573

#310
Gemini Takeaway
Cuisines: Takeaway, Pizza, Chicken Wings
Average price: Under £10
Area: Oxford Road Corridor
Address: 308-310 Oxford Road
Manchester M13 9NS
Phone: 0161 273 3201

#311
Abdul's
Cuisines: Indian, Pakistani,
Fast Food, Takeaway
Average price: £11-25
Area: Oxford Road Corridor
Address: 133-135 Oxford Rd
Manchester M1 7DY
Phone: 0161 273 7339

#312
Byron
Cuisines: Burgers
Average price: £26-45
Address: 115 Deansgate
Manchester M3 2NW
Phone: 0161 832 1222

#313
The Paramount
Cuisines: Pub, Burgers
Average price: Under £10
Area: Oxford Road Corridor
Address: 33-35 Oxford Street
Manchester M1 4BH
Phone: 0161 233 1820

#314
The B Lounge
Cuisines: Pub, European
Average price: £11-25
Area: Piccadilly
Address: 97 Piccadilly
Manchester M1 2DB
Phone: 0161 236 4161

#315
Sanam Sweethouse
Cuisines: Indian, Pakistani, Sweet Shop
Average price: Under £10
Area: Rusholme
Address: 145-151 Wilmslow Road
Manchester M14 5AW
Phone: 0161 224 8824

#316
Noddys Take Away Food Shop
Cuisines: Fast Food, Takeaway
Average price: Under £10
Area: West Didsbury
Address: 573 Wilmslow Road
Manchester M20 3QH
Phone: 0161 434 7600

#317
Kashmiri Spice
Cuisines: Indian
Average price: Under £10
Address: 259 Kingsway
Manchester M19 1AN
Phone: 0161 442 3000

#318
Crazy Cow
Cuisines: Breakfast & Brunch
Average price: £11-25
Area: East Didsbury
Address: 837 Wilmslow Rd
Manchester M20 5WD
Phone: 0161 215 0325

#319
Couture Cafe Bar
Cuisines: Cafe, Coffee & Tea
Average price: £11-25
Area: Oxford Road Corridor
Address: 250 Oxford Road
Manchester M13 9PL
Phone: 0161 275 2675

#320
Changos Burrito Bar
Cuisines: Mexican
Average price: Under £10
Area: Oxford Road Corridor
Address: Oxford Street
Manchester M1 6FQ
Phone: 0161 228 2182

#321
Abduls
Cuisines: Fast Food, Takeaway
Average price: Under £10
Area: Fallowfield
Address: 318 Wilmslow Road
Manchester M14 6XQ
Phone: 0161 248 7573

#322
Croma
Cuisines: Pizza, Italian
Average price: £11-25
Area: Chorlton
Address: 500 Wilbraham Road
Manchester M21 9AP
Phone: 0161 881 1117

#323
Las Iguanas
Cuisines: Lounge, Latin American
Average price: £11-25
Area: City Centre
Address: 84 Deansgate
Manchester M3 2ER
Phone: 0161 819 2606

#324
Subway
Cuisines: Sandwiches
Average price: Under £10
Address: 49 Peter Street
Manchester M2 3NG
Phone: 0161 835 1982

#325
Swadesh
Cuisines: Indian
Average price: £11-25
Area: Chinatown
Address: 98 Portland Street
Manchester M1 4GX
Phone: 0161 236 1313

#326
Happy Seasons
Cuisines: Chinese
Average price: £11-25
Area: Chinatown
Address: 59 Faulkner Street
Manchester M1 4FF
Phone: 0161 236 7189

#327
Tusk
Cuisines: Burgers
Average price: £11-25
Area: Northern Quarter
Address: 78-88 High Street
Manchester M4 1ES
Phone: 0161 828 8700

#328
Saffron
Cuisines: Indian, Pakistani, Buffet
Average price: £11-25
Address: 107 Cheetham Hill Road
Manchester M8 8PY
Phone: 0161 834 1222

#329
KFC
Cuisines: American, Fast Food, Takeaway
Average price: Under £10
Area: Rusholme
Address: Arndale Centre
Manchester M1

#330
The Cod Father
Cuisines: Fish & Chips, British
Average price: Under £10
Area: Fallowfield
Address: 331 Wilmslow Road
Manchester M14 6NW
Phone: 0161 248 9719

#331
Lucky Star
Cuisines: Fast Food, Takeaway
Average price: £11-25
Address: 68 Mauldeth Rd W
Manchester M20 3FQ
Phone: 0161 434 6983

#332
Pacifica Cantonese
Cuisines: Chinese
Average price: £11-25
Address: 5-7 Church Road
Manchester M30 0DL
Phone: 0161 707 8828

#333
Langley Friery
Cuisines: Fish & Chips
Average price: Under £10
Address: 227 Wood Street
Manchester M24 5RA
Phone: 0161 653 6431

#334
Crazy Wendy's
Cuisines: Thai
Average price: £26-45
Area: West Didsbury
Address: 210 Burton Road
Manchester M20 2LW
Phone: 0161 445 5200

#335
Chopsticks Chinese Restaurant
Cuisines: Chinese, Fast Food, Takeaway
Average price: £11-25
Address: 161-169 Chorley Road
Manchester M27 4AE
Phone: 0161 727 9999

#336
Saigon Lotus
Cuisines: Vietnamese, Asian Fusion
Average price: Under £10
Area: Ancoats, Petersfield
Address: 146 Oldham Road
Manchester M4 6BG
Phone: 0161 914 6777

#337
Carluccio's
Cuisines: Italian
Average price: £11-25
Area: Piccadilly
Address: London Road Manchester M1

#338
Doops Coffee House
Cuisines: Coffee & Tea, Sandwiches
Average price: £11-25
Address: 63 Peter Street
Manchester M2 3
Phone: 0161 819 5678

#339
Atlas Shawarma
Cuisines: Fast Food, Takeaway,
Middle Eastern
Average price: Under £10
Area: Rusholme
Address: Manchester M14 5AH
Phone: 07874 675347

#340
Harry Ramsden's
Cuisines: British
Average price: £11-25
Area: Salford Quays
Address: Unit 5 Castlemore Retail Park
Manchester M16 0SN
Phone: 0161 873 8017

#341
Islamabad Grill
Cuisines: Indian
Average price: Under £10
Area: Rusholme
Address: 199-201 Wilmslow Road
Manchester M14 5AQ
Phone: 0161 257 3890

#342
The Post Box
Cuisines: Cafe
Average price: Under £10
Area: Chorlton
Address: 543 Wilbraham Road
Manchester M21 9PP
Phone: 0161 881 4853

#343
Olive & Thyme
Cuisines: Mediterranean
Average price: £26-45
Area: Chorlton
Address: 416-418 Barlow Moor Road
Manchester M21 8AD
Phone: 0161 881 6695

#344
Shans Takeaway
Cuisines: Fast Food, Takeaway
Average price: Under £10
Area: Fallowfield
Address: 312 Wilmslow Road
Manchester M14 6XQ
Phone: 0161 256 4358

#345
Peking Chef
Cuisines: Chinese
Average price: £11-25
Address: 208 Mauldeth Road
Manchester M19 1AJ

#346
University V Grills
Cuisines: Breakfast & Brunch, Greek
Average price: Under £10
Area: Oxford Road Corridor
Address: 12 Oxford Road
Manchester M13 9RN
Phone: 0161 273 2551

#347
Veggie Kitchen
Cuisines: British
Average price: Under £10
Area: Northern Quarter
Address: Piccadilly Garden
Manchester M1 1RG

#348
Mughal Taste
Cuisines: Indian, Pakistani
Average price: Under £10
Address: 53 Bury New Road
Manchester M8 8FX
Phone: 0161 832 0636

#349
Hong Kong Chippy
Cuisines: Fish & Chips
Average price: Under £10
Address: 149 Henrietta Street
Manchester M16 9PS
Phone: 0161 226 4083

#350
Delights
Cuisines: Halal
Average price: Under £10
Area: Rusholme
Address: 72 Wilmslow Road
Manchester M14 5AL
Phone: 0161 224 1555

#351
Jasmine
Cuisines: Arabian
Average price: £11-25
Area: Chorlton
Address: 569 Barlow Moor Road
Manchester M21 8AE
Phone: 0161 881 1442

#352
Zains Krispy Chicken
Cuisines: Fast Food, Takeaway
Average price: Under £10
Area: Rusholme
Address: 113 Wilmslow Rd
Manchester M14 5AN
Phone: 0161 224 4675

#353
Saajan
Cuisines: Indian
Average price: Under £10
Area: Rusholme
Address: 129 Wilmslow Road
Manchester M14 5AW
Phone: 0161 256 3070

#354
Karim's Orient Experience Restaurant
Cuisines: Asian Fusion
Average price: £26-45
Address: 382 Heywood Old Road
Manchester M24
Phone: 0161 653 6677

#355
Smiths
Cuisines: French
Average price: £11-25
Address: 1 Church Road
Manchester M30 0DL
Phone: 0161 788 7343

#356
Shiraz
Cuisines: Persian/Iranian
Average price: £11-25
Address: 299 Palatine Road
Manchester M22 4HH
Phone: 0161 945 8080

#357
Woodhouse Garden Inn
Cuisines: Pub, British
Average price: £26-45
Address: 48 Medlock Road
Manchester M35 9WN
Phone: 0161 681 3782

#358
Khan Saab
Cuisines: Indian, Pakistani
Average price: £11-25
Address: 117 Bury New Road
Manchester M45 6AA
Phone: 0161 766 2148

#359
Tung Fong
Cuisines: Chinese
Average price: £26-45
Address: 2 Worsley Road
Manchester M28 2NL
Phone: 0161 794 5331

#360
Shabaz Indian Take Away
Cuisines: Fast Food, Takeaway
Average price: £11-25
Address: 5 Rufford Parade
Manchester M45 8PL
Phone: 0161 796 1969

#361
Hills Traditional
Cuisines: Fish & Chips
Average price: Under £10
Area: Oldham
Address: 331 Oldham Road
Manchester M24 2DN
Phone: 0161 654 0299

#362
Spice House
Cuisines: Fast Food, Takeaway
Average price: £11-25
Address: 27 Spark Road
Manchester M23 1DQ
Phone: 0161 998 3080

#363
Spicy Hut Restaurant
Cuisines: Indian, Pakistani
Average price: £11-25
Area: Rusholme
Address: 35 Wilmslow Road
Manchester M14 5TB
Phone: 0161 248 6200

#364
Krunchy Fried Chicken
Cuisines: Fast Food, Takeaway
Average price: £11-25
Area: Rusholme
Address: 44, Wilmslow Road
Manchester M14 5TQ
Phone: 0161 256 3694

#365
Chico's Grill House
Cuisines: Fast Food, Takeaway
Average price: Under £10
Area: Longsight
Address: 185 Dickenson Road
Manchester M13 0YN
Phone: 0161 257 2576

#366
Ocean Treasure
Seafood Restaurant
Cuisines: Chinese
Average price: £26-45
Address: Greenside Way
Manchester M24 1SW
Phone: 0161 653 6688

#367
The Slug & Lettuce
Cuisines: British
Average price: £26-45
Area: City Centre
Address: 64-66 Deansgate
Manchester M3 2EN
Manchester M3 4
Phone: 0161 839 0985

#368
Siam Orchid
Cuisines: Thai, Karaoke
Average price: £11-25
Area: Chinatown
Address: 54 Portland Street
Manchester M1 4QU
Phone: 0161 236 1388

#369
Brasserie Chez Gerard
Cuisines: British, Moroccan, French
Average price: £26-45
Address: 2-10 Albert Square
Manchester M2 5
Phone: 0161 834 7633

#370
The Beijing
Cuisines: Chinese
Average price: Under £10
Area: Chinatown
Address: 48 Portland St
Manchester M1 4QU
Phone: 0161 228 0883

#371
Dockers
Cuisines: Fish & Chips
Average price: Under £10
Area: City Centre
Address: 27 Withy Grove
Manchester M4 2BS
Phone: 0161 773997

#372
TGI Fridays
Cuisines: American, Bar, Burgers
Average price: £11-25
Area: City Centre
Address: Cross Street
Manchester M2 7DH
Phone: 0844 692 8903

#373
YeoPan's
Cuisines: Chinese, Fast Food, Takeaway
Average price: £11-25
Area: Chorlton
Address: 522 Wilbraham Road
Manchester M21 9AW
Phone: 0161 881 6888

#374
All Star Lanes
Cuisines: Bowling Alley,
American, Cocktail Bar
Average price: £11-25
Address: 235 Deansgate
Manchester M3 4EN
Phone: 0161 871 3600

#375
Duttons Manchester
Cuisines: Gastropub
Average price: £11-25
Area: City Centre
Address: 2-10 Albert Square
Manchester M2
Phone: 0161 241 6839

#376
Kitchenette
Cuisines: British
Average price: £11-25
Address: 60 Oxford Street
Manchester M1 5EE
Phone: 0161 228 6633

#377
Philpotts
Cuisines: Sandwiches
Average price: Above £46
Address: Lowry House
Manchester M2 1FB
Phone: 0161 835 2111

#378
Krispy Chicken
Cuisines: Fast Food, Takeaway
Average price: Under £10
Area: Rusholme
Address: 113 Wilmslow Road
Manchester M14 5
Phone: 0161 224 4675

#379
McDonalds
Cuisines: Fast Food, Takeaway, American
Average price: Under £10
Address: 7 The Orient
Manchester M17 8EH

#380
Café Cilantro
Cuisines: Vegetarian
Average price: £11-25
Address: 52 Beech Rd
Manchester M21 9EG
Phone: 0871 961 4821

#381
Cheese Hamlet
Cuisines: Deli, Delicatessen
Average price: £11-25
Area: Didsbury Village
Address: 706 Wilmslow Road
Manchester M20 2DW
Phone: 0161 434 4781

#382
Palace Hotel
Cuisines: Hotel, British
Average price: £26-45
Area: Oxford Road Corridor
Address: Oxford Road
Manchester M60 7HA
Phone: 0161 288 1111

#383
Cafe Lloyd
Cuisines: Fish & Chips
Average price: £11-25
Address: 16 Lloyd St
Manchester M2 5ND
Phone: 0161 835 2073

#384
Per Tutti
Cuisines: Italian
Average price: £11-25
Area: Castlefield
Address: 3-11 Liverpool Road
Manchester M3 4NW
Phone: 0161 834 9741

#385
Papa G's
Cuisines: Greek
Average price: £11-25
Area: City Centre
Address: 27 Withy Grove
Manchester M4 2BS
Phone: 0161 834 8668

#386
Lass O'Gowrie
Cuisines: British, Pub
Average price: Under £10
Area: Gay Village
Address: 36 Charles Street
Manchester M1 7DB
Phone: 0161 273 6932

#387
Wood Wine & Deli
Cuisines: Wine Bar, Deli, Delicatessen
Average price: £11-25
Area: Northern Quarter
Address: 44 Tib Street
Manchester M4 1LA
Phone: 0161 478 7100

#388
Wing's
Cuisines: Chinese, Fast Food, Takeaway
Average price: Under £10
Area: City Centre
Address: Arndale Food Court
Manchester M4 3AQ
Phone: 0161 834 9000

#389
Subway
Cuisines: Fast Food, Takeaway
Average price: Under £10
Area: Longsight
Address: Manchester Arndale
Manchester M4 3AB
Phone: 04416 1835 9179

#390
Urban Spice
Cuisines: Fast Food, Takeaway
Average price: Under £10
Area: Oxford Road Corridor
Address: 70 Hathersage Road
Manchester M13 0FN
Phone: 0161 248 9773

#391
Fish Bait Fish Bar
Cuisines: Fish & Chips
Average price: Under £10
Area: West Didsbury
Address: 178 Burton Rd
Manchester M20 1LH
Phone: 0161 448 0128

#392
Due Fratelli
Cuisines: Fast Food, Takeaway
Average price: £11-25
Area: Chorlton
Address: 249 Barlow Moor Road
Manchester M21 7GJ
Phone: 0161 881 6444

#393
La Tasca
Cuisines: Spanish
Average price: £11-25
Address: Unit R7a The Trafford Centre
Manchester M17 8AA

#394
KFC
Cuisines: Fast Food, Takeaway,
Chicken Wings
Average price: £11-25
Address: 9 The Orient
Manchester M17 8EH
Phone: 0161 749 8012

#395
Cafe Greco
Cuisines: Italian, Sandwiches
Average price: Under £10
Area: City Centre
Address: Market Food Court
Manchester M4 3AQ

#396
Rice
Cuisines: Asian Fusion
Average price: £11-25
Address: Unit 5A The Orient
Manchester M17 8AA
Phone: 0161 755 0577

#397
The Deli on Burton Road
Cuisines: Department Stores, Sandwiches
Average price: £26-45
Area: West Didsbury
Address: BUrton Road
Manchester M20 1LH
Phone: 0161 445 2912

#398
Khan's Kebab House
Cuisines: Halal
Average price: £11-25
Address: 426 Wilmslow Road
Manchester M20 3BW
Phone: 0161 448 2700

#399
Coriander
Cuisines: Indian
Average price: Under £10
Address: 432 Wilmslow Road
Manchester M20 3BW
Phone: 0161 438 2984

#400
Ashoka Restaurant
Cuisines: Indian
Average price: £11-25
Area: Oxford Road Corridor
Address: 105-107 Portland Street
Manchester M1 6DF
Phone: 0161 228 7550

#401
La Tasca
Cuisines: Spanish
Average price: £11-25
Address: 132 The Orient
Manchester M17 8EG
Phone: 0161 749 9966

#402
TGI Fridays
Cuisines: American, Wine Bar
Average price: £11-25
Address: Valley Park Road
Manchester M25 3AJ
Phone: 0161 798 7125

#403
Leo's Fish Bar
Cuisines: Fast Food, Takeaway,
Fish & Chips
Average price: Under £10
Area: Northern Quarter
Address: 12 Oldham Street
Manchester M1 1JQ
Phone: 0161 237 3999

#404
The Great Central
Cuisines: British, Pub
Average price: Under £10
Area: Fallowfield
Address: 343 Wilmslow Road
Manchester M14 6NS
Phone: 0161 248 1740

#405
Pret A Manger
Cuisines: Coffee & Tea, Sandwiches
Average price: £26-45
Area: City Centre
Address: 27 Cross Street
Manchester M2 1WL
Phone: 020 7932 5278

#406
Cafe Rouge
Cuisines: French
Average price: £11-25
Area: City Centre
Address: Unit 1 The Printworks
Manchester M4 2BS
Phone: 0161 839 8897

#407
Beef & Pudding
Cuisines: British
Average price: £26-45
Area: City Centre
Address: 37 Booth Street
Manchester M2 4AA
Phone: 0161 237 3733

#408
Sansou
Cuisines: Cafe, Juice Bar
Average price: Under £10
Area: West Didsbury
Address: 108 Barlow Moor Road
Manchester M20 2PN
Phone: 0161 445 3192

#409
Costa Coffee
Cuisines: Cafe
Average price: Under £10
Area: Spinningfields
Address: 18-20 Bridge Street
Manchester M3 3BZ
Phone: 0161 839 7281

#410
Al Bacio
Cuisines: Italian
Average price: £26-45
Area: City Centre
Address: 10-14 S King Street
Manchester M2 6DW
Phone: 0161 832 7669

#411
24 Bar and Grill
Cuisines: Bar, British
Average price: £26-45
Area: Chinatown
Address: 24 Princess Street
Manchester M1 4LY
Phone: 0161 238 4348

#412
Portland Street Restaurant & Bar
Cuisines: Bar, British
Average price: £11-25
Area: Gay Village
Address: Portland Street
Manchester M1
Phone: 0161 246 3435

#413
Bridgewater Bistro
Cuisines: Bistro
Average price: Under £10
Address: 120 Princess Road
Manchester M15 5AT

#414
**Alvinos Caribbean
Takeaway and Bakery**
Cuisines: Takeaway, Caribbean, Bakery
Average price: Under £10
Area: Rusholme
Address: 180 Great Western Street
Manchester M14 4LH
Phone: 0161 226 6407

#415
Chicken Run
Cuisines: Fast Food, Takeaway
Average price: Under £10
Address: 6 Yarburgh Street
Manchester M16 7FJ
Phone: 0161 226 6714

#416
Pizza Hut
Cuisines: Pizza, Italian
Average price: £11-25
Address: White City Way
Manchester M16 0RP

#417
Charcoal Chicken
Cuisines: Steakhouse
Average price: Under £10
Area: Rusholme
Address: 141-143 Wilmslow Road
Manchester M14 5AW
Phone: 0161 225 8800

#418
Shaygan Halal Take Away
Cuisines: Fast Food, Takeaway
Average price: Under £10
Area: Rusholme
Address: 159 Dickenson Road
Manchester M14 5HZ
Phone: 0161 248 5815

#419
Kebab King
Cuisines: Fast Food, Takeaway
Average price: Under £10
Address: 787 Rochdale Rd
Manchester M9 5XD
Phone: 0161 205 7991

#420
Mia's Sandwich Shop
Cuisines: Sandwiches
Average price: Under £10
Address: 1 Taylors Road
Manchester M32 0JJ
Phone: 0161 865 2188

#421
Sayuri Noodle Bar
Cuisines: Chinese, Fast Food, Takeaway
Average price: £11-25
Area: Fallowfield
Address: 351-353 Wilmslow Road
Manchester M14 6XS
Phone: 0800 061 2528

#422
Kyotoya
Cuisines: Japanese
Average price: £11-25
Address: 28 Copson Street
Manchester M20 3HB
Phone: 0161 445 2555

#423
Pizza Express
Cuisines: Pizza, Italian
Average price: £11-25
Address: 130 Bury New Road
Manchester M25 0AA
Phone: 0161798 4794

#424
The Little Chippy
Cuisines: Fast Food, Takeaway
Average price: Under £10
Area: Levenshulme
Address: 929 Stockport Road
Manchester M19
Phone: 0161 225 9595

#425
Carluccios
Cuisines: Italian
Average price: £11-25
Address: The Great Hall
Manchester M17 8AA
Phone: 0161 747 4973

#426
Happy Garden Takeaway
Cuisines: Chinese
Average price: Under £10
Address: 304 Parrs Wood Road
Manchester M20 6JY
Phone: 0161 434 3663

#427
Bob's Fish & Chips
Cuisines: Fish & Chips
Average price: Under £10
Area: Didsbury Village
Address: 1 School Lane
Manchester M20 6SA

#428
Club Phoenix
Cuisines: Pub, Burgers
Average price: Under £10
Area: Oxford Road Corridor
Address: 1 University Precinct
Manchester M13 9RN
Phone: 0161 272 5921

#429
Windmill Carving Room
Cuisines: British
Average price: Under £10
Address: 81 Hulme Rd
Manchester M34 2WZ
Phone: 0161 320 6144

#430
La Olla Restaurant
Cuisines: Spanish
Average price: £11-25
Area: Sale
Address: 15 Northenden Road
Manchester M33 2DH
Phone: 0161 973 3000

#431
Chop Chop
Cuisines: Chinese, Fast Food,
Takeaway, Fish & Chips
Average price: £11-25
Area: Northern Quarter
Address: 50 Great Ancoats Street
Manchester M4 5AB
Phone: 0161 228 2228

#432
Label
Cuisines: Restaurants, Lounge, Club
Average price: £26-45
Area: City Centre
Address: 78 Deansgate
Manchester M3 2FW
Phone: 0161 833 1878

#433
Bistro 1847: Manchester
Cuisines: Vegetarian
Average price: £26-45
Area: City Centre
Address: 58 Mosley St
Manchester M2 3HZ
Phone: 0161 236 1811

#434
Wings Dai Pai Dong
Cuisines: Dim Sum, Fast Food, Takeaway
Average price: Under £10
Area: City Centre
Address: 44 Cross St
Manchester M2 4
Phone: 0161 833 3388

#435
Browns
Cuisines: Bar, British
Average price: £11-25
Area: City Centre
Address: 1 York Street
Manchester M2 2AW
Phone: 0161 819 1055

#436
Axm Club
Cuisines: British, Gay Bar
Average price: £11-25
Area: Gay Village
Address: 100 Bloom Street
Manchester M1 3LY
Phone: 0845 834 0297

#437
Istanbul Express
Cuisines: Fast Food, Takeaway
Average price: Under £10
Area: Gay Village
Address: 29-31 Sackville Street
Manchester M1 3LZ
Phone: 0161 237 5555

#438
Cygnet Sandwich Bar
Cuisines: Sandwiches
Average price: Under £10
Area: Ancoats, Petersfield
Address: 18 Swan Street
Manchester M4 5JN
Phone: 0161 835 2827

#439
Florida Fried Chicken
Cuisines: Chicken Wings, Fast Food,
Takeaway, Burgers
Average price: Under £10
Area: Oxford Road Corridor
Address: 263 Upper Brook Street
Manchester M13 0HR
Phone: 0161 273 4327

#440
Tandoori Nights
Cuisines: Indian, Lounge
Average price: £26-45
Address: 252 Middleton Road
Manchester M8 4WA
Phone: 0161 740 3100

#441
Miramar Chinese Restaurant
Cuisines: Chinese, Fast Food, Takeaway
Average price: £11-25
Area: Levenshulme
Address: 1018 Stockport Road
Manchester M19 3WN
Phone: 0161 224 4986

#442
Five Guys Burgers and Fries
Cuisines: Burgers
Average price: £26-45
Address: Great Hall
Manchester M17 8AA

#443
Bella Italia
Cuisines: Italian
Average price: £11-25
Area: Northern Quarter
Address: 11-13 Piccadilly
Manchester M1 1LY
Phone: 0161 236 2342

#444
Lotus Restaurant
Cuisines: Malaysian
Average price: £11-25
Address: 289 Palatine Road
Manchester M22 4ET
Phone: 0161 945 9711

#445
Battered Cod
Cuisines: Fast Food, Takeaway,
Fish & Chips
Average price: Under £10
Address: 444 Wilmslow Road
Manchester M20 3BW
Phone: 0161 448 7520

#446
Gurkha Grill
Cuisines: Indian
Average price: £26-45
Area: West Didsbury
Address: 198 Burton Road
Manchester M20 1LH
Phone: 0161 445 3461

#447
Chorlton Eatery
Cuisines: Breakfast & Brunch,
Coffee & Tea, British
Average price: £11-25
Area: Chorlton
Address: 565 Barlow Moor Road
Manchester M21 8AE
Phone: 0161 860 0200

#448
Evuna
Cuisines: Spanish, Tapas Bar
Average price: £11-25
Area: Northern Quarter
Address: 79 Thomas Street
Manchester M4 1LW
Phone: 0161 833 1130

#449
Antonio's
Cuisines: Fast Food, Takeaway
Average price: Under £10
Area: Piccadilly
Address: 14-15 Station Approach
Manchester M1 2GH

#450
Krunchy Fried Chicken
Cuisines: Fast Food, Takeaway
Average price: Under £10
Area: Rusholme
Address: 50-52 Wilmslow Road
Manchester M14 5TQ
Phone: 0161 256 3694

#451
Purity
Cuisines: Bar, Club, Steakhouse
Average price: £26-45
Address: 36 Peter Street
Manchester M2 5GP
Phone: 0161 819 7777

#452
Pizza Hut
Cuisines: Pizza
Average price: Under £10
Area: Didsbury Village
Address: 766 Wilmslow Road
Manchester M20 2DR
Phone: 0161 434 9920

#453
Hell Fire Club
Cuisines: Soul Food
Average price: £11-25
Address: Queens Road
Manchester M9 5FF
Phone: 0161 277 9346

#454
Dixie Chickens
Cuisines: Fast Food, Takeaway
Average price: Above £46
Area: Chorlton
Address: 450 Wilbraham Road
Manchester M21 0AG
Phone: 0161 881 7910

#455
Olivien Pizza House
Cuisines: Fast Food, Takeaway
Average price: £11-25
Area: West Didsbury
Address: 126 Burton Road
Manchester M20 1JQ
Phone: 0161 434 5444

#456
New Emperor
Cuisines: Chinese
Average price: £11-25
Area: Chinatown
Address: 52-56 George Street
Manchester M1 4HF
Phone: 0161 228 2883

#457
Avalanche Bar & Restaurant
Cuisines: Italian
Average price: £11-25
Area: City Centre
Address: Booth Street
Manchester M2

#458
Café YumYum
Cuisines: Milkshake Bar,
Coffee & Tea, Sandwiches
Average price: Under £10
Area: City Centre
Address: 18 Cross Street
Manchester M2 7AE
Phone: 0161 839 1336

#459
Pret A Manger
Cuisines: Bakery, Sandwiches,
Coffee & Tea
Average price: Under £10
Address: 34 Oxford Street
Manchester M1 5EL
Phone: 0161 228 7965

#460
Rajas Pizza Bar
Cuisines: Pizza
Average price: Under £10
Area: Chinatown
Address: 84 Portland Street
Manchester M1 4GX
Phone: 0161 237 1122

#461
Louis Vuitton
Cuisines: Cafe
Average price: £11-25
Area: City Centre
Address: Exchange Sq
Manchester M3 1BD
Phone: 0161 828 0400

#462
Go Falafel
Cuisines: Falafel
Average price: Under £10
Area: Rusholme
Address: 10 Mayfair Court
Manchester M22

#463
King Kabana
Cuisines: Fast Food, Takeaway
Average price: Under £10
Area: Rusholme
Address: Unit 1 Walmer St East
Manchester M14 5SS
Phone: 0161 256 4767

#464
De Nada
Cuisines: Portuguese
Average price: £11-25
Area: Chorlton
Address: 127 Manchester Road
Manchester M21 9PG
Phone: 0161 881 6618

#465
New Ashy's
Cuisines: Restaurants
Average price: Under £10
Address: 66 Crumpsall Ln
Manchester M8 5SG
Phone: 0161 740 4447

#466
Bento King
Cuisines: British, Food Delivery Services,
Asian Fusion
Average price: £11-25
Area: Chorlton
Address: 467 Princess Road
Manchester M20 1BH
Phone: 0161 448 1710

#467
Lusitano
Cuisines: Tapas, Wine Bar
Average price: £11-25
Area: Chorlton
Address: 613 Wilbraham Road
Manchester M21 9AN
Phone: 0161 861 8880

#468
Burger King
Cuisines: American
Average price: Under £10
Address: Birchfields Road
Manchester M14 6FS
Phone: 0161 225 7925

#469
Gold Medal Chip Shop
Cuisines: Fish & Chips
Average price: Under £10
Address: 2 Agnew Road
Manchester M18 7AR
Phone: 0161 223 0426

#470
Zal Takeaway
Cuisines: Fast Food, Takeaway
Average price: £11-25
Area: West Didsbury
Address: 123 Burton Road
Manchester M20 1JP
Phone: 0161 438 2000

#471
The Drum
Cuisines: Pub, Restaurants
Average price: £11-25
Address: Chester Road
Manchester M32 8NB
Phone: 0161 866 8876

#472
The Metropolitan
Cuisines: British, Gastropub, Bar
Average price: £11-25
Area: West Didsbury
Address: 2 Lapwing Lane
Manchester M20 2WS
Phone: 0161 438 2332

#473
Arndale Food Court
Cuisines: Bakery, American
Average price: Under £10
Area: City Centre
Address: Manchester Arndale
Manchester M4 3AQ

#474
Evuna
Cuisines: Tapas Bar, Bar
Average price: £26-45
Address: 277-279 Deansgate
Manchester M3 4EW
Phone: 0161 819 2752

#475
Shere Khan
Cuisines: Indian, Pakistani
Average price: £11-25
Address: The Trafford Centre
Manchester M17 8AA
Phone: 0161 749 9900

#476
Passage To India
Cuisines: Indian, Pakistani
Average price: £26-45
Address: 168 Monton Road
Manchester M30 9GA
Phone: 0161 787 9375

#477
Didsbury Fish Bar
Cuisines: Fish & Chips
Average price: Under £10
Area: Didsbury Village
Address: 1 School Lane
Manchester M20 6SA
Phone: 0161 445 4207

#478
Pond Quay
Cuisines: Chinese
Average price: Under £10
Address: 15 Crofts Bank Road
Manchester M41 0TZ
Phone: 0161 748 0890

#479
Fuel
Cuisines: Coffee & Tea, Vegetarian
Average price: Under £10
Address: 448 Wilmslow Road
Manchester M20 3BW
Phone: 0161 448 9702

#480
Rice
Cuisines: Asian Fusion
Average price: £11-25
Area: City Centre
Address: 79 Deansgate
Manchester M3 2BW
Phone: 0161 833 0113

#481
Pizza Hut
Cuisines: Pizza
Average price: £11-25
Area: City Centre
Address: Arndale Ctr
Manchester M2 1NP
Phone: 0161 839 8307

#482
Annies Restaurant
Cuisines: British
Average price: Above £46
Area: City Centre
Address: 5 Old Bank Street
Manchester M2 7PE
Phone: 0161 839 4423

#483
Jigsaw Sandwich Bar
Cuisines: Coffee & Tea, Sandwiches
Average price: £26-45
Address: 121 Market Street
Manchester M46 0DF
Phone: 0161 1942 887333

#484
New Samsi
Cuisines: Japanese, Supermarket
Average price: £26-45
Area: Gay Village
Address: 36 Whitworth Street
Manchester M1 3NR
Phone: 0161 279 0022

#485
Martins
Cuisines: Bakery, Sandwiches
Average price: Under £10
Area: Ladybarn
Address: 104 Mauldeth Road
Manchester M14 6SQ
Phone: 0161 445 1994

#486
Panicos Kebab House
Cuisines: Fast Food, Takeaway,
Greek, Sandwiches
Average price: Under £10
Area: Chorlton
Address: 418 Barlow Moor Rd
Manchester M21 8AD
Phone: 0161 861 0613

#487
Starbucks
Cuisines: Coffee & Tea, Sandwiches
Average price: £11-25
Area: Castlefield, Spinningfields
Address: Quay St
Manchester M3 3HN
Phone: 0161 834 0836

#488
Fresh Bites
Cuisines: Fast Food, Takeaway
Average price: Under £10
Area: Northern Quarter
Address: 71 Oldham Street
Manchester M4 1LW
Phone: 0161 839 7444

#489
Nando's
Cuisines: Portuguese, Chicken Wings
Average price: £11-25
Area: City Centre
Address: Manchester Arndale
Manchester M4 3AQ
Phone: 0161 834 3073

#490
Giraffe
Cuisines: Desserts, Breakfast & Brunch
Average price: £11-25
Area: Spinningfields
Address: 3 Hardman Square
Manchester M3 3AB
Phone: 0161 839 0009

#491
Archie's
Cuisines: Fast Food, Takeaway
Average price: Under £10
Area: Oxford Road Corridor
Address: 72 Oxford Road
Manchester M1 5NH
Phone: 0161 237 1736

#492
Eastern Pearl Take Away
Cuisines: Fast Food, Takeaway
Average price: £11-25
Area: Didsbury Village
Address: 434 Wilmslow Road
Manchester M20 3BW
Phone: 0161 434 1869

#493
Koreana
Cuisines: Korean
Average price: £11-25
Area: City Centre
Address: 40a King Street West
Manchester M3 2WY
Phone: 0161 832 4330

#494
Design A Sandwich
Cuisines: Fast Food, Takeaway,
Coffee & Tea, Sandwiches
Average price: Under £10
Area: City Centre
Address: 13d Barton Arcade
Manchester M3 2BB
Phone: 0161 839 1900

#495
Dexter's Grill & Bar
Cuisines: American,
Steakhouse, Burgers
Average price: Above £46
Address: 11 The Orient
Manchester M17 8EH
Phone: 0161 1942 887333

#496
Cadishead Charcoal Grill
Cuisines: Fast Food, Takeaway
Average price: Under £10
Address: 192c Liverpool Road
Manchester M44 6FE
Phone: 0161 776 9889

#497
All Bar One
Cuisines: Lounge, European
Average price: £11-25
Area: City Centre
Address: 73 King Street
Manchester M2 4NG
Phone: 0161 830 1811

#498
Wasabi
Cuisines: Japanese, Sushi Bar, Bar
Average price: £11-25
Area: Chinatown
Address: 63 Faulkner Street
Manchester M1 4FF
Phone: 0161 228 7288

#499
Pret A Manger
Cuisines: Coffee & Tea,
Sandwiches, Desserts
Average price: £11-25
Address: 34 Brazennose Street
Manchester M2 5EA
Phone: 0161 228 228 7965

#500
Maxwells Chippy
Cuisines: Fish & Chips
Average price: Under £10
Area: Gay Village
Address: 31 Bloom Street
Manchester M1 3JE
Phone: 0161 236 9038

#1
Museum of Science & Industry
Category: Museum, Art Gallery
Address: Liverpool Road
Manchester M3 4FP
Phone: 0161 832 2244

#2
Band on the Wall
Category: Bar, Music Venues,
Jazz & Blues
Address: 25 Swan Street
Manchester M4 5JZ
Phone: 0161 834 1786

#3
Manchester Art Gallery
Category: Art Gallery
Address: Mosley Street
Manchester M2 3JL
Phone: 0161 235 8888

#4
Night & Day
Category: Bar, Music Venues
Address: 26 Oldham Street
Manchester M1 1JN
Phone: 0161 236 4597

#5
Imperial War Museum North
Category: Museum
Address: Trafford Wharf Road
Manchester M17 1TZ
Phone: 0161 836 4000

#6
Manchester Craft
and Design Centre
Category: Arts & Crafts, Art Gallery
Address: 17 Oak St
Manchester M4 5JD
Phone: 0161 832 4274

#7
Dulcimer
Category: Bar, Music Venues
Address: 567 Wilbraham Road
Manchester M21 0AE
Phone: 0161 860 6444

#8
The Deaf Institute
Category: Lounge, Music Venues
Address: 135 Grosvenor Street
Manchester M1 7HE
Phone: 0161 276 9350

#9
The Briton's Protection
Category: Pub, Music Venues
Address: 50 Great Bridgewater Street
Manchester M1 5LE
Phone: 0161 236 5895

#10
Old Trafford
Category: Stadium
Address: Sir Matt Busby Way
Manchester M16 0RA
Phone: 0161 868 8000

#11
O2 Apollo Manchester
Category: Music Venues, Theatre,
Comedy Club
Address: Stockport Road
Manchester M12 6AP
Phone: 0844 477 7677

#12
Nexus Art Cafe
Category: Music Venues,
Lounge, Coffee & Tea
Address: 2 Dale Street
Manchester M1 1JW
Phone: 0161 236 0100

#13
Manchester Academy 2
Category: Music Venues, Bar
Address: Oxford Road
Manchester M13 9PR
Phone: 0161 275 2930

#14
St Ann's Church
Category: Music Venues, Church
Address: St Ann's Street
Manchester M2 7LF
Phone: 0161 834 1161

#15
Contact
Category: Theatre, Music Venues
Address: Oxford Road
Manchester M15 6JA
Phone: 0161 274 0600

#16
Manchester Museum
Category: Museum, Art Gallery
Address: Oxford Road
Manchester M13 9PL
Phone: 0161 275 2634

#17
Manchester Academy
Category: Music Venues
Address: Oxford Road
Manchester M13 9PR
Phone: 0161 275 2930

#18
Trafford Centre
Category: Cinema, Shopping Centre
Address: 130 Peel Avenue
Manchester M17 8AA
Phone: 0161 746 7777

#19
**Manchester Craft
& Design Centre**
Category: Art Gallery
Address: 776 Chester Road
Manchester M32 0QH
Phone: 07024 069543

#20
The Castle Hotel
Category: Pub, Music Venues
Address: 66 Oldham Street
Manchester M4 1LE
Phone: 0161 237 9485

#21
Common
Category: Bar, Music Venues
Address: 39 - 41 Edge Street
Manchester M4 1HW
Phone: 0161 832 9245

#22
Phones 4u Arena
Category: Theatre, Stadium,
Music Venues
Address: Victoria Station
Manchester M3 1AR
Phone: 0161 950 5000

#23
The Star and Garter
Category: Pub, Club, Music Venues
Address: 18-20 Fairfield Street
Manchester M1 2QF
Phone: 0161 273 6726

#24
The Roadhouse
Category: Music Venues
Address: 8 Newton Street
Manchester M1 2AN
Phone: 0161 237 9789

#25
Retro Bar
Category: Music Venues, Dive Bar
Address: 78 Sackville Street
Manchester M1 3NJ
Phone: 0161 274 4892

#26
The Temple
Category: Music Venues, Dive Bar
Address: 100 Great Bridgewater Street
Manchester M1 5JW
Phone: 0161 278 1610

#27
Odeon
Category: Cinema
Address: 27 Withy Grove
Manchester M4 2BS
Phone: 0871 224 4007

#28
Manchester City Football Club
Category: Stadium
Address: Rowsley Street
Manchester M11 3FF
Phone: 0161 438 7650

#29
**Manchester Food
and Drink Festival**
Category: Festival
Address: Albert Sq
Manchester M2 5DB
Phone: 0161 839 4353

#30
Cornerhouse
Category: Cinema, Bar, Cafe
Address: 70 Oxford Street
Manchester M1 5NH
Phone: 0161 200 1500

#31
Manchester Opera House
Category: Theatre, Opera & Ballet
Address: Quay Street
Manchester M3 3HP
Phone: 0161 823 1700

#32
**Hop & Grape Manchester
Academy 3**
Category: Music Venues, Bar
Address: Oxford Rd
Manchester M13 9PR
Phone: 0161 275 2930

#33
Richard Goodall Gallery
Category: Art Gallery
Address: 59 Thomas Street
Manchester M4 1NA
Phone: 0161 832 3435

#34
Royal Northern College of Music
Category: Music Venues,
Cultural Center, Theatre
Address: 124 Oxford Road
Manchester M13 9RD
Phone: 0161 907 5200

#35
The Ram
Category: Music Venues, Pub
Address: 393 Wilmslow Road
Manchester M20 4WA
Phone: 0161 283 9296

#36
The Ritz
Category: Club, Music Venues, Bar
Address: Whitworth Street W
Manchester M1 5WW
Phone: 0161 236 3234

#37
Cineworld
Category: Cinema
Address: Wilmslow Road
Manchester M20 5PG
Phone: 0871 200 2000

#38
Grand Central
Category: Music Venues, Pub
Address: 80 Oxford Road
Manchester M1 5NH
Phone: 0161 236 0890

#39
Eastern Bloc Records
Category: Music Venues, Cafe
Address: 5A Stevenson Square
Manchester M1 1DN
Phone: 0161 228 6555

#40
Richard Goodall Gallery
Category: Art Gallery, Museum
Address: 103 High Street
Manchester M4 1HQ
Phone: 0161 834 3330

#41
Dancehouse Theatre
Category: Theatre
Address: 10a Oxford Rd
Manchester M1 5QA
Phone: 0161 237 9753

#42
**The Frog and Bucket
Comedy Club**
Category: Social Club, Comedy Club
Address: 102 Oldham Street
Manchester M4 1LJ
Phone: 0161 236 9805

#43
The Garratt
Category: Pub, Music Venues
Address: 127 Princess Street
Manchester M1 7AG
Phone: 0161 237 5111

#44
Twenty Twenty Two
Category: Bar, Art Gallery,
Music Venues
Address: 20 Dale Street
Manchester M1 1EZ
Phone: 0161 237 9360

#45
The Printworks
Category: Arcade, Cinema, Bar
Address: 27 Withy Grove
Manchester M4 2BS
Phone: 0161 829 8000

#46
The Ruby Lounge
Category: Club, Music Venues
Address: 28-34 High Street
Manchester M4 1QB
Phone: 0161 834 1392

#47
CUBE
Category: Art Gallery
Address: 113-115 Portland Street
Manchester M1 6DW
Phone: 0161 237 5525

#48
People's History Museum
Category: Museum
Address: Left Bank
Manchester M3 3ER
Phone: 0161 838 9190

#49
Z-Arts
Category: Theatre, Art Gallery,
Music Venues
Address: 335 Stretford Road
Manchester M15 5ZA
Phone: 0161 226 1912

#50
Victoria Baths
Category: Museum,
Venues & Event Space
Address: Hathersage Road
Manchester M13 0FE
Phone: 0161 224 2020

#51
Manchester 235
Category: Gambling, Chinese, Bar
Address: 2 Watson Street
Manchester M3 4LP
Phone: 0161 828 0300

#52
**Manchester Metropolitan
Students Union**
Category: Social Club, Lounge
Address: Grosvenor Square
Manchester M15 6BH
Phone: 0161 247 1162

#53
Chetham's School of Music
Category: Specialty School,
Music Venues, Recording Studio
Address: Long Millgate
Manchester M3 1SB
Phone: 0161 834 9644

#54
Whitworth Art Gallery
Category: Art Gallery
Address: Oxford Road
Manchester M15 6ER
Phone: 0161 275 7450

#55
Sunshine Studio
Category: Dance School,
Theatre, Sports Club
Address: 52 Newton Street
Manchester M1 1ED
Phone: 0161 228 6814

#56
Charlies Karaoke Bar
Category: Karaoke, Venues & Event Space,
Music Venues
Address: 1 Harter Street
Manchester M1 6
Phone: 0161 237 9898

#57
The Three Minute Theatre
Category: Theatre
Address: 35-39 Oldham Street
Manchester M1 1JG
Phone: 0161 834 4517

#58
**Manchester United Museum
and Tour Centre**
Category: Museum
Address: Sir Matt Busby Way
Manchester M16 0RA
Phone: 0870 442 1994

#59
John Rylands Library
Category: Library, Museum
Address: 150 Deansgate
Manchester M3 3EH
Phone: 0161 306 0555

#60
Club Academy
Category: Music Venues
Address: Oxford Road
Manchester M13 9PR
Phone: 0161 275 2930

#61
National Squash Centre
Category: Stadium
Address: Rowsley Street
Manchester M11 3FF
Phone: 0161 220 3800

#62
Nicolas
Category: Winerie
Address: 8 Barton Arcade
Manchester M3 2BB
Phone: 0161 834 7328

#63
The Whim Wham Cafe
Category: Jazz & Blues, Bar, British
Address: Arch 64 Whitworth Street West
Manchester M1 5WQ
Phone: 0161 236 0930

#64
Pitcher & Piano
Category: Pub, Music Venues
Address: Arch 9 and 10
Manchester M1 5LH
Phone: 0161 839 6117

#65
Belle Vue Greyhound Stadium
Category: Stadium
Address: Kirkmanshulme Lane
Manchester M18 7BA
Phone: 0870 840 7557

#66
FAC 251: The Factory
Category: Club, Music Venues
Address: 112-118 Princess St
Manchester M1 7EN
Phone: 0161 272 7251

#67
Sound Control
Category: Club, Music Venues
Address: 1 New Wakefield Street
Manchester M1 5NP
Phone: 0161 236 0340

#68
Dry Bar
Category: Bar, Music Venues
Address: 29-30 Oldham St
Manchester M1 1JN
Phone: 0161 236 9840

#69
Manchester Jewish Museum
Category: Museum, Art Gallery
Address: 190 Cheetham Hill Road
Manchester M8 8LW
Phone: 0161 834 9879

#70
Showcase Cinema
Category: Cinema
Address: Hyde Road
Manchester M12 5AL
Phone: 0871 220 1000

#71
Venus
Category: Club, Music Venues
Address: 42 Maybrook House
Manchester M3 2EQ
Phone: 0161 834 7288

#72
Alliance Française
de Manchester
Category: Social Club
Address: 55 Portland Street
Manchester M1 3HP
Phone: 0161 236 7117

#73
Incognito Gallery
Category: Art Gallery
Address: 5 Stevenson Square
Manchester M1 1DN
Phone: 0161 228 7999

#74
Genting Club
Category: Gambling, Lounge
Address: 110 Portland Street
Manchester M1 4RL
Phone: 0161 228 0077

#75
Castlefield Events Arena
Category: Music Venues, Local Flavour
Address: 101 Liverpool Road
Manchester M3 4JN
Phone: 0161 834 4026

#76
The Gallery Café
Category: Coffee & Tea, Art Gallery
Address: Mosley Street
Manchester M2 3JL
Phone: 0161 235 8888

#77
Lowry Art Gallery
Category: Art Gallery
Address: Pier 8
Manchester M50 3AZ
Phone: 0161 876 2121

#78
Gallery Of Costume
Category: Museum
Address: Wilmslow Road
Manchester M14 5LL
Phone: 0161 224 5217

#79
Matt and Phreds
Category: Club, Music Venues
Address: 64 Tib Street
Manchester M4 1LW
Phone: 0161 839 7187

#80
Waterside Arts Centre
Category: Art Gallery, Theatre
Address: 1 Waterside Plaza
Manchester M33 7ZF
Phone: 0161 912 5616

#81
Bouzouki Restaurant
Category: Greek, Music Venues
Address: 88 Princess Street
Manchester M1 6NG
Phone: 0161 236 9282

#82
**Museum Of The Greater
Manchester Police**
Category: Museum
Address: Newton Street
Manchester M1 1LN
Phone: 0161 856 3287

#83
The Venue
Category: Club, Music Venues
Address: 29 Jacksons Row
Manchester M2 5WD
Phone: 0161 834 3793

#84
Pitcher & Piano
Category: Pub, Music Venues
Address: Lower Mosley Street
Manchester M1 5LH
Phone: 0161 839 6117

#85
Manchester Irish Festival
Category: Festival
Address: Albert Square
Manchester M2 5RT
Phone: 0161 228 0662

#86
Generation Pop
Category: Art Gallery
Address: E3 New York Street
Manchester M1 4BD
Phone: 0161 848 0880

#87
National Winter Ales Festival
Category: Festival
Address: 371 Oldham Road
Manchester M40 8RR
Phone: 01727 867201

#88
Platt Chapel
Category: Music Venues, Venues & Event
Space, Party & Event Planning
Address: 186 Wilmslow Road
Manchester M14 5LL
Phone: 0161 478 4203

#89
Espionage Manchester
Category: Theatre, Florist
Address: Quay Street Manchester M3
Phone: 07502 000072

#90
**The Kurdish Creative
Film Centre**
Category: Festival, Cinema
Address: 46-50 Oldham Street
Manchester M1 1
Phone: 0161 234 2781

#91
**Museum of Transport
Greater Manchester**
Category: Museum
Address: Boyle Street
Manchester M8 8UW
Phone: 0161 205 2122

#92
Bridgewater Hall
Category: Music Venues, Bar,
Opera & Ballet
Address: Lower Mosley Street
Manchester M2 3WS
Phone: 0844 907 9000

#93
Castlefield Gallery
Category: Art Gallery
Address: 2 Hewitt St
Manchester M15 4GB
Phone: 0161 832 8034

#94
Kraak
Category: Art Gallery, Music Venues
Address: 11 Stevenson Square
Manchester M1 1DB
Phone: 07855 939129

#95
Colin Jellicoe
Category: Art Gallery
Address: 82 Portland Street
Manchester M1 4QX
Phone: 0161 236 2716

#96
Gamerbase
Category: Arcade
Address: 90 Market Street
Manchester M1 1PB
Phone: 0161 834 2312

#97
Picturehouse
Category: Bar, Music Venues
Address: 25 Swan St
Manchester M4 5JZ
Phone: 0161 834 1786

#98
Odeon Trafford Centre
Category: Cinema
Address: 201 The Dome
Manchester M17 8DF
Phone: 0871 224 4007

#99
Lounge 31
Category: Bar, Music Venues
Address: 31 Withy Grove
Manchester M4 2BJ
Phone: 0161 819 4710

#100
Electric Circus
Category: Gambling
Address: 110 Portland Street
Manchester M1 4RL
Phone: 0161 228 0077

#101
Goethe-Institut
Category: Social Club, Library
Address: 56 Oxford Street
Manchester M1 6EU
Phone: 0161 237 1077

#102
Mint Casino
Category: Gambling, Lounge
Address: 40-44 Princess Street
Manchester M1 6DE
Phone: 0161 236 3034

#103
Masako Art & Flowers
Category: Art Gallery, Florist
Address: 17 Ellesmere St
Manchester M15 5
Phone: 0161 839 5175

#104
**KinoFilm European
Short Film**
Category: Festival
Address: Unit 7 St Wilfred's Enterprise
Centre Manchester M15 5BJ
Phone: 07954 360989

#105
The Lenagan Library
Category: Library, Universities, Cinema
Address: University of Manchester Oxford
Road Manchester M13 9QS
Phone: 0161 275 4985

#106
Creative Recycling
Category: Art Gallery
Address: 40 Beech Road
Manchester M21 9EL
Phone: 0161 881 4422

#107
Pados House
Category: Theatre
Address: St Marys Rd
Manchester M25
Phone: 0161 773 7729

#108
Wendy J Levy Contemporary Art
Category: Art Gallery
Address: 17 Warburton Street
Manchester M20 6WA
Phone: 0161 446 4880

#109
The International 3
Category: Art Gallery
Address: 8 Fairfield St
Manchester M1 2
Phone: 0161 237 3336

#110
Phoenix Gallery
Category: Art Gallery
Address: 17 Ellesmere Street
Manchester M15 4JY
Phone: 0161 839 2232

#111
Powerleague Trafford
Category: Football, Stadium
Address: Trafford Way
Manchester M17 8DD
Phone: 0161 755 9720

#112
The Press Club
Category: Social Club
Address: 2 Queens Street
Manchester M2 5JB
Phone: 0161 834 8562

#113
Novus Contemporary Art
Category: Art Gallery
Address: Burton Road
Manchester M20 2LW
Phone: 0161 438 3888

#114
Ladbrokes
Category: Gambling
Address: 44 Portland Street
Manchester M1 4GS
Phone: 0800 022 3454

#115
Odeon Cinema
Category: Cinema
Address: 90 Great Bridgewater Street
Manchester M1 5JW
Phone: 0871 224 4007

#116
Bigshots
Category: Arcade
Address: Piccadilly Station
Manchester M1 2BN
Phone: 0161 237 3484

#117
**Prestwich Church
Institute & Mens Club**
Category: Social Club,
Venues & Event Space
Address: Bury New Road
Manchester M25 1AR
Phone: 0161 773 6057

#118
Castle Gallery
Category: Art Gallery
Address: Trafford Centre
Manchester M17 8AA
Phone: 0161 748 7237

#119
Sandbar
Category: Pub, Music Venues
Address: 120 Grosvenor Street
Manchester M1 7HL
Phone: 0161 273 1552

#120
Central Methodist Hall
Category: Music Venues,
Venues & Event Space
Address: Oldham Street
Manchester M1 1JQ
Phone: 0161 236 5194

#121
Stretford Ex Servicemens Club
Category: Social Club
Address: 30 Talbot Road
Manchester M16 0PF
Phone: 0161 872 2732

#122
Altrincham Rehearsal Studio
Category: Dance Studio, Music Venues
Address: Southmoor Road
Manchester M23 9DS
Phone: 0161 946 0008

#123
Contemporary Six, The Gallery
Category: Art Gallery, Arts & Crafts
Address: The Royal Exchange Arcade
Manchester M2 7EA
Phone: 0161 835 2666

#124
Spice UK
Category: Social Club, Sports & Leisure
Address: 13 Thorpe St
Manchester M16 9PR
Phone: 0161 873 8788

#125
Antwerp Mansion
Category: Music Venues
Address: Wilmslow Rd
Manchester M14 5BT
Phone: 07429 578193

#126
Phifer Network
Category: Social Club
Address: 2 Ladybarn Crescent
Manchester M14 6UU
Phone: 07741 606128

#127
The Firework Shop
Category: Wedding Planning
Address: Lowerwhittle farm
Manchester OL10 2QF
Phone: 01706 629926

#128
AMBA Lifestyle
Category: Art Gallery
Address: 15 Market Place
Manchester M24 6AE
Phone: 0161 222 3633

#129
Club V
Category: Music Venues
Address: 111 Deansgate
Manchester M3 2BQ
Phone: 0161 834 9975

#130
Happystorm Theatre
Category: Theatre
Address: 47 Chorlton St
Manchester M1 3FY
Phone: 07547 711839

#131
Dry Live
Category: Club, Music Venues
Address: 28-30 Oldham Street
Manchester M1 1JN
Phone: 0161 236 1444

#132
**Manchester
Photographic Gallery**
Category: Art Gallery
Address: 45 Dale Street
Manchester M1 2HF
Phone: 0161 236 7224

#133
Philharmonic String Quartet
Category: Music Venues, Theatre,
Wedding Planning
Address: 307 Vicus 73 Liverpool Road
Manchester M3 4AQ
Phone: 07545 991621

#134
Hit and Run
Category: Club, Music Venues
Address: Area 51 Eclipse House
Manchester M1 5WZ
Phone: 0161 236 1316

#135
The Edge Theatre & Arts Centre
Category: Theatre
Address: The Edge Theatre & Arts Centre
Manchester Road Manchester M21 9JG
Phone: 0161 282 9776

#136
The Magic of Alex D Fisher
Category: Music Venues, Theatre
Address: 77 Wilton road
Manchester M8 4PD
Phone: 07961 050230

#137
Fitzroy Social Club
Category: Social Club
Address: Durham Street
Manchester M43 6DT
Phone: 0161 370 2400

#138
A1 Ostrich Feathers Manchester
Category: Wedding Planning
Address: Failsworth Antique Mill
Manchester M35
Phone: 0161 219 1082

#139
Ladbrokes
Category: Gambling
Address: 2 Station Approach
Manchester M60 7
Phone: 0800 022 3454

#140
UK Talent Searcher
Category: Theatre
Address: 682 bolton road
Manchester M27 8FH
Phone: 07986 013049

#141
Grosvenor Casino
Category: Casino
Address: Parrswood Entertainment Centre
Manchester M20 5PG
Phone: 0161 669 7165

#142
Social Circle
Category: Social Club
Address: 515 Parrs Wood Road
Manchester M20 5
Phone: 07767 686177

#143
Yvonne Dixon Events
Category: Wedding Planning
Address: 403 Moorside Road
Manchester M41 5SD
Phone: 0161 202 9084

#144
Starlite Productions
Category: Venues & Event Space,
Wedding Planning
Address: 6 Lodge Road
Manchester M26 1AL
Phone: 0161 959 6250

#145
Sand Limeand Soda
Category: Art Gallery
Address: 26g vernon mill
Manchester SK1
Phone: 07951 356328

#146
Cats Drama
Category: Theatre
Address: 54 Colshaw Road
Manchester M23 2QQ
Phone: 0161 945 1051

#147
The Firework Shop
Category: Wedding Planning
Address: Lower Whittle Farm
Manchester OL10 2QF
Phone: 07805 837854

#148
Grosvenor Casino
Category: Casino
Address: 35 George Street
Manchester M1 4HQ
Phone: 0161 236 7121

#149
Actors Centre North
Category: Specialty School, Theatre
Address: 21-31 Oldham St
Manchester M1 1JG
Phone: 0161 819 2513

#150
Tracey Cartledge Mosaic Studio
Category: Art Gallery
Address: 44 Ellesmere Street
Manchester M15 4JY
Phone: 0161 860 0387

#151
Premier Musicians
Category: Venues & Event Space, Wedding
Planning, Music Venues
Address: 307 Vicus 73 Liverpool Road
Manchester M3 4AQ
Phone: 07545 991621

#152
Castlefield Quartet
Category: Venues & Event Space, Wedding
Planning, Theatre
Address: 307 Vicus 73 Liverpool Road
Manchester M3 4AQ
Phone: 07545 991621

#153
Manchester Pride
Category: Arcade
Address: Ducie Street
Manchester M1 2JW
Phone: 0161 236 7474

#154
Desipride Entertainment
Category: Music Venues
Address: 10 Thorncombe Road
Manchester M16 7YB
Phone: 07814 005501

#155
ukshadicom
Category: Social Club
Address: 13 flat4 rectory road crumpsel
Manchester M8 5EA
Phone: 07405 660941

#156
Honest Policy
Category: Social Club
Address: 29 cawdor road
Manchester M14 6LS
Phone: 07709 840065

#157
Medium May
Category: Psychics & Astrologers
Address: 14 Ringwood Avenue
Manchester M12 5TP
Phone: 0161 248 5338

#158
**Levenshulme Bowling
& Social Club**
Category: Social Club
Address: 1 Burnage Range
Manchester M19 2HQ
Phone: 0161 224 4122

#159
Royal British Legion
Category: Social Club, Music Venues
Address: 225 Bury Old Road
Manchester M25 1JE
Phone: 0161 773 5736

#160
Capitol Theatre
Category: Theatre
Address: Cavendish Street
Manchester M15 6BH
Phone: 0161 247 1305

#161
Koolkarts
Category: Kids Activities
Address: 127 Chorley Road
Manchester M27 4AA
Phone: 0161 950 9829

#162
Mariyka's Dance Studio
Category: Dance School
Address: 25-27 Rutland Street
Manchester M27 6AU
Phone: 0161 728 3142

#163
Aukesson Art
Category: Art Gallery
Address: 43 Bucklow Drive
Manchester M22 4WA
Phone: 07533 765999

#164
The Yard Theatre
Category: Theatre
Address: Old Birley Street
Manchester M15 5RF
Phone: 0161 226 7696

#165
Hough End Hall
Category: Castle
Address: 95 Nell Lane
Manchester M21 7RL
Phone: 0161 861 9986

#166
Walkden Labour Club
Category: Social Club
Address: 1 Cecil Street
Manchester M28 3BR
Phone: 0161 790 2915

#167
St. Josephs Players
Category: Theatre
Address: High Legh Old Hall Mill Lane
Manchester M46 0RG
Phone: 01942 674784

#168
Olivers's Personal Portraits
Category: Art Gallery
Address: 21 Farleigh close
Manchester BL5 3ES
Phone: 07850 662758

#169
The Lowry
Category: Art Gallery, Theatre
Address: Pier 8 Salford M50 3AZ
Phone: 0161 876 2121

#170
Heaven
Category: Bar, Club, Music Venues
Address: 36 Peter Street
Manchester M2 5GP
Phone: 0161 819 7798

#171
**Manchester
Geographical Society**
Category: Social Club
Address: 6 Mount Street
Manchester M2 5NS
Phone: 0161 834 2965

#172
Tib Lane Gallery
Category: Art Gallery
Address: 14a Tib Lane
Manchester M2 4JA
Phone: 0161 834 6928

#173
Urban Talent
Category: Theatre
Address: 1 Oxford Court
Manchester M2 3WQ
Phone: 0161 228 6866

#174
St. James Club
Category: Social Club
Address: 45 Spring Garden
Manchester M2 2BG
Phone: 0161 829 3000

#175
Canyon Associates
Category: Arcade
Address: 6 Hewitt Street
Manchester M15 4GB
Phone: 0161 245 4600

#176
Actors Direct
Category: Theatre
Address: 109 Portland Street
Manchester M1 6DN
Phone: 0161 237 1904

#177
Silent Way
Category: Theatre
Address: 384 Deansgate
Manchester M3 4LA
Phone: 0161 832 2111

#178
Nigel Martin Smith
Category: Theatre
Address: 28 Queen Street
Manchester M2 5LF
Phone: 0161 834 4500

#179
Art Lounge
Category: Art Gallery
Address: 8 The Triangle
Manchester M4 3TR
Phone: 0161 832 8228

#180
Guide Bridge Theatre
Category: Theatre
Address: Audenshaw Road
Manchester M34 5HJ
Phone: 0161 330 8078

#181
Pitcher & Piano
Category: Pub, Music Venues
Address: Great Bridgwater Square
Manchester M2 3WS
Phone: 0161 228 7888

#182
Lime Management
Category: Theatre
Address: 1 Oxford Court
Manchester M2 3WQ
Phone: 0161 236 0827

#183
Nidges Casting Agency
Category: Theatre
Address: Half Moon Chambers
Manchester M2 1HN
Phone: 0161 832 8259

#184
Blyth Gallery
Category: Art Gallery
Address: 3 Brazil Street
Manchester M1 3PJ
Phone: 0161 236 1004

#185
Actors Group
Category: Theatre
Address: 21-31 Oldham Street
Manchester M1 1JG
Phone: 0161 834 4466

#186
Breaking Cycles
Category: Theatre
Address: 8 Lower Ormond Street
Manchester M1 5QF
Phone: 0161 237 1655

#187
Alexander Forbes
Category: Insurance, Art Gallery
Address: 30-32 Charlotte Street
Manchester M1 4FD
Phone: 0161 228 0721

#188
Intercity Casting
Category: Theatre
Address: Portland Street
Manchester M1 3LF
Phone: 0161 238 4950

#189
NQ Live
Category: Club, Music Venues
Address: Tib Street
Manchester M4 1LN
Phone: 0161 834 8188

#190
Leaf Street
Category: Theatre
Address: 75 Rockdove Avenue
Manchester M15 5EH
Phone: 0161 232 7326

#191
The Engine House
Category: Theatre, Music Venues
Address: 3 Cambridge St
Manchester M1 5BY
Phone: 07874 152338

#192
Musicans Ltd String Quartet
Category: Theatre
Address: 38 City Road East
Manchester M15 4QL
Phone: 07957 994889

#193
Electriks
Category: Theatre
Address: 24 Lever Street 3rd Floor
Manchester M1 1DZ
Phone: 0161 278 5650

#194
J B Associates
Category: Theatre
Address: 1-3 Stevenson Square
Manchester M1 1DN
Phone: 0161 237 1808

#195
Ear To The Ground (North)
Category: Arcade
Address: 11-13 Spear Street
Manchester M1 1JU
Phone: 0161 237 9786

#196
Hyper Media
Category: Arcade
Address: 59 Piccadilly
Manchester M1 2AQ
Phone: 0161 660 7055

#197
Orpheus String Quartet
Category: Venues & Event Space,
Wedding Planning, Theatre
Address: 307 Vicus 73 Liverpool Road
Manchester M3 4AQ
Phone: 07545 991621

#198
Amber
Category: Theatre
Address: 5 Newton Street
Manchester M1 1HL
Phone: 0161 228 0236

#199
Natural Eye Gallery
Category: Art Gallery
Address: 17 Oak Street
Manchester M4 5JD
Phone: 0161 834 3883

#200
**Ivc Social Sporting
& Cultural Activities**
Category: Social Club
Address: 94-96 Grosvenor Street
Manchester M1 7HL
Phone: 0161 273 2316

#201
KMC
Category: Theatre
Address: 48 Great Ancoats Street
Manchester M4 5AB
Phone: 0161 237 3009

#202
T R C Management
Category: Theatre
Address: 23 New Mount Street
Manchester M4 4DE
Phone: 0161 953 4091

#203
Sparklestreet HQ
Category: Theatre
Address: 18 Sparkle Street
Manchester M1 2NA
Phone: 0161 273 3435

#204
Charabanc Music Management
Category: Theatre
Address: 18 Sparkle Street
Manchester M1 2NA
Phone: 0161 273 5554

#205
T1 Telecoms
Category: Theatre
Address: 2 Jersey Street
Manchester M4 6JB
Phone: 0161 237 1411

#206
Artzu Gallery
Category: Art Gallery
Address: Great Ancoats Street
Manchester M4 5AD
Phone: 0161 228 3001

#207
Proper Job Theatre Company
Category: Theatre
Address: 41 Old Birley Street
Manchester M15 5RF
Phone: 0161 227 9787

#208
Manchester Jazz Festival
Category: Theatre
Address: 37 Ducie Street
Manchester M1 2JW
Phone: 0161 228 0662

#209
The Acting Studio
Category: Theatre
Address: 121 Princess Street
Manchester M1 7AD
Phone: 0161 228 0445

#210
S K Sports & Leisure
Category: Stadium
Address: 10a Lockett Street
Manchester M8 8EE
Phone: 0161 834 0351

#211
Direct 2 U
Category: Arcade
Address: 57a Derby Street
Manchester M8 8HW
Phone: 0161 832 7452

#212
Bullet Management
Category: Theatre
Address: Charlton Place
Manchester M12 6HS
Phone: 0161 274 3000

#213
Dance Initiative Greater Manchester
Category: Theatre
Address: Zion Arts Centretretford Road
Manchester M15 5ZA
Phone: 0161 232 7179

#214
Grosvenor Casino
Category: Casino
Address: 2 Ramsgate Street
Manchester M8 9SG
Phone: 0161 831 6370

#215
Icon Actors Management
Category: Theatre
Address: Tanzaro House
Manchester M12 6FZ
Phone: 0161 273 3344

#216
Temperance World Media
Category: Theatre
Address: 12 Hyde Road
Manchester M12 6BQ
Phone: 0161 275 9000

#217
The Manchester Young People's Theatre
Category: Theatre
Address: Devas Street
Manchester M15 6JA
Phone: 01604 704900

#218
Polish Parish Club
Category: Social Club
Address: 196 Lloyd Street North
Manchester M14 4QB
Phone: 0161 226 2544

#219
Creative Recycling Handcrafted
Category: Art Gallery
Address: 42 ST. Hildas Road
Manchester M16 9PQ
Phone: 0161 848 0488

#220
One21 Designs
Category: Theatre
Address: Suite 10 4th Floor
Manchester M12 6JH
Phone: 0161 273 3121

#221
West Indian Sports & Social Club
Category: Social Club
Address: Westwood Street
Manchester M14 4SW
Phone: 0161 226 7236

#222
Grand Central Square
Category: Pub, Cinema
Address: Wellington Road
South Stockport SK1 3TA
Phone: 0161 477 6080

#223
Feelgood Theatre Productions
Category: Theatre
Address: 21 Lindum Avenue
Manchester M16 9NQ
Phone: 0161 862 9212

#224
English Martyrs Parish Centre
Category: Social Club
Address: Alexandra Road South
Manchester M16 8GF
Phone: 0161 226 1107

#225
Old Trafford Conservative Club
Category: Social Club
Address: 124 Seymour Grove
Manchester M16 0FF
Phone: 0161 881 1339

#226
Cambos
Category: Social Club
Address: 17 Albert Street
Manchester M1 3HZ
Phone: 0161 237 1723

#227
IndyManBeerCon - Independent Manchester Beer Convention
Category: Festival
Address: Hathersage Road
Manchester M13 0FE
Phone: 0161 224 2020

#228
Polish Circle Club
Category: Social Club
Address: 433 Cheetham Hill Road
Manchester M8 0PF
Phone: 0161 740 9432

#229
Darley Lawn Tennis & Social Club
Category: Social Club
Address: Wood Road North
Manchester M16 9QG
Phone: 0161 881 3203

#230
Gorton Villa Social
Category: Social Club
Address: 34 Gortonvilla Walk
Manchester M12 5ES
Phone: 0161 223 2879

#231
Rusholme Conservative Club
Category: Social Club
Address: Antwerp House
Manchester M14 5RF
Phone: 0161 224 1897

#232
Whizzkiddzz
Category: Arcade
Address: 5 Grosvenor Road
Manchester M16 8JP
Phone: 0161 226 1071

#233
Greater Manchester Bangladesh Association
Category: Social Club
Address: 19a Birch Lane
Manchester M13 0NW
Phone: 0161 225 4012

#234
Pantoworld
Category: Theatre
Address: 29 Milverton Road Victoria Park
Manchester M14 5PJ
Phone: 0161 225 9339

#235
Bunny Lewis Enterprises
Category: Theatre
Address: 41 Alexandra Road South
Manchester M16 8GH
Phone: 0161 227 9879

#236
St Kentigerns Social Club
Category: Social Club
Address: Hart Road
Manchester M14 7BB
Phone: 0161 224 2033

#237
Abraham Moss Centre Theatre
Category: Theatre
Address: 140 Crescent Road
Manchester M8 5UF
Phone: 0161 908 8327

#238
Longsight & District Sports & Social Club
Category: Social Club
Address: Kirkmanshulme Lane
Manchester M12 4WB
Phone: 0161 224 3213

#239
Railway Club
Category: Social Club
Address: 837-839 Chester Road
Manchester M32 0RN
Phone: 0161 865 6755

#240
Royal British Legion
Category: Social Club
Address: 86 Belle Vue Street
Manchester M12 5PP
Phone: 0161 223 0688

#241
Crumpsall Constitutional Club
Category: Social Club
Address: 2 Lansdowne Road
Manchester M8 5SH
Phone: 0161 740 1252

#242
Movin Music
Category: Theatre
Address: 33 Albany Road
Manchester M21 0BH
Phone: 0161 881 9227

#243
Artys
Category: Art Gallery
Address: 412 Wilbraham Road
Manchester M21 0SD
Phone: 0161 861 7177

#244
Trafford Park Heritage Shop
Category: Museum
Address: Eleventh St
Manchester M17 1JF
Phone: 0161 848 9173

#245
Edward Cervenka
Category: Theatre
Address: 30 Wyverne Road
Manchester M21 0ZN
Phone: 0161 881 4314

#246
Lip Service
Category: Theatre
Address: 116 Longford Road
Manchester M21 9NP
Phone: 0161 881 2638

#247
Bar Baroque
Category: Music Venues
Address: 478 Wilbraham Rd
Manchester M21 9AS
Phone: 0161 881 9130

#248
Barnes Green Catholic Social Club
Category: Social Club
Address: 6 Factory Lane
Manchester M9 8AB
Phone: 0161 205 1053

#249
Conservative & Unionist Club
Category: Social Club
Address: 746 Rochdale Road
Manchester M9 4BP
Phone: 0161 205 5252

#250
Lithuanian Social Club
Category: Social Club
Address: 121 Middleton Road
Manchester M8 4JY
Phone: 0161 740 5039

#251
Rhythm & Rhyme
Category: Arcade
Address: 58 Corkland Road
Manchester M21 8XH
Phone: 0161 860 0911

#252
Trafford Athletic Club
Category: Stadium
Address: Ryebank Road
Manchester M21 9TA
Phone: 0161 881 4488

#253
The Clayton Conservative Club Company
Category: Social Club
Address: 625 Ashton New Road
Manchester M11 4RX
Phone: 0161 223 1128

#254
The Buzz
Category: Arcade
Address: Mauldeth Road West
Manchester M21 7SP
Phone: 0870 240 1170

#255
Lauriston Club
Category: Social Club
Address: 12 Manchester Road
Manchester M21 9JG
Phone: 0161 881 3096

#256
Crumpsall Labour Club
Category: Social Club
Address: 98 Wilton Road
Manchester M8 4PX
Phone: 0161 740 3373

#257
Simpson Memorial Community Association
Category: Social Club
Address: Moston Lane
Manchester M9 4HF
Phone: 0161 205 1575

#258
Devil Child Promotions
Category: Arcade
Address: 27 Lichfield Drive
Manchester M25 0HX
Phone: 0161 798 4236

#259
The Voiceover Gallery
Category: Theatre
Address: 34 Stockton Road
Manchester M21 9ED
Phone: 0161 881 8844

#260
**Troydale Tenants
& Residents Association**
Category: Social Club
Address: 5 Dolwen Walk
Manchester M40 2FR
Phone: 0161 682 9846

#261
G M B Whitehouse Club
Category: Social Club
Address: 193 Middleton Road
Manchester M8 4JZ
Phone: 0161 740 1732

#262
Stretford Bridge Club
Category: Social Club
Address: 66 Derbyshire Lane
Manchester M32 8BF
Phone: 0161 865 2846

#263
St Richards Social Club
Category: Social Club
Address: 10-12 Sutcliffe Avenue
Manchester M12 5TN
Phone: 0161 224 1405

#264
Club & Institute Union
Category: Social Club
Address: 534 Hyde Road
Manchester M18 7AA
Phone: 0161 223 1686

#265
Avanti Display
Category: Theatre
Address: 46 Nell Lane
Manchester M21 7SN
Phone: 0161 860 7267

#266
Withington Conservative Club
Category: Social Club
Address: 16 Mauldeth Road
Manchester M20 4ND
Phone: 0161 434 2879

#267
Music Hall
Category: Social Club
Address: 29 Old Church Street
Manchester M40 2JN
Phone: 0161 681 7665

#268
HM Music Promotions
Category: Arcade
Address: 55 Bluestone Road
Manchester M40 9JB
Phone: 0161 688 6738

#269
Royal British Legion
Category: Social Club
Address: Slade Lane
Manchester M19 2EX
Phone: 0161 248 6010

#270
Withington Public Hall Institute
Category: Social Club
Address: 2 Burton Road
Manchester M20 3ED
Phone: 0161 445 2672

#271
**Newton Heath Catholic
Mens Club**
Category: Social Club
Address: 137 Culcheth Lane
Manchester M40 1LY
Phone: 0161 681 7003

#272
Royal British Legion
Category: Social Club
Address: Ross Avenue
Manchester M19 2HW
Phone: 0161 224 4716

#273
St James Conservative Club
Category: Social Club
Address: 572 Gorton Lane
Manchester M18 8EH
Phone: 0161 223 0455

#274
Plush UK
Category: Arcade
Address: 64 Victoria Road
Manchester M32 0AB
Phone: 0161 864 4746

#275
Amber Club
Category: Social Club
Address: 1143 Oldham Road
Manchester M40 2FU
Phone: 0161 681 3892

#276
Deus Ex Machina
Theatre Company
Category: Theatre
Address: 18 Elder Mount Road
Manchester M9 8BT
Phone: 0161 795 4709

#277
Royal British Legion
Category: Social Club
Address: Beverly Road
Manchester M14 6TZ
Phone: 0161 224 6210

#278
The Manchester Song
& Dance Company
Category: Theatre
Address: 12 Barnhill Road
Manchester M25 9NH
Phone: 0161 798 4365

#279
Young Gifted & Green
Category: Arcade
Address: 6 Wald Avenue
Manchester M14 6TE
Phone: 0161 225 0706

#280
Stretford Conservative Club
Category: Social Club
Address: 20 King Street
Manchester M32 8AE
Phone: 0161 865 1292

#281
The Manchester Bridge Club
Category: Social Club
Address: 30 Palatine Road
Manchester M20 3JJ
Phone: 0161 445 3712

#282
Pupfish
Category: Theatre
Address: 9 Brixton Avenue
Manchester M20 1JF
Phone: 0161 610 7529

#283
Royal British Legion Ladybarn
Category: Social Club
Address: & District Club
Manchester M14 6TE
Phone: 0161 225 8105

#284
Mccafferty Illustrations
Category: Theatre
Address: Flat 2 41 Alan Road Withington
Manchester M20 4WG
Phone: 0161 434 2201

#285
Pro Music UK
Category: Theatre
Address: 30 Victoria Avenue
Manchester M19 2PE
Phone: 0161 224 6236

#286
Proper Job Theatre Company
Category: Theatre
Address: 1 Hoscar Drive
Manchester M19 2LS
Phone: 0161 249 0564

#287
Swinton Masonic Hall
Category: Social Club
Address: Hospital Road
Manchester M27 4EY
Phone: 0161 794 5377

#288
Manchester Maccabi
Community & Sports Club
Category: Social Club
Address: Bury Old Road
Manchester M25 0EG
Phone: 0161 492 0040

#289
G M Buses Social Club
Category: Social Club
Address: 301 Mount Road
Manchester M19 3ET
Phone: 0161 224 1176

#290
**Higher Openshaw
Working Men's Club**
Category: Social Club
Address: 49 Stanley Street
Manchester M11 1LE
Phone: 0161 370 1048

#291
Sonic Tonic
Category: Arcade
Address: 204 Barlow Road
Manchester M19 3HF
Phone: 0161 224 6587

#292
Eccles Liberal Club
Category: Social Club
Address: 34 Wellington Road
Manchester M30 0NP
Phone: 0161 789 3047

#293
**West Didsbury
Conservative Club**
Category: Social Club
Address: 173 Burton Road
Manchester M20 2LN
Phone: 0161 445 3917

#294
**Prestwich Amateur Dramatic
& Operatic Society**
Category: Theatre
Address: 23 ST. Marys Road
Manchester M25 1AQ
Phone: 0161 773 7729

#295
**Failsworth Home Guard
Old Comrades**
Category: Social Club
Address: Poplar Street
Manchester M35 0HY
Phone: 0161 681 1891

#296
Goldengate Promotions
Category: Arcade
Address: 3 Danesmoor Road
Manchester M20 3JT
Phone: 0161 283 7273

#297
Sale Harriers Manchester
Category: Social Club
Address: 16 Whitethorn Avenue
Manchester M19 1EU
Phone: 0161 432 1831

#298
Animount Systems
Category: Theatre
Address: The Old Town Hall Lapwing Lane
Manchester M20 2WR
Phone: 0161 448 9990

#299
Carlton Club
Category: Social Club
Address: 279 Bury Old Road
Manchester M25 1JA
Phone: 0161 773 2284

#300
Openshaw A E U Club & Institute
Category: Social Club
Address: Toxteth Street
Manchester M11 1EZ
Phone: 0161 370 2069

#301
Heaton Park Sports & Social Bar
Category: Social Club
Address: 315 Bury Old Road
Manchester M25 1JA
Phone: 0161 773 1091

#302
P Snowden
Category: Social Club
Address: Overdale
Manchester M27 5WZ
Phone: 0161 281 5694

#303
**Victoria Avenue East
Ex Service Mens Club**
Category: Social Club
Address: White Moss Road
Manchester M9 6EF
Phone: 0161 740 5832

#304
Gorton Working Mens Club
Category: Social Club
Address: 2 Thornwood Avenue
Manchester M18 7HW
Phone: 0161 223 3509

#305
Cricket Club
Category: Social Club
Address: Wilmslow Road
Manchester M20 2ZY
Phone: 0161 445 5347

#306
Heaton Hall
Category: Art Gallery
Address: Heaton Park
Manchester M25 2SW
Phone: 0161 773 1231

#307
Royal British Legion
Category: Social Club
Address: Manchester Road
Manchester M43 6SF
Phone: 0161 370 1367

#308
Joku Entertainment
Category: Arcade
Address: Barton Dock Road
Manchester M41 7BQ
Phone: 0161 747 7779

#309
Royal British Legion
Category: Social Club
Address: Victoria Avenue
Manchester M9 0RA
Phone: 0161 740 6138

#310
Royal British Legion Swinton
Category: Social Club
Address: Cheetham Road
Manchester M27 4UQ
Phone: 0161 794 2422

#311
Swinton Catholic Club
Category: Social Club
Address: 11 Worsley Road
Manchester M27 5WN
Phone: 0161 794 3365

#312
Taylor's
Category: Social Club
Address: Barton Lane
Manchester M30 0FR
Phone: 0161 789 3016

#313
**Middleton & Chadderton
Sea Cadets**
Category: Social Club
Address: 265 Oldham Road
Manchester M35 0AS
Phone: 0161 681 8697

#314
Droylsden Working Men's Club
Category: Social Club
Address: Lloyd Street
Manchester M43 6UB
Phone: 0161 301 4722

#315
Droylsden Catholic Club
Category: Social Club
Address: Sunnyside Road
Manchester M43 7WW
Phone: 0161 370 2046

#316
Prestwich Liberal Club
Category: Social Club
Address: 509 Bury New Road
Manchester M25 3AJ
Phone: 0161 773 3518

#317
Royal British Legion
Category: Social Club
Address: 609 Bolton Road
Manchester M27 4EJ
Phone: 0161 794 3511

#318
Failsworth Liberal Club
Category: Social Club
Address: 339 Oldham Road
Manchester M35 0AN
Phone: 0161 681 1606

#319
Medlock Gymnastics Academy
Category: Social Club, Sports & Leisure
Address: Greenside Trading Centre
Greenside Lane Manchester M43 7AJ
Phone: 0161 371 7666

#320
Audenshaw Masonic Club
Category: Social Club
Address: Manchester Road
Manchester M34 5GB
Phone: 0161 370 2235

#321
Moston Ward Labour Club
Category: Social Club
Address: 841 Moston Lane
Manchester M40 5RT
Phone: 0161 681 4665

#322
Swinton Conservative Club
Category: Social Club
Address: 1 The Parade
Manchester M27 4BH
Phone: 0161 794 1784

#323
Droylsden Little Theatre
Category: Theatre
Address: Market Street
Manchester M43 7AY
Phone: 0161 370 7713

#324
Swinton & Pendlebury
Labour Club
Category: Social Club
Address: 10 Station Road
Manchester M27 6AF
Phone: 0161 794 2556

#325
Salisbury Conservative Club
Category: Social Club
Address: Ashton Road
Manchester M43 7BW
Phone: 0161 370 2314

#326
Borough Social Club
Category: Social Club
Address: 167 Station Road
Manchester M27 6BU
Phone: 0161 794 1239

#327
Folly Lane A R L F Club
Category: Social Club
Address: Station Road
Manchester M27 6AH
Phone: 0161 728 2205

#328
Cosmo Bingo & Social Club
Category: Social Club
Address: 241 Liverpool Road
Manchester M30 0QN
Phone: 0161 789 3524

#329
Royal British Legion
Category: Social Club
Address: 109 Moston Lane East
Manchester M40 3GJ
Phone: 0161 681 3703

#330
Patricroft Conservative Club
Category: Social Club
Address: 1 Edison Road
Manchester M30 7AW
Phone: 0161 789 3729

#331
Wanderscan
Category: Theatre
Address: 22 Parkside
Manchester M24 1NL
Phone: 0161 653 1460

#332
Cat's Dance & Fitness
Category: Theatre
Address: 35 St Josephs Avenue
Manchester M45 6NT
Phone: 0161 796 7064

#333
Patricroft Working Mens Club
Category: Social Club
Address: 17 Legh Street
Manchester M30 0UT
Phone: 0161 789 3989

#334
Talbot Catholic Club
Category: Social Club
Address: 12 Eldon Place
Manchester M30 8QE
Phone: 0161 789 1021

#335
Urmston Masonic Hall
Category: Social Club
Address: 15 Westbourne Road
Manchester M41 0XQ
Phone: 0161 748 6533

#336
Urmston Mens' Club & Institute
Category: Social Club
Address: 81 Higher Road
Manchester M41 9AP
Phone: 0161 748 9022

#337
New Moston Club
Category: Social Club
Address: Parkfield Road North
Manchester M40 3RQ
Phone: 0161 681 1632

#338
J M Leisure
Category: Theatre
Address: 580 Manchester Old Road
Manchester M24 4PJ
Phone: 0161 653 2029

#339
Taxplan
Category: Theatre
Address: 234 Manchester New Road
Manchester M24 1NP
Phone: 0161 643 3215

#340
Urmston Social Club
Category: Social Club
Address: 1 & 3 Old Crofts Bank
Manchester M41 7AA
Phone: 0161 748 3666

#341
The Stockport Motor Club
Category: Theatre
Address: 18 Lynwood Road
Manchester M19 1RJ
Phone: 0161 432 9161

#342
G M B Cringlewood Social Club
Category: Social Club
Address: Yew Tree Lane
Manchester M23 0DN
Phone: 0161 998 2561

#343
Moorside Social Club
Category: Social Club
Address: 207 Moorside Road
Manchester M27 9LD
Phone: 0161 794 1934

#344
**Unsworth South Social
Working Mens Club**
Category: Social Club
Address: Derwent Avenue
Manchester M45 8HU
Phone: 0161 766 5915

#345
Flat & Round Records
Category: Arcade
Address: 26 Wilton Street
Manchester M45 7EU
Phone: 0161 766 8781

#346
**Northenden Players
Theatre Club**
Category: Social Club
Address: Boat Lane
Manchester M22 4HR
Phone: 0161 945 4160

#347
Brackley Conservative Club
Category: Social Club
Address: 1 Hazelhurst Fold
Manchester M28 2JU
Phone: 0161 794 1735

#348
Cineworld
Category: Cinema
Address: Wilmslow Road
Manchester M20 5PG
Phone: 0871 200 2000

#349
Faze 2
Category: Arcade
Address: 61 Church Road
Manchester M22 4WD
Phone: 0161 998 9966

#350
Gallery
Category: Art Gallery
Address: 59 Flixton Road
Manchester M41 5AN
Phone: 0161 748 4109

#351
Royal British Legion
Category: Social Club
Address: 10 Royle Green Road
Manchester M22 4NG
Phone: 0161 998 4684

#352
H Donn
Category: Art Gallery
Address: 138-142 Bury New Road
Manchester M45 6AD
Phone: 0161 766 8819

#353
Fresh Management
Category: Theatre
Address: 891 Kingsway
Manchester M20 5PB
Phone: 0161 434 8333

#354
Philip Partridge Entertainment
Category: Arcade
Address: 34 Winwood Road
Manchester M20 5PE
Phone: 0161 448 2672

#355
Royal British Legion
Category: Social Club
Address: Grosvenor Street
Manchester M34 3WN
Phone: 0161 336 4340

#356
Denton West End Social Club
Category: Social Club
Address: Grosvenor Street
Manchester M34 3WN
Phone: 0161 337 9816

#357
Flixton Ex Servicemen's
Association
Category: Social Club
Address: Flixton Road
Manchester M41 6QY
Phone: 0161 748 2617

#358
Flixton Conservative Club
Category: Social Club
Address: Flixton Road
Manchester M41 5DF
Phone: 0161 748 2846

#359
Our Lady Parochial Centre
Category: Social Club
Address: Wood Street
Manchester M24 4DH
Phone: 0161 643 6303

#360
Denton Villa Football
& Netball Club
Category: Social Club
Address: 32 Jackson Garden
Manchester M34 2EH
Phone: 0161 336 8681

#361
New Millbeck Club
Category: Social Club
Address: Millbeck Road
Manchester M24 4HR
Phone: 0161 653 5448

#362
Woodside Working Mens
Social Club
Category: Social Club
Address: Higher Wood Street
Manchester M24 5SW
Phone: 0161 643 3212

#363
Colour Of Sport
Category: Theatre
Address: 36 Radcliffe New Road
Manchester M45 7GY
Phone: 0161 796 6842

#364
Brooklands Trade
& Labour Club
Category: Social Club
Address: Carrswood Road
Manchester M23 9HQ
Phone: 0161 998 5838

#365
Rome Fine Arts
Category: Art Gallery
Address: 284 Stand Lane
Manchester M26 1JE
Phone: 0161 766 9991

#366
Denton Workingmen's
Club& Institute
Category: Social Club
Address: 3 Frederick Street
Manchester M34 3JB
Phone: 0161 336 2227

#367
Conservative Club
Category: Social Club
Address: 45 Manchester Road
Manchester M34 2AF
Phone: 0161 336 2085

#368
Denton Labour Party Holdings
Category: Social Club
Address: Ashton Road
Manchester M34 3JF
Phone: 0161 336 2883

#369
Denton Liberal Club
Category: Social Club
Address: 1 Bowden Street
Manchester M34 2AB
Phone: 0161 336 2307

#370
St Bernadettes Social Centre
Category: Social Club
Address: Selby Avenue
Manchester M45 8UT
Phone: 0161 766 2116

#371
Winston Conservative Club
Category: Social Club
Address: Hall Lane
Manchester M23 1AQ
Phone: 0161 945 1450

#372
Boarshaw Working Mens Club
Category: Social Club
Address: 1 Dixon Street
Manchester M24 6GB
Phone: 0161 643 2820

#373
Cheshire Arts Theatre
Category: Theatre
Address: 20 Birch Grove
Manchester M34 5DN
Phone: 0161 320 4268

#374
Sacred Heart Parish Centre
Category: Social Club
Address: 92 Floatshall Road
Manchester M23 1HP
Phone: 0161 998 4626

#375
Waterfall Theatre Co
Category: Theatre
Address: 39a Porlock Road
Manchester M23 1LZ
Phone: 0161 998 8844

#376
**Hebers Working Mens
Club & Institute**
Category: Social Club
Address: 231 Hollin Lane
Manchester M24 5LU
Phone: 0161 643 3636

#377
PC Rescued
Category: Theatre
Address: 10 Erlesmere Avenue
Manchester M34 3FD
Phone: 0161 320 5518

#378
Stanycliffe Social Centre
Category: Social Club
Address: Stanycliffe Lane
Manchester M24 2PB
Phone: 0161 643 2276

#379
St. Johns Catholic Mens Club
Category: Social Club
Address: Greenwood Road
Manchester M22 8AU
Phone: 0161 998 5807

#380
**Cessxpress Intermusic'N'Sports
Pleasure Leisure Company**
Category: Arcade
Address: 10 Tamar Drive
Manchester M23 2QB
Phone: 0161 087 2968

#381
St. Marys Catholic Social Club
Category: Social Club
Address: Pine Street
Manchester M26 2WQ
Phone: 0161 723 2181

#382
**Kearsley & Ringley
Conservative Club**
Category: Social Club
Address: 52 Ringley Road
Manchester M26 1FS
Phone: 01204 571796

#383
**Benchill & District
Conservative Club**
Category: Social Club
Address: Crossacres Road
Manchester M22 5BS
Phone: 0161 437 4980

#384
D Bradley
Category: Arcade
Address: 50 Ringley Road Stoneclough
Manchester M26 1FS
Phone: 01204 400508

#385
Greenbrow Social Club
Category: Social Club
Address: Greenbrow Road
Manchester M23 2TU
Phone: 0161 437 3329

#386
Radcliffe British Legion Club
Category: Social Club
Address: 50 Water Street
Manchester M26 4DF
Phone: 0161 723 2586

#387
Royal British Legion
Category: Social Club
Address: Wilfred Road
Manchester M28 3AJ
Phone: 0161 790 2434

#388
Longley Road Club
Category: Social Club
Address: 17 Longley Road
Manchester M28 3JA
Phone: 0161 790 2446

#389
Wythenshawe Forum Trust
Category: Stadium
Address: Forum Square
Manchester M22 5RX
Phone: 0161 935 4000

#390
Walkden Science Club
Category: Social Club
Address: Bolton Road
Manchester M28 3AX
Phone: 0161 799 0881

#391
Buckingham Bingo Club
Category: Social Club
Address: 10-12 New Ellesmere Approach
Manchester M28 3EE
Phone: 0161 790 6655

#392
Urmston Conservative Club
Category: Social Club
Address: Moorfield Walk
Manchester M41 0TT
Phone: 0161 748 2108

#393
Bridge For All Teaching Group
Category: Social Club
Address: 425 Bolton Road
Manchester M26 3QG
Phone: 0161 724 5670

#394
The Royal British Legion
Category: Social Club
Address: Victoria Street
Manchester M28 1HQ
Phone: 0161 790 2928

#395
St. Anthony's Parish Centre
Category: Social Club
Address: Portway Road
Manchester M22 0NT
Phone: 0161 437 6588

#396
Higher Irlam Social Club
Category: Social Club
Address: Cutnook Lane
Manchester M44 6JS
Phone: 0161 775 2868

#397
Pictor Framing Studio
Category: Art Gallery
Address: 29 Chaddock Lane
Manchester M28 1DE
Phone: 0161 790 8008

#398
Pentdale
Category: Theatre
Address: 32 Windmill Road
Manchester M28 3RP
Phone: 0161 790 8346

#399
Irlam Steel Recreation Club
Category: Social Club
Address: Liverpool Road
Manchester M44 6AJ
Phone: 0161 775 2346

#400
Holy Family
Category: Social Club
Address: Chaddock Lane
Manchester M28 1DN
Phone: 0161 790 1898

#401
Armitage Social Club
Category: Social Club
Address: Madams Wood Road
Manchester M28 0JU
Phone: 0161 790 5293

#402
Entertainment Trade Management
Category: Theatre
Address: 122 Mosley Common Rd
Manchester M28 1AN
Phone: 0161 799 9513

#403
Irlam Catholic Men's Social Club
Category: Social Club
Address: 617 Liverpool Road
Manchester M44 5BE
Phone: 0161 777 9512

#404
Royal British Legion
Category: Social Club
Address: Woodhouse Lane
Manchester M22 9TF
Phone: 0161 437 2952

#405
The Aviation Shop
Category: Social Club
Address: LVL 13 Term 1 Multi Storey Car P
Manchester M90 1QX
Phone: 0161 489 2444

#406
Irlam Conservative Club
Category: Social Club
Address: Astley Road
Manchester M44 6AB
Phone: 0161 775 2499

#407
Astley Conservative Club
Category: Social Club
Address: 90-94 Higher Green Lane
Manchester M29 7HZ
Phone: 01942 882009

#408
Astley Labour Club
Category: Social Club
Address: Manchester Road
Manchester M29 7DY
Phone: 01942 882977

#409
Top Club
Category: Social Club
Address: Manchester Road West
Manchester M38 9EG
Phone: 0161 790 5241

#410
Partington Social Club
Category: Social Club
Address: 2 Warburton Lane
Manchester M31 4NR
Phone: 0161 776 1318

#411
Cadishead Labour Club
Category: Social Club
Address: Fir Street
Manchester M44 5AG
Phone: 0161 775 2045

#412
Conservative Club
Category: Social Club
Address: 5 Stanley Street
Manchester M29 8AE
Phone: 01942 882713

#413
R A O B Club
Category: Social Club
Address: Castle Street
Manchester M29 8EG
Phone: 01942 884707

#414
Sacred Heart Parochial
Club & Centre
Category: Social Club
Address: Lodge Road
Manchester M46 9BN
Phone: 01942 882464

#415
Atherton Liberal Club
Category: Social Club
Address: 30 Flapper Fold Lane
Manchester M46 0FA
Phone: 01942 882240

#416
Atherton Sports & Social Club
Category: Social Club
Address: Formby Avenue
Manchester M46 9PZ
Phone: 01942 888811

#417
Atherton Laburnam Rovers F C
Category: Stadium
Address: Spa Road
Manchester M46 9NQ
Phone: 01942 883950

#418
Atherton Village Club
Category: Social Club
Address: Leigh Road
Manchester M46 0PA
Phone: 07979 633453

#419
Lyme Park
Category: Botanical Garden
Address: Disley Disley SK12 2NR
Phone: 01633 762023

#420
**National Trust: Quarry Bank Mill
and Styal Estate**
Category: Cultural Center
Address: Styal Wilmslow SK9 4LA
Phone: 01625 527468

#421
Plaza Theatre
Category: Music Venues, Theatre
Address: Mersey Square
Stockport SK1 1SP
Phone: 0161 477 7779

#422
Salford Museum & Art Gallery
Category: Museum, Art Gallery
Address: The Crescent Salford M5 4WU
Phone: 0161 778 0800

#423
Red Cinema
Category: Cinema
Address: The Lowry Designer Outlet
Salford M50 3AG
Phone: 0870 998 1878

#424
**Bolton Museum, Art Gallery
and Aquarium**
Category: Art Gallery, Aquarium
Address: Le Mans Crescent Bolton BL1
1SE**Phone:** 01204 332211

#425
Knutsford Wine Bar
Category: Wine Bar, Music Venues
Address: 41a King Street
Knutsford WA16 6DW
Phone: 01565 750459

#426
Palace Theatre
Category: Theatre, Music Venues
Address: Oxford Street
Manchester M1 6FT
Phone: 0161 245 6600

#427
The Quays Theatre
Category: Theatre, Bar
Address: 140 The Quays
Salford M50 3AG
Phone: 0870 787 5780

#428
Witchwood Public House
Category: Pub, Music Venues
Address: 152 Old St
Ashton Under Lyne OL6 7SF
Phone: 0161 344 0321

#429
Lancashire County Cricket Club
Category: Sports Club, Stadium
Address: Talbot Road
Manchester M16 0PX
Phone: 0161 282 4000

#430
Cineworld Bolton
Category: Cinema
Address: 15 The Valley
Bolton BL1 8TS
Phone: 0870 777 2775

#431
Chorley Little Theatre
Category: Theatre, Cinema
Address: Dole Lane
Chorley PR7 2RL
Phone: 01257 275123

#432
Eureka
Category: Museum
Address: Discovery Road
Halifax HX1 2NE
Phone: 01422 330069

#433
Chads Theatre Co
Category: Theatre
Address: Mellor Road
Cheadle SK8 5AU
Phone: 0161 486 1788

#434
Justicia Craft Centre
Category: Arts & Crafts
Address: 81 Knowsley Street
Bolton BL1 2BJ
Phone: 01204 363308

#435
The Birdcage Manchester
Category: Club, Music Venues
Address: Withy Grove
Manchester M4 3AQ
Phone: 0161 832 1700

#436
Jodrell Bank Centre for Astrophysics
Category: Museum, Landmark
Address: Jodrell Bank
Manchester SK11 9DL
Phone: 01477 571339

#437
County Gallery
Category: Framing, Art Gallery
Address: 32-34 Railway Street
Altrincham WA14 2RE
Phone: 0161 928 9942

#438
Lyme Hall
Category: Museum
Address: Disley Stockport SK12 2NR
Phone: 01663 766492

#439
Ordsall Hall Museum
Category: Museum
Address: Ordsall Lane
Salford M5 3AN
Phone: 0161 872 0251

#440
Air Raid Shelters Tour
Category: Local Flavour, Art Gallery
Address: 61 Great Underbank
Stockport SK1 1NE
Phone: 0161 474 1940

#441
Hat Works
Category: Museum
Address: Wellington Mill
Stockport SK3 0EU
Phone: 0845 833 0975

#442
Bury Art Gallery & Museum
Category: Art Gallery
Address: Moss Street
Bury BL9 0DF
Phone: 0161 253 5878

#443
The Cinnamon Club
Category: Jazz & Blues, European
Address: The Bowdon Room
Trafford WA14 2TQ
Phone: 0161 926 8992

#444
Cadishead Conservative Club
Category: Social Club
Address: Grange Place
Manchester M44 5UN
Phone: 0161 775 2433

#445
Quarry Bank Mill
Category: Museum
Address: Styal
Manchester SK9 4LA
Phone: 01625 527468

#446
Pavillion Garden
Category: Venues & Event Space,
Swimming Pool, Festival, Park
Address: St John's Road
Buxton SK17 6XN
Phone: 01298 23114

#447
Bolton Albert Hall
Category: Venues & Event Space,
Music Venues, Theatre
Address: Victoria Square
Bolton BL1 1RJ
Phone: 01204 334433

#448
Games Workshop
Category: Sports & Leisure,
Hobby Shop, Social Club
Address: 31 St Mary Street
Cardiff CF10 1PU
Phone: 029 2064 4917

#449
Carlton Club
Category: Social Club
Address: 113 Carlton Road
Manchester M16 8BE
Phone: 0161 881 3042

#450
Filmworks
Category: Cinema
Address: Withy Grove
Manchester M4 2BS
Phone: 0870 010 2030

#451
Un-Convention Festival
Category: Festival
Address: 20 Huddart Close
Salford M5 3RS
Phone: 0161 872 3767

#452
Savoy Cinema
Category: Cinema
Address: Heaton Moor Road
Stockport SK4 4HY
Phone: 0161 432 2114

#453
Powerleague
Category: Social Club, Football
Address: Stadium Way
Wigan WN5 0UN
Phone: 01942 210080

#454
**Museum Of The
Manchester Regiment**
Category: Museum
Address: Wellington Road
Ashton-under-Lyne OL6 6DL
Phone: 0161 342 3078

#455
Thackeray Music
Category: Theatre, Music & DVDs
Address: 7 Woodlands Road
Stockport SK4 3AF
Phone: 0161 432 3351

#456
**Woodhouses Working
Mens Club**
Category: Social Club
Address: 62-64 Medlock Road
Manchester M35 9WN
Phone: 0161 681 3562

#457
Portland Basin Museum
Category: Museum
Address: Portland Place
Ashton-under-Lyne OL7 0QA
Phone: 0161 343 2878

#458
ConservativeClub
Category: Social Club
Address: Mellor Street
Stockport SK8 5AT
Phone: 0161 485 1087

#459
Stalybridge Labour Club
Category: Social Club,
Venues & Event Space
Address: Acres Lane
Stalybridge SK15 2JR
Phone: 0161 338 4796

#460
Busy Bee Networking Group
Category: Social Club
Address: 5 Cedar Rd
Altrincham WA15 9
Phone: 07870 601168

#461
The Heywood
Category: Social Club, Pub
Address: 1 Tower Street
Heywood OL10 3AA
Phone: 01706 369710

#462
Astley Green Colliery Museum
Category: Museum
Address: Higher Green Lane
Astley Green
Manchester M29 7JB
Phone: 01772 431937

#463
George Lawton Hall
Category: Theatre
Address: Stamford St
Mossley OL5 0HR
Phone: 01457 832223

#464
**Warrington Museum
& Art Gallery**
Category: Museum, Art Gallery
Address: Museum Street / Bold Street
Warrington WA1 1JB
Phone: 01925 442399

#465
Micklehurst Cricket Club
Category: Social Club, Sports Club
Address: Castle Lane Ashton
Under Lyne SK15 3QG
Phone: 01457 832163

#466
Harlequin Theatre
Category: Theatre
Address: Queen Street
Northwich CW9 5JN
Phone: 01606 44235

#467
JB's
Category: Music Venues
Address: Grains Road
Shaw OL2 8JB
Phone: 01706 841460

#468
Morley Green Club
Category: Social Club
Address: Mobberley Road
Wilmslow SK9 5NT
Phone: 01625 525224

#469
Vue Entertainment
Category: Cinema
Address: The Linkway
Bolton BL6 6JA
Phone: 01204 668809

#470
Bradshaw Conservative Club
Category: Social Club
Address: Lee Gate
Bolton BL2 3ET
Phone: 01204 416947

#471
Uppermill Conservative Club
Category: Social Club
Address: 74 High Street
Oldham OL3 6AP
Phone: 01457 873077

#472
Astley Bridge Cricket Club
Category: Social Club, Sports & Leisure
Address: Moss Bank Way
Bolton BL1 6PZ
Phone: 01204 415515

#473
Astley Bridge Conservative Club
Category: Social Club
Address: Moss Bank Way
Bolton BL8 8NP
Phone: 01204 301233

#474
**Astley Hall Museum
and Art Gallery**
Category: Museum, Art Gallery
Address: Astley Park
Chorley PR7 1NP
Phone: 01257 515555

#475
Lowton Civic Hall
Category: Venues & Event Space,
Recreation Center, Cultural Center
Address: Hesketh Meadow Lane
Warrington WA3 2AH
Phone: 01942 672971

#476
Parr Hall Concert Hall
Category: Theatre
Address: Palmyra Square
South Warrington WA1 1BL
Phone: 01925 442345

#477
Stockport Story
Category: Museum
Address: 30-31 Market Place
Stockport SK1 1ES
Phone: 0161 480 1460

#478
The Halliwell Jones Stadium
Category: Stadium
Address: Winwick Road
Warrington WA2 7NE
Phone: 01925 248880

#479
Cubecure
Category: Art Gallery
Address: 16 Peel Street
Huddersfield HD7 6BW
Phone: 01484 842305

#480
**Powerleague
Manchester South**
Category: Stadium
Address: The Range Stadium Whalley
Range High School Wilbraham Road
Manchester M16 8GW
Phone: 0161 881 8442

#481
John Bull Chop House
Category: Pub, Music Venues
Address: 2 Coopers Row
Wigan WN1 1PQ
Phone: 01942 242862

#482
Irish Democratic League
Category: Social Club
Address: George Street
Rossendale BB4 5RX
Phone: 01706 214787

#483
Legoland Discovery Centre
Category: Toy Shop, Arcade
Address: Barton Square
Trafford M17 8AS
Phone: 0871 222 2662

#484
The Boulevard
Category: Pub, Music Venues
Address: 17A Wallgate
Wigan WN1 1LD
Phone: 01942 497165

#485
Halifax Playhouse
Category: Theatre
Address: King Cross Street
Halifax HX1 2SH
Phone: 01422 365998

#486
Cineworld Stockport
Category: Cinema
Address: 4 Grand Central Square
Stockport SK1 3TA
Phone: 0870 777 2775

#487
Antrobus Village Hall
Category: Venues & Event Space
Address: Knutsford Road
Northwich CW9 6LB
Phone: 07544 567708

#488
Bury Met Theatre
Category: Theatre
Address: Market Street
Bury BL9 0BW
Phone: 0161 761 2216

#489
Cosmo Bingo Club
Category: Arcade
Address: 62 Market Street
Stalybridge SK15 2AB
Phone: 0161 338 5277

#490
Castle Gallery
Category: Art Gallery
Address: 75 Deansgate
Manchester M2 7
Phone: 0161 839 3800

#491
Vue Bury
Category: Cinema
Address: Park 66 Bury BL9 8RS
Phone: 0871 224 0240

#492
Cineworld Cinema
Category: Cinema
Address: Fold Way
Ashton-under-Lyne OL7 0PG
Phone: 0871 200 2000

#493
Bolton Museum & Art Gallery
Category: Museum
Address: Victoria Square
Bolton BL1 1RJ
Phone: 01204 332211

#494
The Lowry Gift Shop
Category: Cinema, Gift Shop
Address: Pier 8 Salford Quays
Manchester M50 3AZ
Phone: 0870 787 5780

#495
Salt Museum
Category: Museum
Address: 162 London Road
Northwich CW9 8AB
Phone: 01606 41331

#496
OdeonCinema
Address: 100 Westbrook Centre
Warrington WA5 8UD
Phone: 0871 224 4007

#497
The Original Art Shop
Category: Art Gallery
Address: Market Street
Manchester M4 3AT
Phone: 0161 834 3370

#498
The Art Surgery
Category: Art Gallery, Photographers
Address: 33-35 Tib Street
Manchester M4 1LX
Phone: 0161 819 2888

#499
Odeon Rochdale
Category: Cinema
Address: Sandbrook Park
Rochdale OL11 1RY
Phone: 0871 224 4007

#500
New Century Hall
Category: Venues & Event Space
Address: Corporation Street
Manchester M60 4ES
Phone: 0161 827 5198

#1
Band on the Wall
Category: Bar, Music Venues,
Jazz & Blues
Average price: Modest
Area: Northern Quarter
Address: 25 Swan Street
Manchester M4 5JZ
Phone: 0161 834 1786

#2
The Marble Arch
Category: Pub, Gastropub
Average price: Modest
Area: Ancoats, Petersfield
Address: 73 Rochdale Road
Manchester M4 4HY
Phone: 0161 832 5914

#3
Cornerhouse
Category: Cinemas, Bar, Cafe
Average price: Modest
Area: Oxford Road Corridor
Address: 70 Oxford Street
Manchester M1 5NH
Phone: 0161 200 1500

#4
Sandbar
Category: Pub, Music Venues
Average price: Modest
Area: Oxford Road Corridor
Address: 120 Grosvenor Street
Manchester M1 7HL
Phone: 0161 273 1552

#5
Matt and Phreds
Category: Club, Jazz & Blues,
Music Venues
Average price: Modest
Area: Northern Quarter
Address: 64 Tib Street
Manchester M4 1LW
Phone: 0161 839 7187

#6
Sinclair's Oyster Bar
Category: Pub, British
Average price: Inexpensive
Area: City Centre
Address: 2 Cathedral Gates
Manchester M3 1SW
Phone: 0161 834 0430

#7
Pi
Category: British, Pub
Average price: Modest
Area: Chorlton
Address: 99 Manchester Road
Manchester M21 9GA
Phone: 0161 882 0000

#8
FAB Café
Category: Lounge, Club, Dive Bar
Average price: Modest
Area: Chinatown
Address: 109 Portland Street
Manchester M1 6DN
Phone: 0161 212 2997

#9
The Deaf Institute
Category: Lounge, Music Venues
Average price: Modest
Area: Oxford Road Corridor
Address: 135 Grosvenor Street
Manchester M1 7HE
Phone: 0161 276 9350

#10
Chaophraya
Category: Thai, Bar
Average price: Expensive
Area: City Centre
Address: Chapel Walks Manchester
Manchester M2 1HN
Phone: 0161 832 8342

#11
Big Hands
Category: Pub, Lounge, Dive Bar
Average price: Modest
Area: Oxford Road Corridor
Address: 296 Oxford Road
Manchester M13 9NS
Phone: 0161 272 7309

#12
Trof
Category: Bar, British
Average price: Modest
Area: City Centre
Address: 6-8 Thomas Street
Manchester M4 1EU
Phone: 0161 833 3197

#13
Nexus Art Cafe
Category: Music Venues, Lounge
Average price: Inexpensive
Area: Northern Quarter
Address: 2 Dale Street
Manchester M1 1JW
Phone: 0161 236 0100

#14
Manchester Academy 2
Category: Music Venues, Bar
Average price: Modest
Area: Oxford Road Corridor
Address: Oxford Road
Manchester M13 9PR
Phone: 0161 275 2930

#15
Sam's Chop House
Category: British, Pub
Average price: Modest
Area: City Centre
Address: Blackpool Hold
Manchester M2 1HN
Phone: 0161 834 3210

#16
St Ann's Church
Category: Music Venues
Area: City Centre
Address: St Ann's Street
Manchester M2 7LF
Phone: 0161 834 1161

#17
Soup Kitchen
Category: Bar, Cafe
Average price: Modest
Area: Northern Quarter
Address: 31-33 Spear Street
Manchester M1 1DF
Phone: 0161 236 5100

#18
The Font
Category: Pub, Lounge
Average price: Inexpensive
Area: Oxford Road Corridor
Address: 7-9 New Wakefield Street
Manchester M1 5NP
Phone: 0161 236 0944

#19
Manchester Academy
Category: Music Venues
Average price: Modest
Area: Oxford Road Corridor
Address: Oxford Road
Manchester M13 9PR
Phone: 0161 275 2930

#20
The Ox
Category: Hotel, Gastropub, Bar
Average price: Expensive
Area: Castlefield
Address: Liverpool Road
Manchester M3 4NQ
Phone: 0161 839 7740

#21
The Old Wellington
Category: Gastropub, Pub, British
Average price: Modest
Area: City Centre
Address: 4 Cathedral Gates
Manchester M3 1SW
Phone: 0161 839 5179

#22
Sankeys
Category: Club
Average price: Expensive
Area: Ancoats, Petersfield
Address: Radium Street
Manchester M4 6AY
Phone: 0161 236 5444

#23
Kro Bar
Category: Pub, European
Average price: Modest
Area: Oxford Road Corridor
Address: 325 Oxford Road
Manchester M13 9PG
Phone: 0161 274 3100

#24
Dukes 92
Category: Pub, British
Average price: Modest
Area: Castlefield
Address: 18 Castle Street
Manchester M3 4LZ
Phone: 0161 839 3522

#25
Room
Category: Bar, European
Average price: Expensive
Area: City Centre
Address: 81 King Street
Manchester M2 4AH
Phone: 0161 839 2005

#26
The Metropolitan
Category: British, Gastropub, Bar
Average price: Modest
Area: West Didsbury
Address: 2 Lapwing Lane
Manchester M20 2WS
Phone: 0161 438 2332

#27
Michael Caines Restaurant
Category: British, Champagne Bar
Average price: Expensive
Area: Piccadilly
Address: 107 Piccadilly
Manchester M1 2DB
Phone: 0161 200 5678

#28
The Bay Horse
Category: Pub
Average price: Modest
Area: Northern Quarter
Address: 35-37 Thomas Street
Manchester M4 1NA
Phone: 0161 661 1041

#29
The Ruby Lounge
Category: Club, Music Venues
Average price: Modest
Area: Northern Quarter
Address: 28-34 High Street
Manchester M4 1QB
Phone: 0161 834 1392

#30
The Art of Tea
Category: Tea Room, Bar
Average price: Modest
Area: Didsbury Village
Address: 47 Barlow Moor Road
Manchester M20 6TW
Phone: 0161 448 9323

#31
English Lounge
Category: Pub, British, Burgers
Average price: Modest
Area: Northern Quarter
Address: 64-66 High Street
Manchester M4 1EA
Phone: 0161 832 4824

#32
The Castle Hotel
Category: Pub, Music Venues
Average price: Modest
Area: Northern Quarter
Address: 66 Oldham Street
Manchester M4 1LE
Phone: 0161 237 9485

#33
Common
Category: Bar, Music Venues
Average price: Modest
Area: Northern Quarter
Address: 39 - 41 Edge Street
Manchester M4 1HW
Phone: 0161 832 9245

#34
Phones 4u Arena
Category: Theatre, Music Venues
Average price: Expensive
Area: City Centre
Address: Victoria Station
Manchester M3 1AR
Phone: 0161 950 5000

#35
Corbieres
Category: Wine Bar, Pizza, Dive Bar
Average price: Inexpensive
Area: City Centre
Address: 2 Half Moon Street
Manchester M2 7PB
Phone: 0161 834 3381

#36
The Alchemist
Category: European, Cocktail Bar
Average price: Expensive
Area: Spinningfields
Address: 3 Hardman Street
Manchester M3 3HF
Phone: 0161 817 2950

#37
Marble Beerhouse
Category: Pub, Brewerie
Average price: Modest
Area: Chorlton
Address: 57 Manchester Road
Manchester M21 9PW
Phone: 0161 881 9206

#38
Bar Fringe
Category: Pub
Average price: Modest
Area: Ancoats, Petersfield
Address: 8 Swan Street
Manchester M4 5JN
Phone: 0872 107 7077

#39
The Star and Garter
Category: Pub, Club, Music Venues
Average price: Inexpensive
Area: Piccadilly
Address: 18-20 Fairfield Street
Manchester M1 2QF
Phone: 0161 273 6726

#40
The Roadhouse
Category: Music Venues
Average price: Modest
Area: Northern Quarter
Address: 8 Newton Street
Manchester M1 2AN
Phone: 0161 237 9789

#41
The Woodstock
Category: Pub, Gastropub
Average price: Modest
Area: Didsbury Village
Address: 139 Barlow Moor Road
Manchester M20 2DY
Phone: 0161 448 7951

#42
Cord Bar
Category: Cocktail Bar
Average price: Modest
Area: Northern Quarter
Address: 8 Dorsey Street
Manchester M4 1LU
Phone: 0161 832 9494

#43
The Crown and Kettle
Category: Pub
Average price: Modest
Area: Ancoats, Petersfield
Address: 2 Oldham Road
Manchester M4 5FE
Phone: 0161 236 2923

#44
Retro Bar
Category: Music Venues, Dive Bar
Average price: Inexpensive
Area: Gay Village
Address: 78 Sackville Street
Manchester M1 3NJ
Phone: 0161 274 4892

#45
The Railway
Category: Pub
Average price: Inexpensive
Area: West Didsbury
Address: 3 Lapwing Lane
Manchester M20 2WS
Phone: 0161 445 9839

#46
The City Arms
Category: Pub
Average price: Modest
Area: City Centre
Address: 48 Kennedy Street
Manchester M2 4BQ
Phone: 0161 236 4610

#47
Java Bar Espresso
Category: Coffee & Tea, Bar
Average price: Inexpensive
Area: Oxford Road Corridor
Address: 1 - 3 Station Approach Oxford
Road Manchester M1 6FU
Phone: 0161 236 3656

#48
Thirsty Scholar
Category: Pub
Average price: Modest
Area: Oxford Road Corridor
Address: 50 New Wakefield Street
Manchester M1 5NP
Phone: 0161 236 6071

#49
Canal Street
Category: Bar, Club, Local Flavour
Average price: Inexpensive
Area: Gay Village
Address: Canal Street
Manchester M1 3

#50
O'Sheas Irish Bar
Category: Pub
Average price: Modest
Area: Oxford Road Corridor
Address: 80 Princess Street
Manchester M1 6NF
Phone: 0161 236 3906

#51
Horse & Jockey
Category: Pub
Average price: Expensive
Area: Chorlton
Address: 9 Chorlton Green
Manchester M21 9HS
Phone: 0161 860 7794

#52
The Spoon Inn
Category: Wine Bar
Average price: Modest
Area: Chorlton
Address: 364 Barlow Moor Road
Manchester M21 8AZ
Phone: 0161 881 2400

#53
Hardy's Well
Category: Pub
Average price: Inexpensive
Area: Rusholme
Address: 257 Wilmslow Road
Manchester M14 5LN
Phone: 0161 224 8034

#54
The Oast House
Category: Pub
Average price: Modest
Area: Spinningfields
Address: Crown Square
Manchester M3 3AY
Phone: 0161 829 3830

#55
Folk Café Bar
Category: Bar, Cafe
Average price: Modest
Area: West Didsbury
Address: 169-171 Burton Road
Manchester M20 2LN
Phone: 0161 445 2912

#56
Efes Taverna
Category: Turkish, Bar
Average price: Inexpensive
Area: Oxford Road Corridor
Address: 46 Princess Street
Manchester M1 6HR
Phone: 0161 236 1824

#57
**Hop & Grape Manchester
Academy 3**
Category: Music Venues, Bar
Average price: Modest
Area: Oxford Road Corridor
Address: Oxford Rd
Manchester M13 9PR
Phone: 0161 275 2930

#58
The Drawing Room
Category: Lounge, Wine Bar
Average price: Modest
Area: West Didsbury
Address: Burton Road
Manchester M20 2LW
Phone: 0161 283 6244

#59
Royal Northern College of Music
Category: Music Venues, Theatre
Average price: Modest
Area: Oxford Road Corridor
Address: 124 Oxford Road
Manchester M13 9RD
Phone: 0161 907 5200

#60
South
Category: Club
Average price: Expensive
Address: 4a S King St
Manchester M2 6DQ
Phone: 0161 831 7756

#61
Odd
Category: Pub
Average price: Modest
Area: Northern Quarter
Address: 30-32 Thomas Street
Manchester M4 1ER
Phone: 0161 833 0070

#62
Kro Piccadilly
Category: Bar, European, British
Average price: Modest
Area: Piccadilly
Address: 1 Piccadilly Gardens
Manchester M1 1RG
Phone: 0161 244 5765

#63
Ape & Apple
Category: Pub
Average price: Modest
Area: City Centre
Address: 28 John Dalton Street
Manchester M2 6HQ
Phone: 0161 839 9624

#64
Taurus
Category: Wine Bar, Gay Bar
Average price: Modest
Area: Gay Village
Address: 1 Canal Street
Manchester M1 3HE
Phone: 0161 236 4593

#65
Reserve
Category: Off Licence, Wine Bar
Average price: Modest
Area: West Didsbury
Address: 176 Burton Road
Manchester M20 1LH
Phone: 0161 438 0101

#66
The Blue Pig
Category: Bar, Persian/Iranian
Average price: Modest
Area: Northern Quarter
Address: 69 High St Manchester
Manchester M4 1FS
Phone: 0161 832 0630

#67
Wasabi
Category: Japanese, Sushi Bar, Bar
Average price: Modest
Area: Chinatown
Address: 63 Faulkner Street
Manchester M1 4FF
Phone: 0161 228 7288

#68
The Northern
Category: Pub
Average price: Modest
Area: Northern Quarter
Address: 56 Tib Street
Manchester M4 1LW
Phone: 0161 835 2548

#69
Walrus
Category: Lounge, Tapas
Average price: Modest
Area: Northern Quarter
Address: 78-88 High Street
Manchester M4 1ES
Phone: 0161 828 8700

#70
Seven Oaks
Category: Pub, Sports Bar
Average price: Inexpensive
Area: Chinatown
Address: 5 Nicholas Street
Manchester M1 4HL
Phone: 0161 237 1233

#71
The Molly House
Category: Pub, Specialty Food,
Coffee & Tea
Average price: Modest
Area: Gay Village
Address: 26/28 Richmond Street
Manchester M1 3NB
Phone: 0161 237 9329

#72
The Fat Loaf
Category: Pub
Average price: Expensive
Area: Didsbury Village
Address: 846 Wilmslow Road
Manchester M20 2RN
Phone: 0161 438 0319

#73
Apotheca Lounge
Average price: Modest
Area: Northern Quarter
Address: 17 Thomas Street
Manchester M4 1FS
Phone: 0161 834 9411

#74
Dusk til Pawn
Category: Cocktail Bar, Pub
Average price: Modest
Area: Northern Quarter
Address: Stevenson Square
Manchester M1 1FB
Phone: 0161 236 5355

#75
Squirrels Bar
Category: Bar
Average price: Inexpensive
Area: Fallowfield
Address: 1 Moseley Road
Manchester M14 6HX
Phone: 0161 248 3050

#76
Hula
Category: Bar
Average price: Modest
Area: Northern Quarter
Address: 11 Stevenson Square
Manchester M1 1DB
Phone: 0161 228 7421

#77
Hangingditch Wine Merchants
Category: Wine Bar, Off Licence
Average price: Modest
Area: City Centre
Address: 42-44 Victoria Street
Manchester M3 1ST
Phone: 0161 832 8222

#78
Copacabana
Category: Mexican, Club, Bar
Area: Northern Quarter
Address: Dale Street
Manchester M1 2HF
Phone: 0161 237 3441

#79
Kosmonaut
Category: Bar, Food
Average price: Modest
Area: Northern Quarter
Address: 10 Tariff Street
Manchester M1 2FF

#80
Boggart microbar
Category: Bar
Average price: Inexpensive
Area: Northern Quarter
Address: High Street
Manchester M4 3AJ
Phone: 0161 277 9666

#81
Zinc Bar and Grill
Category: British, Bar, American
Average price: Expensive
Area: City Centre
Address: The Triangle
Manchester M4 3TR
Phone: 0161 827 4200

#82
Dog & Partridge
Category: Pub
Average price: Modest
Area: Didsbury Village
Address: 665-667 Wilmslow Road
Manchester M20 6RA
Phone: 0161 445 5322

#83
Via Fossa
Category: Gay Bar
Average price: Modest
Area: Gay Village
Address: 28 Canal Street
Manchester M1 3EZ
Phone: 0161 236 6523

#84
Eastern Bloc Records
Category: Music Venues, Cafe
Average price: Modest
Area: Northern Quarter
Address: 5A Stevenson Square
Manchester M1 1DN
Phone: 0161 228 6555

#85
Hard Rock Cafe
Category: American, Bar
Average price: Modest
Area: City Centre
Address: 27 Withy Grove
Manchester M4 2BS
Phone: 0161 831 6700

#86
Terrace
Category: Bar
Average price: Modest
Area: Northern Quarter
Address: 43 Thomas Street
Manchester M4 1NA
Phone: 0161 819 2345

#87
Velvet Bar & Restaurant
Category: British, Lounge, Hotel
Average price: Modest
Area: Gay Village
Address: 2 Canal Street
Manchester M1 3HE
Phone: 0161 236 9003

#88
Mr Thomas's Chop House
Category: British, Pub
Average price: Expensive
Area: City Centre
Address: 52 Cross Street
Manchester M2 7AR
Phone: 0161 832 2245

#89
Mint Lounge
Category: Lounge, Club
Average price: Modest
Area: Northern Quarter
Address: 46-50 Oldham Street
Manchester M4 1LE
Phone: 0161 228 1495

#90
Bluu
Category: Lounge, British
Average price: Modest
Area: Northern Quarter
Address: 85 High Street
Manchester M4 1BD
Phone: 0161 839 7195

#91
Black Dog Ballroom
Category: Lounge, Snooker & Pool Hall,
American
Average price: Modest
Area: Northern Quarter
Address: 43 Oldham Street
Manchester M1 1JG
Phone: 0161 839 0664

#92
The Liar's Club
Category: Pub, Club, Cocktail Bar
Average price: Modest
Address: 19A Back Bridge Street
Manchester M2 3PB
Phone: 0161 834 5111

#93
Proof
Category: Lounge
Average price: Modest
Area: Chorlton
Address: 30a Manchester Road
Manchester M21 9PH
Phone: 0161 8629 3333

#94
One Lounge Bar
Category: Cocktail Bar
Average price: Exclusive
Area: West Didsbury
Address: 1 Lapwing Lane
Manchester M20 2NT
Phone: 0161 448 0101

#95
Las Iguanas
Category: Lounge, Latin American
Average price: Modest
Area: City Centre
Address: 84 Deansgate
Manchester M3 2ER
Phone: 0161 819 2606

#96
The Bank
Category: Pub, British
Average price: Modest
Area: Chinatown, City Centre
Address: 57 Mosley Street
Manchester M2 3FF
Phone: 0872 107 7077

#97
Bem Brasil
Category: Brazilian, Wine Bar
Average price: Expensive
Area: Northern Quarter
Address: 58 Lever Street
Manchester M1 1FJ
Phone: 0161 923 6888

#98
The Mark Addy
Category: Pub
Average price: Modest
Area: City Centre
Address: Stanley Street
Manchester M3 5EJ
Phone: 0161 832 4080

#99
Joshua Brooks
Category: Club, Pub
Average price: Modest
Area: Oxford Road Corridor
Address: 106 Princess Street
Manchester M1 6NG
Phone: 0161 273 7336

#100
Lammars
Category: Lounge, Tapas Bar
Average price: Modest
Area: Northern Quarter
Address: 57 Hilton Street
Manchester M1 2EJ
Phone: 0161 237 9058

#101
The Frog and Bucket
Comedy Club
Category: Comedy Club, Bar
Average price: Modest
Area: Northern Quarter
Address: 102 Oldham Street
Manchester M4 1LJ
Phone: 0161 236 9805

#102
BarMC
Category: Lounge, Hotel
Average price: Modest
Address: 107 Piccadilly
Manchester M1 2DB
Phone: 0161 200 5665

#103
The Footage
Category: Pub, Burgers, Club
Average price: Inexpensive
Area: Oxford Road Corridor
Address: 137 Grosvenor Street
Manchester M1 7DZ
Phone: 0161 275 9164

#104
Black Dog Ballroom NWS
Category: Barbeque, Snooker & Pool Hall
Average price: Modest
Area: Oxford Road Corridor
Address: 11-13 New Wakefield Street
Manchester M1 5NP
Phone: 0161 236 4899

#105
Crown & Anchor
Category: Pub
Average price: Modest
Area: Northern Quarter
Address: 41 Hilton Street
Manchester M1 2EE
Phone: 0161 228 1142

#106
Twenty Twenty Two
Category: Bar, Art Gallery, Music Venues
Average price: Modest
Area: Northern Quarter
Address: 20 Dale Street
Manchester M1 1EZ
Phone: 0161 237 9360

#107
Grinch
Category: Wine Bar, Pizza
Average price: Modest
Area: City Centre
Address: 5-7 Chapel Walks
Manchester M2 1HN
Phone: 0161 907 3210

#108
All Bar One
Category: Lounge, European
Average price: Modest
Area: City Centre
Address: 73 King Street
Manchester M2 4NG
Phone: 0161 830 1811

#109
The Waterhouse
Category: Pub, British
Average price: Inexpensive
Area: City Centre
Address: 67-71 Princess Street
Manchester M2 4EG
Phone: 0161 200 5380

#110
The Printworks
Category: Arcade, Cinemas, Bar
Average price: Expensive
Area: City Centre
Address: 27 Withy Grove
Manchester M4 2BS
Phone: 0161 829 8000

#111
Tribeca
Category: Pub, Lounge, Cocktail Bar
Average price: Modest
Area: Gay Village
Address: 50 Sackville Street
Manchester M1 3WF
Phone: 0161 236 8300

#112
The Salutation
Category: Pub
Average price: Inexpensive
Area: Oxford Road Corridor
Address: 12 Higher Chatham Street
Manchester M15 6ED
Phone: 0161 272 7832

#113
Volta Eaterie & Bar
Category: Gastropub, Pub
Average price: Expensive
Area: West Didsbury
Address: 167 Burton Rd
Manchester M20 2LN
Phone: 0161 448 8887

#114
The Fitzgerald
Category: Club
Average price: Modest
Area: Northern Quarter
Address: 11 Stevenson Square
Manchester M1 1DB

#115
Cruz 101
Category: Club, Gay Bar
Average price: Modest
Area: Gay Village
Address: 101 Princess Street
Manchester M1 6DD
Phone: 0161 950 0101

#116
Marble
Category: Pub
Average price: Modest
Area: Northern Quarter
Address: 57 Thomas Street
Manchester M4 1NA
Phone: 0161 832 0521

#117
Noho Bar
Category: Lounge, Cocktail Bar
Average price: Modest
Area: Northern Quarter
Address: Spear Street
Manchester M1 1FB
Phone: 0161 236 5381

#118
New Union Hotel
Category: Bar, Hotel
Average price: Modest
Area: Oxford Road Corridor
Address: 111 Princess St
Manchester M1 6JB
Phone: 0161 228 1492

#119
Satan's Hollow
Category: Club, Bar
Average price: Inexpensive
Area: Oxford Road Corridor
Address: 101 Princess St
Manchester M1 6DD
Phone: 0161 236 0666

#120
The Bulls Head
Category: Pub
Average price: Modest
Area: Piccadilly
Address: 84 London Road
Manchester M1 2PN
Phone: 0161 236 1724

#121
Great John Street Hotel
Category: Hotel, Bar
Average price: Modest
Area: Castlefield
Address: Great John Street
Manchester M3 4FD
Phone: 0161 831 3211

#122
The Old Monkey
Category: Pub
Average price: Modest
Area: Chinatown
Address: 90-92 Portland Street
Manchester M1 4GX
Phone: 0161 228 6262

#123
Bakerie
Category: Wine Bar, Bakery
Average price: Modest
Area: Northern Quarter
Address: 43-45 Lever Street
Manchester M1 1FN
Phone: 0161 236 9014

#124
Manchester Metropolitan Students Union
Category: Social Club, Lounge
Area: Oxford Road Corridor
Address: Grosvenor Square
Manchester M15 6BH
Phone: 0161 247 1162

#125
Chetham's School of Music
Category: Music Venues
Area: City Centre
Address: Long Millgate
Manchester M3 1SB
Phone: 0161 834 9644

#126
5th Avenue
Category: Club
Average price: Inexpensive
Area: Gay Village
Address: 121 Princess St
Manchester M1 7AG
Phone: 0161 236 2754

#127
Fletcher Moss
Category: Pub
Average price: Modest
Area: Didsbury Village
Address: 1 William St
Manchester M20 6RQ
Phone: 0161 438 0073

#128
The Angel
Category: Pub
Average price: Expensive
Area: Ancoats, Petersfield
Address: 6 Angel Street
Manchester M4 3BQ
Phone: 0161 833 4786

#129
Revolution
Category: Bar, British
Average price: Modest
Area: Oxford Road Corridor
Address: 88-94 Oxford Street
Manchester M1 5WH
Phone: 0161 237 5377

#130
Rosso Restaurant
Category: Italian, Cocktail Bar
Average price: Expensive
Area: City Centre
Address: 43 Spring Gardens
Manchester M2 2BG
Phone: 0161 832 1400

#131
Club Alterego
Category: Club
Average price: Modest
Area: Oxford Road Corridor
Address: 105-107 Princess Street
Manchester M1 6DD
Phone: 0161 236 9266

#132
The Green
Category: Bar, Golf
Average price: Modest
Area: Piccadilly
Address: 26 Ducie Street
Manchester M1 2DQ
Phone: 0161 228 0681

#133
The Salisbury
Category: Pub
Average price: Modest
Area: Oxford Road Corridor
Address: 2 Wakefield Street
Manchester M1 5NE
Phone: 0161 236 5590

#134
The Crescent
Category: Pub
Average price: Exclusive
Area: Salford University Campus
Address: 20 The Crescent
Manchester M5 4PF
Phone: 0161 736 5600

#135
The Warehouse Project
Category: Club
Average price: Expensive
Area: Salford Quays
Address: Trafford Wharf Road
Manchester M17 1AB

#136
Charlies Karaoke Bar
Category: Karaoke, Venues & Event
Spaces, Music Venues
Average price: Exclusive
Area: Oxford Road Corridor
Address: 1 Harter Street
Manchester M1 6
Phone: 0161 237 9898

#137
Baa Bar
Category: Lounge, Club
Average price: Modest
Area: Fallowfield
Address: 258 Wilmslow Rd
Manchester M14 6JR
Phone: 0161 224 9559

#138
Night & Day
Category: Bar, Music Venues
Average price: Modest
Area: Northern Quarter
Address: 26 Oldham Street
Manchester M1 1JN
Phone: 0161 236 4597

#139
Revolution
Category: Lounge, Club
Average price: Modest
Area: City Centre
Address: Arkwright House Parsonage
Gardens Manchester M3 2LF
Phone: 0161 839 9675

#140
The Pub/Zoo
Category: Pub, Club
Average price: Inexpensive
Area: Oxford Road Corridor
Address: 126 Grosvenor Street
Manchester M1 7HL
Phone: 0161 273 1471

#141
Churchills Public House
Category: Pub, Karaoke
Average price: Modest
Area: Gay Village
Address: 37 Chorlton Street
Manchester M1 3HN
Phone: 0161 236 5529

#142
Moon Under Water
Category: Pub, British
Average price: Inexpensive
Area: City Centre
Address: 68-74 Deansgate
Manchester M3 2FN
Phone: 0161 834 5882

#143
Slug & Lettuce
Category: Pub, British
Area: Didsbury Village
Address: 651 Wilmslow Road
Manchester M20 6QZ
Phone: 0161 434 1011

#144
The Font
Category: Lounge, Burgers
Average price: Inexpensive
Area: Fallowfield
Address: 236 Wilmslow Road
Manchester M14 6LE
Phone: 0161 248 4820

#145
Lime
Category: Bar
Average price: Expensive
Area: City Centre
Address: 2 Booth Street
Manchester M2 4AT
Phone: 0161 233 2929

#146
The Whiskey Jar
Category: Bar
Average price: Modest
Area: Northern Quarter
Address: 14 Tariff Street
Manchester M1 2FF
Phone: 0161 237 5686

#147
Ford Madox Brown
Category: Pub
Average price: Inexpensive
Area: Oxford Road Corridor
Address: Oxford Road
Manchester M13 9NG
Phone: 0161 256 6660

#148
Sandinista
Category: Tapas Bar, Lounge
Average price: Modest
Area: City Centre
Address: 2 Old Bank Street
Manchester M2 7PF
Phone: 0161 832 9955

#149
Ducie Bridge
Category: Pub
Average price: Modest
Area: City Centre
Address: 152 Corporation Street
Manchester M4 4DU
Phone: 0161 831 9725

#150
Club Academy
Category: Music Venues
Area: Oxford Road Corridor
Address: Oxford Road
Manchester M13 9PR
Phone: 0161 275 2930

#151
Chez Gerard
Category: Wine Bar, French
Average price: Expensive
Area: City Centre
Address: 2 -8 Commerical Union House
Manchester M2 6LP
Phone: 0161 834 7633

#152
Wahlbar
Category: Bar
Average price: Modest
Area: Fallowfield
Address: 310 Wilmslow Road
Manchester M14 6XQ
Phone: 0161 637 3736

#153
Electrik
Category: Bar
Average price: Modest
Area: Chorlton
Address: 559 Wilbraham Rd
Manchester M20 0AE
Phone: 0161 881 3315

#154
Liquorice
Category: Cocktail Bar
Average price: Modest
Area: City Centre
Address: 50 Pall Mall
Manchester M2 1AQ
Phone: 0161 832 4600

#155
Mother Mac's
Category: Pub
Average price: Expensive
Area: Northern Quarter
Address: 33 Back Piccadilly
Manchester M1 1HP
Phone: 0161 236 1507

#156
Gusto
Category: Italian, Bar
Average price: Modest
Area: Didsbury Village
Address: 756 Wilmslow Road
Manchester M20 2DW
Phone: 0161 445 8209

#157
The Font
Category: Lounge
Average price: Modest
Area: Chorlton
Address: 115-117 Manchester Road
Manchester M21 9PG
Phone: 0161 871 2022

#158
Tib Street Tavern
Category: Pub, Sports Bar
Average price: Modest
Area: Northern Quarter
Address: 74 Tib St
Manchester M4 1LG
Phone: 0161 834 1600

#159
Panacea
Category: Lounge, Champagne Bar
Average price: Exclusive
Area: City Centre
Address: 14 John Dalton St
Manchester M2 6JP
Phone: 0161 833 1111

#160
Scubar
Category: Club, Lounge
Average price: Inexpensive
Area: Oxford Road Corridor
Address: 136 York St
Manchester M1 7XN
Phone: 0161 274 3189

#161
The Living Room
Category: Wine Bar, British, Club
Average price: Expensive
Area: City Centre
Address: 80 Deansgate
Manchester M3 2ER
Phone: 0161 832 0083

#162
Grand Pacific
Category: Asian Fusion, Bar
Average price: Exclusive
Area: Oldham
Address: 1 The Avenue
Manchester M3 3AP
Phone: 0161 831 0288

#163
Harvey Nichols
Category: British, Bar
Average price: Exclusive
Area: City Centre
Address: 21 New Cathedral Street
Manchester M1 1AD
Phone: 0161 828 8898

#164
FAC 251: The Factory
Category: Club, Music Venues
Average price: Inexpensive
Area: Oxford Road Corridor
Address: 112-118 Princess St
Manchester M1 7EN
Phone: 0161 272 7251

#165
O'Neills
Category: Pub
Average price: Inexpensive
Area: Didsbury Village
Address: 655-657 Wilmslow Road
Manchester M20 6RA
Phone: 0161 448 7941

#166
Prohibition
Category: Lounge
Average price: Modest
Area: City Centre
Address: 2-10 St Mary's St
Manchester M3 2LB
Phone: 0161 831 9326

#167
Rampant Lion
Category: Pub
Average price: Modest
Area: Longsight
Address: 17 Anson Road
Manchester M14 5BZ

#168
Islington Mill
Category: Music Venues
Average price: Modest
Area: Salford University Campus
Address: James St
Manchester M3 5HW
Phone: 07947 649896

#169
Sound Control
Category: Club, Music Venues
Average price: Modest
Area: Oxford Road Corridor
Address: 1 New Wakefield Street
Manchester M1 5NP
Phone: 0161 236 0340

#170
Vine Inn
Category: Pub, British
Average price: Modest
Area: City Centre
Address: 42-46 Kennedy Street
Manchester M2 4BQ
Phone: 0161 237 9740

#171
Corridor
Category: Lounge
Average price: Modest
Area: City Centre
Address: 6-8 Barlows Croft
Manchester M3 5DY
Phone: 0161 832 6699

#172
Siam Orchid
Category: Thai, Karaoke
Average price: Modest
Area: Chinatown
Address: 54 Portland Street
Manchester M1 4QU
Phone: 0161 236 1388

#173
Dry Bar
Category: Bar, Music Venues
Average price: Modest
Area: Northern Quarter
Address: 29-30 Oldham St
Manchester M1 1JN
Phone: 0161 236 9840

#174
The Shakespeare
Category: Pub, Food
Average price: Inexpensive
Area: City Centre
Address: 16 Fountain Street
Manchester M2 2AA
Phone: 0161 834 5515

#175
Wetherspoons
Category: Pub, British
Average price: Modest
Area: Northern Quarter
Address: 49 Piccadilly
Manchester M1 2AP
Phone: 0161 236 9206

#176
The Lloyd's Hotel
Category: Pub
Average price: Modest
Area: Chorlton
Address: 617 Wilbraham Road
Manchester M21 9AN
Phone: 0161 862 6990

#177
The Piccadilly
Category: British, Pub
Average price: Modest
Area: Northern Quarter
Address: 60 - 75 Piccadilly
Manchester M1 2BS
Phone: 0872 107 7077

#178
G-A-Y Manchester
Category: Gay Bar
Average price: Inexpensive
Area: Piccadilly
Address: Canal Street
Manchester M1 3

#179
The Grove
Category: Pub, Snooker & Pool Hall
Average price: Inexpensive
Area: Oxford Road Corridor
Address: 316 Oxford Road
Manchester M13 9WJ
Phone: 0161 273 1702

#180
Pure
Category: Club
Average price: Expensive
Area: City Centre
Address: The Printworks
Manchester M4 2BS
Phone: 0161 819 7770

#181
The Union Bar
Category: Bar
Average price: Modest
Area: Oxford Road Corridor
Address: Steve Biko Bldg Oxford Rd
Manchester M13 9PR
Phone: 0161 275 2930

#182
Coyotes Bar
Category: Gay Bar
Average price: Modest
Area: Gay Village
Address: 14 Chorlton Street
Manchester M1 3HW
Phone: 0161 236 4007

#183
Royal Oak
Category: Pub
Average price: Expensive
Area: Didsbury Village
Address: 729 Wilmslow Road
Manchester M20 6WF
Phone: 0161 434 4788

#184
Walkabout
Category: Pub, Club
Average price: Modest
Area: Castlefield, Spinningfields
Address: 13 Quay Street
Manchester M3 3
Phone: 0870 850 4508

#185
Baa Bar
Category: Dive Bar, Club
Average price: Modest
Area: Piccadilly
Address: Arch 11 Deansgate Locks
Manchester M1 5LH
Phone: 0161 832 4446

#186
The Oxford
Category: Pub, Lounge
Average price: Inexpensive
Area: Oxford Road Corridor
Address: 423 Oxford Road
Manchester M13 9WG
Phone: 0161 273 1490

#187
Manto Cafe
Category: Bar
Average price: Modest
Area: Gay Village
Address: 46 Canal Street
Manchester M1 3WD
Phone: 0161 236 2667

#188
Arabesque
Category: Hookah Bar
Area: Northern Quarter
Address: 68 Newton Street
Manchester M1 1EE
Phone: 0161 228 0336

#189
Bowling Green
Category: Pub
Average price: Inexpensive
Area: Chorlton
Address: Brookburn Road
Manchester M21 9ES
Phone: 0161 860 2800

#190
Tiger Tiger
Category: Club, Lounge
Average price: Expensive
Area: City Centre
Address: Units 5-6 The Printworks
Manchester M4 2BS
Phone: 0161 385 8080

#191
Venus
Category: Club, Music Venues
Area: City Centre
Address: 42 Maybrook House
Manchester M3 2EQ
Phone: 0161 834 7288

#192
Cubacafe Bar
Category: Bar
Average price: Modest
Area: Northern Quarter
Address: 43 Port St
Manchester M1 2EQ
Phone: 0161 236 3630

#193
The Queen Of Hearts
Category: Dive Bar
Average price: Inexpensive
Area: Fallowfield
Address: 256 Wilmslow Road
Manchester M14 6LB
Phone: 0161 249 0271

#194
Genting Club
Category: Gambling, Lounge
Average price: Expensive
Area: Oxford Road Corridor
Address: 110 Portland Street
Manchester M1 4RL
Phone: 0161 228 0077

#195
Castlefield Events Arena
Category: Music Venues
Area: Castlefield
Address: 101 Liverpool Road
Manchester M3 4JN
Phone: 0161 834 4026

#196
**University of Manchester
Student's Union**
Category: University, Pub
Average price: Inexpensive
Address: Oxford Road
Manchester M13 9PR
Phone: 0161 275 2930

#197
Revolution
Category: Club, Lounge
Average price: Expensive
Area: Fallowfield
Address: 311-313 Wilmslow Road
Manchester M14 6NW
Phone: 0161 256 4754

#198
The Bar
Category: Bar, British
Average price: Modest
Area: Chorlton
Address: 533 Wilbraham Rd
Manchester M21 0UE
Phone: 0161 861 7576

#199
Tandle Hill Tavern
Category: Pub, British
Average price: Inexpensive
Area: Oldham
Address: 14 Thornham Lane
Manchester M24 2SD
Phone: 01706 345297

#200
Bouzouki Restaurant
Category: Greek, Music Venues
Average price: Modest
Area: Oxford Road Corridor
Address: 88 Princess Street
Manchester M1 6NG
Phone: 0161 236 9282

#201
The Beagle
Category: Street Vendor, Pub
Average price: Modest
Area: Chorlton
Address: 456-458 Barlow Moor Road
Manchester M21 0BQ
Phone: 0161 881 8596

#202
M20 Bar
Category: Lounge
Average price: Expensive
Area: West Didsbury
Address: 158 Burton Rd
Manchester M20 1LH
Phone: 0161 445 6800

#203
Waxy O'Connors
Category: Bar
Average price: Expensive
Area: City Centre
Address: 27 Withy Grove
Manchester M4 2BS
Phone: 0161 831 0885

#204
Old Monkey
Category: Bar
Average price: Modest
Area: Chinatown
Address: 90 Portland Street
Manchester M1
Phone: 0161 228 6262

#205
Opus
Category: Club
Average price: Expensive
Area: City Centre
Address: 27 Withy Grove
Manchester M4 2BS
Phone: 0161 834 2414

#206
Zombie Shack
Category: Cocktail Bar
Average price: Modest
Area: Oxford Road Corridor
Address: 50 New Wakefield Street
Manchester M1 5NP
Phone: 0161 236 6071

#207
The Paramount
Category: Pub, Burgers
Average price: Inexpensive
Area: Oxford Road Corridor
Address: 33-35 Oxford Street
Manchester M1 4BH
Phone: 0161 233 1820

#208
The B Lounge
Category: Pub, European
Average price: Modest
Area: Piccadilly
Address: 97 Piccadilly
Manchester M1 2DB
Phone: 0161 236 4161

#209
The Sedge Lynn
Category: Pub
Average price: Expensive
Area: Chorlton
Address: 21a Manchester Road
Manchester M21 9PN
Phone: 0161 860 0141

#210
The Famous Trevor Arms
Category: Pub
Area: Chorlton
Address: 135 Beech Road
Manchester M21 9EQ
Phone: 0161 636 0250

#211
The Famous Crown
Category: Pub
Average price: Exclusive
Area: Didsbury Village
Address: 770 Wilmslow Rd
Manchester M20 2DR
Phone: 0161 434 7085

#212
Label
Category: Lounge, Club
Average price: Expensive
Area: City Centre
Address: 78 Deansgate
Manchester M3 2FW
Phone: 0161 833 1878

#213
The Liquor Store
Category: Bar
Average price: Modest
Area: City Centre
Address: 40 Blackfriars Street
Manchester M3 2EG
Phone: 0161 834 6239

#214
The Hare and Hounds
Category: Pub
Average price: Inexpensive
Area: Northern Quarter
Address: 46 Shudehill
Manchester M4 1
Phone: 0161 832 4737

#215
Monrose Hotel
Category: Hotel, Bar
Area: Piccadilly
Address: 38 London Road
Manchester M1 2PF
Phone: 0161 236 0564

#216
Lava Cafe Bar
Category: Sports Bar
Area: Castlefield
Address: Castle Quay
Manchester M15 4NJ
Phone: 0161 833 2444

#217
The Station
Category: Pub
Average price: Expensive
Area: Didsbury Village
Address: 682 Wilmslow Road
Manchester M20 2DN
Phone: 0161 445 9761

#218
Legends Manchester
Category: Pub
Average price: Inexpensive
Area: Oxford Road Corridor
Address: 6 Whitworth Street
Manchester M1 3QW
Phone: 0161 236 5400

#219
Café North
Category: Coffee & Tea, Bar
Average price: Modest
Area: Northern Quarter
Address: 66 Shudehill
Manchester M4 4AA
Phone: 0161 839 4916

#220
Room
Category: Bar, British
Area: City Centre
Address: 81 King Street
Manchester M2 4ST
Phone: 0161 839 2005

#221
Burton Arms Hotel
Category: Pub, Bed & Breakfast
Area: Northern Quarter
Address: 31 Swan Street
Manchester M4 5JZ
Phone: 0161 834 3455

#222
Vina Karaoke Bar
Category: Karaoke, Club, Dive Bar
Area: Chinatown
Address: 34 Charlotte Street
Manchester M1 4FD
Phone: 0161 237 9838

#223
Platt Chapel
Category: Music Venues
Area: Rusholme
Address: 186 Wilmslow Road
Manchester M14 5LL
Phone: 0161 478 4203

#224
The Ducie Arms
Category: Pub
Average price: Modest
Area: Oxford Road Corridor
Address: 52 Devas Street
Manchester M15 6HS
Phone: 0161 273 2279

#225
Morley Cheeks
Category: Pub
Average price: Modest
Area: Chorlton
Address: 575 Barlow Moor Road
Manchester M21 8AE
Phone: 0161 860 7878

#226
Beggar's Bush
Category: Bar, British
Area: Chorlton
Address: 48 Beech Road
Manchester M21 9EQ
Phone: 0161 861 7393

#227
Long Legs Table Dancing
Category: Adult Entertainment
Area: Chinatown
Address: 46 George Street
Manchester M1 4HF
Phone: 0161 237 3977

#228
The Bijou Club, Manchester
Category: Club
Area: City Centre
Address: 1-7 Chapel Street
Manchester M3 7NJ
Phone: 0161 834 6377

#229
Kahlua Coffee House
Category: Mexican, Cocktail Bar
Area: Northern Quarter
Address: 104 High Street
Manchester M4 1HQ
Phone: 0161 833 0035

#230
Kyoto Lounge
Category: Lounge
Area: Oxford Road Corridor
Address: 131 Grosevenor Street
Manchester M1 7HE
Phone: 07771 744909

#231
Parrswood Hotel
Category: Pub
Average price: Inexpensive
Area: East Didsbury
Address: 356 Parrswood Road
Manchester M20 6JD
Phone: 0161 445 1783

#232
New York-New York
Category: Bar
Average price: Modest
Area: Gay Village
Address: 94-98 Bloom Street
Manchester M1 3LY
Phone: 0161 236 6556

#233
The Courtyard Bar
Category: Pub
Average price: Inexpensive
Area: Oxford Road Corridor
Address: Chester Streer
Manchester M1 5SH

#234
Shotz Cafe
Category: Hookah Bar
Average price: Inexpensive
Area: Rusholme
Address: 114-116 Wilmslow Road
Manchester M14 5AJ
Phone: 0161 879 2694

#235
Rotana Cafe
Category: Hookah Bar
Average price: Inexpensive
Area: Rusholme
Address: 122 Wilmslow Rd
Manchester M14 5AH
Phone: 0161 249 0930

#236
Norwegian Blue
Category: Bar, Club
Average price: Modest
Area: City Centre
Address: 27 Withy Grove
Manchester M4 2BS
Phone: 0161 839 1451

#237
MTwenty
Category: Lounge
Area: West Didsbury
Address: 158 Burton Rd
Manchester M20 1LH
Phone: 07773 016539

#238
The Green Finch
Category: Pub
Average price: Inexpensive
Area: West Didsbury
Address: 108 Palatine Road
Manchester M20 3ZA
Phone: 0161 448 9397

#239
Henry J Beans
Category: American, Bar
Area: City Centre
Address: Unit 18 Dantzic Street
Manchester M4 2AD
Phone: 0161 827 7820

#240
The Burlington Room
Category: Lounge
Area: Oxford Road Corridor
Address: The University of Manchester
Manchester M13 9PL
Phone: 0161 275 2392

#241
Sachas Hotel
Category: Hotel, Bar
Average price: Inexpensive
Area: Northern Quarter
Address: 12 Tib St
Manchester M4 1SH
Phone: 0161 228 1234

#242
Circle Club
Category: Wine Bar, Champagne Bar
Average price: Expensive
Area: City Centre
Address: 13 Barton Arcade
Manchester M3 2BB
Phone: 0161 288 8118

#243
Lloyds Bar
Category: Pub
Average price: Modest
Area: City Centre
Address: 27 Withy Grove
Manchester M4 2BS
Phone: 0161 817 2980

#244
Lawn Club
Category: Club
Average price: Modest
Area: Spinningfields
Address: Hardman Square
Manchester M3 3EB
Phone: 07857 964334

#245
Waldorf Hotel
Category: Pub
Average price: Modest
Area: Piccadilly
Address: 12 Gore Street
Manchester M1 3AQ
Phone: 0161 228 3269

#246
Kraak
Category: Music Venues
Average price: Modest
Area: Northern Quarter
Address: 11 Stevenson Square
Manchester M1 1DB
Phone: 07855 939129

#247
TGI Fridays
Category: American, Bar
Average price: Modest
Area: City Centre
Address: Cross Street
Manchester M2 7DH
Phone: 0844 692 8903

#248
Jolly Angler
Category: Pub
Area: Piccadilly
Address: 47 Ducie Street
Manchester M1 2JW
Phone: 0161 236 5307

#249
Albaghdady Cafe
Category: Hookah Bar
Area: Rusholme
Address: 118 Wilmslow Rd
Manchester M14 5AJ
Phone: 0161 248 8868

#250
The Beech Inn
Category: Pub
Average price: Modest
Area: Chorlton
Address: 72 Beech Road
Manchester M21 9EG
Phone: 0161 881 1180

#251
Albert Inn
Category: Pub
Area: Didsbury Village
Address: 454 Wilmslow Road
Manchester M20 3BG
Phone: 0161 445 5747

#252
BarCa
Category: Bar
Average price: Modest
Area: Castlefield
Address: 8 & 9 Catalan Square
Manchester M3 4RU
Phone: 0161 839 7099

#253
The Orange Grove
Category: Pub
Average price: Inexpensive
Area: Rusholme
Address: 304 Wilmslow Road
Manchester M14 6NL
Phone: 0161 224 1148

#254
Gullivers
Category: Pub
Average price: Inexpensive
Area: Northern Quarter
Address: 109 Oldham Street
Manchester M4 1LW
Phone: 07807 884399

#255
Mulligans
Category: Pub
Average price: Modest
Area: City Centre
Address: 12 Southgate
Manchester M3 2RB
Phone: 0161 832 9233

#256
Thistle Manchester Hotel
Category: Hotel, Bar
Area: Piccadilly
Address: 3-5 Portland Street
Manchester M1 6DP
Phone: 0870 333 9139

#257
The Milton Club
Category: Bar, Club
Average price: Expensive
Area: Castlefield
Address: 244 Milton Hall
Manchester M3 4BQ
Phone: 0161 850 2353

#258
Cast
Category: Bar
Area: Oxford Road Corridor
Address: 97 Oxford Street
Manchester M1 6ET
Phone: 0161 237 9407

#259
Lass O'Gowrie
Category: British, Pub
Average price: Inexpensive
Area: Gay Village
Address: 36 Charles Street
Manchester M1 7DB
Phone: 0161 273 6932

#260
Wood Wine & Deli
Category: Wine Bar
Average price: Modest
Area: Northern Quarter
Address: 44 Tib Street
Manchester M4 1LA
Phone: 0161 478 7100

#261
Picturehouse
Category: Bar, Music Venues
Area: Northern Quarter
Address: 25 Swan St
Manchester M4 5JZ
Phone: 0161 834 1786

#262
**The Martin Harris Centre
for Music and Drama**
Category: Theatre, Music Venues
Area: Oxford Road Corridor
Address: Bridgeford St
Manchester M13 9PL
Phone: 0161 275 2930

#263
Blue Bell Inn
Category: Pub
Average price: Inexpensive
Area: Levenshulme
Address: 170 Barlow Road
Manchester M19 3HF
Phone: 0161 224 1723

#264
Odder Bar
Category: Bar
Average price: Modest
Area: Oxford Road Corridor
Address: 14 Oxford Road
Manchester M1 5QA
Phone: 0161 238 9132

#265
Edwards
Category: Lounge
Average price: Modest
Area: Piccadilly
Address: 11 Portland St
Manchester M1 3HU
Phone: 0161 237 0631

#266
All Bar One
Category: Wine Bar
Area: City Centre
Address: 73-79 King Street
Manchester M2 4NG
Phone: 0161 830 1811

#267
Arora Hotel Manchester
Category: Hotel, Bar
Average price: Expensive
Area: Chinatown
Address: 18-24 Princess St
Manchester M1 4LG
Phone: 0161 236 8999

#268
Lounge 31
Category: Bar, Music Venues
Average price: Modest
Area: City Centre
Address: 31 Withy Grove
Manchester M4 2BJ
Phone: 0161 819 4710

#269
Overdraught
Category: Club, Dive Bar
Average price: Inexpensive
Area: Gay Village
Address: 121 Princess St
Manchester M1 7AG
Phone: 0161 237 0811

#270
Gardens Hotel
Category: Hotel, Bar
Average price: Inexpensive
Area: Northern Quarter
Address: 55 Piccadilly
Manchester M1 2AP
Phone: 0161 236 5155

#271
Harry's Bar
Category: Lounge
Area: Gay Village
Address: Sackville Street
Manchester M1 3QJ
Phone: 0872 107 7077

#272
Sanctuary
Category: Pub
Area: Didsbury Village
Address: 653 Wilmslow Road
Manchester M20 6QZ
Phone: 0161 445 9130

#273
Cheshire Cat
Category: Pub, Food
Average price: Modest
Area: Fallowfield
Address: 256 Wilmslow Road
Manchester M14 6LB
Phone: 0161 249 0271

#274
Bloom Bar
Category: Bar
Average price: Modest
Area: Spinningfields
Address: Spinningfields Estate
Manchester M3 3AP

#275
Old Granada Studios
Category: Festival, Music Venues
Average price: Inexpensive
Area: Spinningfields
Address: Quay Street
Manchester M3 3JE

#276
MOJO
Category: Pub, Lounge
Area: Spinningfields
Address: 59A Bridge Street
Manchester M3 3BQ
Phone: 0845 611 8643

#277
24 Bar and Grill
Category: Bar, British
Average price: Expensive
Area: Chinatown
Address: 24 Princess Street
Manchester M1 4LY
Phone: 0161 238 4348

#278
Electric Circus
Category: Gambling
Average price: Expensive
Area: Oxford Road Corridor
Address: 110 Portland Street
Manchester M1 4RL
Phone: 0161 228 0077

#279
Mint Casino
Category: Casino, Lounge
Area: Oxford Road Corridor
Address: 40-44 Princess Street
Manchester M1 6DE
Phone: 0161 236 3034

#280
El Capo
Category: Cocktail Bar
Average price: Modest
Area: Northern Quarter
Address: 12 Tariff Street
Manchester M1 2FF
Phone: 0161 237 3154

#281
Portland Street Restaurant & Bar
Category: Bar, British
Average price: Modest
Area: Gay Village
Address: Portland Street
Manchester M1
Phone: 0161 246 3435

#282
Spektrum
Category: Club
Area: Ancoats, Petersfield
Address: Radium St
Manchester M4 6AY
Phone: 0161 236 5444

#283
256 Wilmslow Road
Category: Pub
Average price: Modest
Area: Fallowfield
Address: 256 Wilmslow Road
Manchester M14 6LB
Phone: 0161 249 0271

#284
Lansdowne Hotel
Category: Hotel, Bar
Area: Fallowfield
Address: 346-348 Wilmslow Road
Manchester M14 6AB
Phone: 0161 224 6244

#285
**Rileys Sports Bar
ChorltonCumHardy**
Category: Snooker & Pool Hall,
Sports Bar
Area: Chorlton
Address: 302B Barlow Moor Road
Manchester M21 8AY
Phone: 0161 860 4960

#286
Union Inn
Category: Pub
Area: Levenshulme
Address: Stockport Road
Manchester M19 3AD
Phone: 0161 224 1271

#287
The Violet Hour
Category: Cocktail Bar
Average price: Expensive
Area: West Didsbury
Address: 236 Burton Road
Manchester M20 2LW

#288
Mitre Hotel
Category: Hotel, Bar
Average price: Modest
Area: City Centre
Address: Cathedral Gates
Manchester M3 1SW
Phone: 0161 834 4128

#289
Club Phoenix
Category: Pub
Average price: Inexpensive
Area: Oxford Road Corridor
Address: 1 University Precinct
Manchester M13 9RN
Phone: 0161 272 5921

#290
**Ramada
Manchester Piccadilly Hotel**
Category: Hotel, Bar
Area: Northern Quarter
Address: Piccadilly Plz
Manchester M60 1QR
Phone: 0844 815 9024

#291
Bar 4 Eighty
Category: Pub
Area: Chorlton
Address: 480 Wilbraham Road
Manchester M21 9AS
Phone: 0161 861 9558

#292
The Spread Eagle
Category: Pub
Average price: Modest
Area: Chorlton
Address: 526 Wilbraham Road
Manchester M21 9LD
Phone: 0161 861 0385

#293
Orchid Lounge
Category: Karaoke, Bar
Area: Chinatown
Address: 54 Portland St
Manchester M1 4QU
Phone: 0161 236 1388

#294
The Rembrandt Bar and Hotel
Category: Hotel, Bar
Average price: Modest
Area: Gay Village
Address: 33 Sackville St
Manchester M1 3LZ
Phone: 0161 236 1311

#295
Browns
Category: Bar, British
Average price: Modest
Area: City Centre
Address: 1 York Street
Manchester M2 2AW
Phone: 0161 819 1055

#296
Axm Club
Category: British, Gay Bar
Average price: Modest
Area: Gay Village
Address: 100 Bloom Street
Manchester M1 3LY
Phone: 0845 834 0297

#297
Expo Lounge
Category: Lounge
Average price: Modest
Area: Didsbury Village
Address: 766 Wilmslow Road
Manchester M20 2DR

#298
Cafe Casablanca
Category: Hookah Bar
Area: Rusholme
Address: 100 Wilmslow Road
Manchester M14 5AJ
Phone: 0161 256 2555

#299
Fiddlers Green
Category: Pub
Average price: Inexpensive
Area: Levenshulme
Address: 881 Stockport Road
Manchester M19 3PG
Phone: 0161 224 2254

#300
Yates's
Category: Bar
Average price: Inexpensive
Area: Gay Village
Address: 49 Portland Street
Manchester M1 3HG
Phone: 0161 228 0162

#301
The Royal Oak
Category: Pub
Average price: Inexpensive
Area: Chorlton
Address: 440 Barlow Moor Road
Manchester M21 0AE
Phone: 0161 860 7438

#302
Grey Horse Inn
Category: Pub
Average price: Inexpensive
Area: Chinatown
Address: 80 Portland Street
Manchester M1 4QX
Phone: 0161 236 1874

#303
Mansion Club
Category: Club
Area: Castlefield
Address: Longworth St
Manchester M3 4BQ
Phone: 0161 832 3038

#304
Entourage
Category: Club, Champagne Bar
Average price: Expensive
Area: City Centre
Address: The Printworks
Manchester M4 2
Phone: 0161 839 1344

#305
The Eagle Bar
Category: Gay Bar
Average price: Modest
Area: Gay Village
Address: Bloom St
Manchester M1 3

#306
Napoleons Night Club
Category: Club
Average price: Inexpensive
Area: Gay Village
Address: 35 Bloom Street
Manchester M1 3LY
Phone: 0161 236 8800

#307
BED
Category: Lounge
Area: Gay Village
Address: 50 Sackville Street
Manchester M1 3WF
Phone: 0161 236 8300

#308
Piccadilly Lounge
Category: Lounge, British
Area: Piccadilly
Address: 1 Auburn St
Manchester M1 3DG
Phone: 0161 242 1030

#309
The Wheatsheaf
Category: Pub
Area: Northern Quarter
Address: 30 Oak Street
Manchester M4 5JE
Phone: 0871 230 5513

#310
The Cavendish Bar
Category: Pub
Area: Oxford Road Corridor
Address: 44 Cavendish Street
Manchester M15 6BQ
Phone: 0161 226 7600

#311
Kro Bar
Category: Pub
Average price: Inexpensive
Area: Oxford Road Corridor
Address: 60 Pencroft Way
Manchester M15 6SZ
Phone: 0161 232 9796

#312
Lusitano
Category: Tapas, Wine Bar
Average price: Modest
Area: Chorlton
Address: 613 Wilbraham Road
Manchester M21 9AN
Phone: 0161 861 8880

#313
The Laundrette
Category: Cocktail Bar
Average price: Modest
Area: Chorlton
Address: 32 Beech Road
Manchester M21 9EL
Phone: 0161 881 5777

#314
Verso
Category: Lounge
Average price: Inexpensive
Area: West Didsbury
Address: 110 Burton Rd
Manchester M20 1LP
Phone: 0161 438 6633

#315
Old House At Home
Category: Pub
Area: West Didsbury
Address: 61-63 Burton Road
Manchester M20 1HB
Phone: 0161 446 2315

#316
The Thompsons Arms
Category: Club, Pub
Average price: Inexpensive
Area: Gay Village
Address: 23 Sackville Street
Manchester M1 3LZ
Phone: 0161 228 3012

#317
Blue Parrot Bar and Grille
Category: Bar
Average price: Modest
Area: Piccadilly
Address: 11 Westminster House
Manchester M1 3DY
Phone: 0161 236 8359

#318
Contact
Category: Theatre, Music Venues
Average price: Modest
Area: Oxford Road Corridor
Address: Oxford Road
Manchester M15 6JA
Phone: 0161 274 0600

#319
Paddys Goose
Category: Pub
Area: Gay Village
Address: 29 Bloom Street
Manchester M1 3JE
Phone: 0161 236 1246

#320
Wetherspoons
Category: British, Pub
Area: Oxford Road Corridor
Address: 33-36 Oxford Street
Manchester M1 4BH
Phone: 0161 233 1820

#321
Area 51 Club
Category: Club
Average price: Modest
Area: Piccadilly
Address: Whitworth St West
Manchester M1 5WZ
Phone: 0161 236 1316

#322
Port Street Beer House
Category: Pub
Average price: Modest
Area: Northern Quarter
Address: 39-41 Port Street
Manchester M1 2EQ
Phone: 0161 237 9949

#323
The Great Central
Category: British, Pub
Average price: Inexpensive
Area: Fallowfield
Address: 343 Wilmslow Road
Manchester M14 6NS
Phone: 0161 248 1740

#324
K2 Karaoke Nightclub
Category: Karaoke, Club, Bar
Area: Chinatown
Address: 52 George Street
Manchester M1 4HF
Phone: 0871 230 4226

#325
View
Category: Club, Gay Bar
Area: Gay Village
Address: 40 Chorlton Street
Manchester M1 3HW
Phone: 0161 236 9033

#326
Victorias Gentlemens Club
Category: Adult Entertainment
Average price: Expensive
Area: City Centre
Address: Dantzic Street
Manchester M4 2AD
Phone: 0161 832 4444

#327
Central Methodist Hall
Category: Music Venues,
Venues & Event Spaces
Area: Northern Quarter
Address: Oldham Street
Manchester M1 1JQ
Phone: 0161 236 5194

#328
Bar21
Category: Bar, Italian, American
Area: Northern Quarter
Address: 10 Thomas Street
Manchester M4 1DH
Phone: 0161 832 2769

#329
W A K Films
Category: Pub
Average price: Exclusive
Area: Ancoats, Petersfield
Address: Jersey Street
Manchester M4 6JG
Phone: 0161 279 0546

#330
Royal Oak Hotel
Category: Pub
Area: Chorlton
Address: 440 Barlow Moor Road
Manchester M21 0BQ
Phone: 0161 860 7438

#331
Dulcimer
Category: Bar, Music Venues
Average price: Modest
Area: Chorlton
Address: 567 Wilbraham Road
Manchester M21 0AE
Phone: 0161 860 6444

#332
Bar Rogue & Bar Wave
Category: Bar, Club
Area: Gay Village
Address: Portland Street
Manchester M1 3LA
Phone: 0161 228 7007

#333
Palace Theatre
Category: Theatre, Music Venues
Average price: Expensive
Area: Oxford Road Corridor
Address: Oxford Street
Manchester M1 6FT
Phone: 0161 245 6600

#334
Richmond Park Bar
Category: Pub
Average price: Inexpensive
Area: Fallowfield
Address: Whitworth Lane
Manchester M14 6YY

#335
JD Wetherspoons
Category: Pub, British
Area: Northern Quarter
Address: 49 Piccadilly
Manchester M1 1
Phone: 0161 236 9206

#336
Fridays
Category: Bar
Area: Northern Quarter
Address: Tib Street
Manchester M4 1SH
Phone: 0161 228 1234

#337
The Shack
Category: Bar
Average price: Modest
Area: Northern Quarter
Address: 26-28 Hilton House
Manchester M1 2EH
Phone: 0161 236 6009

#338
Merchant Hotel
Category: Hotel, Bar
Area: Northern Quarter
Address: Back Piccadilly
Manchester M1 1HP
Phone: 0161 236 2939

#339
The Brewer's Arms
Category: Pub
Area: Ladybarn
Address: 151 Ladybarn Lane
Manchester M14 6RQ
Phone: 0161 224 5576

#340
Chalk Bar and Grill
Category: Bar
Average price: Expensive
Area: Didsbury Village
Address: 784-788 Wilmslow Road
Manchester M20 2DR
Phone: 0161 445 1042

#341
Sackville Lounge
Category: Gay Bar
Average price: Modest
Area: Gay Village
Address: Sackville Street
Manchester M1

#342
The Lower Turks Head
Category: Pub
Average price: Modest
Area: Northern Quarter
Address: Short Street
Manchester M1 1JG

#343
Knott Bar
Category: Pub, British,
Average price: Modest
Area: Castlefield
Address: 374 Deansgate
Manchester M3 4LY
Phone: 0161 839 9229

#344
Bar Pop
Category: Gay Bar, Club
Average price: Inexpensive
Area: Gay Village
Address: 10 Canal Street
Manchester M1 3EZ

#345
Sanctuary On Sackville
Category: British, Wine Bar, Lounge
Area: Gay Village
Address: 46 Sackville Street
Manchester M1
Phone: 0161 237 5551

#346
Bakerie
Category: Wine Bar
Average price: Modest
Area: Northern Quarter
Address: 51 Lever Street
Manchester M1 1FN

#347
Shamrock Inn
Category: Pub
Area: Ancoats, Petersfield
Address: 17 Bengal Street
Manchester M4 6AQ
Phone: 0161 238 8578

#348
Woolton Hall Bar
Category: Pub
Average price: Inexpensive
Area: Fallowfield
Address: Whitworth Lane
Manchester M14 6WS

#349
Antwerp Mansion
Category: Music Venues
Area: Rusholme
Address: Wilmslow Rd
Manchester M14 5BT
Phone: 07429 578193

#350
The Long Bar
Category: Wine Bar, Lounge,
Champagne Bar
Average price: Modest
Area: Spinningfields
Address: Spinningfield Estate
Manchester M3 3JE
Phone: 07917 058924

#351
The Lost Dene
Category: Pub
Area: Spinningfields
Address: 144 Deansgate
Manchester M3 3EE
Phone: 0161 839 9035

#352
Club V
Category: Music Venues
Area: City Centre
Address: 111 Deansgate
Manchester M3 2BQ
Phone: 0161 834 9975

#353
Mud Crab
Category: Burgers, Bar
Area: City Centre
Address: 5-7 Chapel Walks
Manchester M2 1HN
Phone: 0161 907 3210

#354
Red Hot Karaoke!!
Category: Karaoke
Area: City Centre
Address: 48 Deansgate
Manchester M3 2EG
Phone: 07984 627576

#355
Montpellier
Category: Bar, Cafe
Area: Northern Quarter
Address: 36 Back Turner Street
Manchester M4
Phone: 0161 832 3146

#356
Dry Live
Category: Club, Music Venues
Average price: Modest
Area: Northern Quarter
Address: 28-30 Oldham Street
Manchester M1 1JN
Phone: 0161 236 1444

#357
Philharmonic String Quartet
Category: Music Venues, Theatre
Area: Castlefield
Address: 307 Vicus 73 Liverpool Road
Manchester M3 4AQ
Phone: 07545 991621

#358
Hit and Run
Category: Club, Music Venues
Area: Piccadilly
Address: Area 51 Eclipse House
Manchester M1 5WZ
Phone: 0161 236 1316

#359
Dubai Cafe
Category: Coffee & Tea, Hookah Bar
Area: Rusholme
Address: 86 Wilmslow Road
Manchester M14 5AL
Phone: 0161 224 9040

#360
Booze Manchester
Category: Off Licence, Pub
Average price: Exclusive
Area: Longsight
Address: Cariocca Business Park
Manchester M12 4AH
Phone: 07799 338875

#361
Fallow Cafe
Category: British, Pub
Area: Fallowfield
Address: 2a Landcross Road
Manchester M14 6NA
Phone: 0161 224 0467

#362
MantraSound Disco
Category: DJs, Karaoke
Average price: Modest
Area: Fallowfield
Address: Fallowfield
Manchester M14
Phone: 01691 649044

#363
The Stoker's Arms
Category: Pub
Area: Didsbury Village
Address: 657 Wilmslow Road
Manchester M20 6RA
Phone: 0161 448 7941

#364
Parrswood Hotel
Category: British, Pub
Area: East Didsbury
Address: 356 Parrswood Road
Manchester M20
Phone: 0161 445 1783

#365
Bar Six 2
Category: Bar
Area: Stockport
Address: 62 Middle Hillgate
Manchester SK1 3EH
Phone: 07531 730304

#366
Red House Pub
Category: Pub
Area: Ashton Under Lyne
Address: lees road
Manchester OL6
Phone: 0161 343 5594

#367
Sparking Clog
Category: Pub
Average price: Inexpensive
Area: Bolton
Address: Radcliffe Moor Road
Manchester M26 3WY
Phone: 0161 723 5690

#368
Regent Inns
Category: Hotel, Pub
Average price: Inexpensive
Area: Castlefield, Spinningfields
Address: 13 Quay Street
Manchester M3 3HN
Phone: 0870 765 1221

#369
The Lost Dene
Category: Pub
Area: City Centre
Address: 19-23 King Street
Manchester M2 6AN
Phone: 0161 839 9035

#370
White Lion Hotel
Category: Pub
Area: Castlefield
Address: 43 Liverpool Road
Manchester M3 4NQ
Phone: 0161 832 7373

#371
Grosvenor Casino
Category: Casino
Area: Chinatown
Address: 35 George Street
Manchester M1 4HQ
Phone: 0161 236 7121

#372
Long Legs Table Dancing
Category: Adult Entertainment
Area: Chinatown
Address: 46 George Street
Manchester M1 4HF
Phone: 0161 237 3977

#373
Uber Lounge
Category: Cocktail Bar
Area: Castlefield
Address: 8-9
Manchester M3 4RU
Phone: 0161 839 7099

#374
Sub61
Category: Bar
Area: Castlefield
Address: Artillery Street
Manchester M3
Phone: 07910 431115

#375
Alibi
Category: Bar
Area: Gay Village
Address: Unit 1 the Circus Development
Cnr Oxford Str & Portland Str
Manchester M1
Phone: 0845 604 9904

#376
Wetherspoons
Category: Pub, British
Area: City Centre
Address: Princess Street
Manchester M2 4EG
Phone: 0161 200 5380

#377
The Old Monkey
Category: Pub
Area: City Centre
Address: 90-92 Portland Street
Manchester M1 4GX
Phone: 0161 228 6262

#378
Holmes Place Health Club
Category: Gym, Pub
Average price: Modest
Area: City Centre
Address: 4 The Printworks
Manchester M4 2BS
Phone: 0161 831 9922

#379
Stockport Garrick Theatre
Category: Theatre, Music Venues
Address: Exchange Street
Stockport, Greater Manchester
Phone: 0161 480 5866

#380
Gallery Oldham
Category: Art Gallery
Address: Oldham Cultural Quater
Oldham OL1 1AL
Phone: 0161 770 4653

#381
Forum Theatre
Category: Theatre
Average price: Modest
Address: The Precinct
Stockport SK6 4EA
Phone: 0161 430 6570

#382
City Shisha Lounge
Category: Hookah Bar
Area: City Centre
Address: 85 Greengate
Manchester M3 7NA
Phone: 0161 637 7764

#383
Bar Rogue & Bar Wave
Category: Bar
Average price: Inexpensive
Area: Gay Village
Address: Portland Street
Manchester M1 3LA
Phone: 0161 228 7007

#384
Lola's
Category: Cocktail Bar
Area: Northern Quarter
Address: 17 Tariff Street
Manchester M1 2EJ
Phone: 0161 228 7813

#385
Premier Musicians
Category: Venues & Event Spaces,
Wedding Planning, Music Venues
Area: Castlefield
Address: 307 Vicus 73 Liverpool Road
Manchester M3 4AQ
Phone: 07545 991621

#386
**Companion
Manchester Escorts**
Category: Adult Entertainment
Area: Oxford Road Corridor
Address: Oxford Road
Manchester M13 9PL
Phone: 07714 751329

#387
Marrakesh Cafe
Category: Hookah Bar
Area: Rusholme
Address: 119 Wilmslow Road
Manchester M14 5AN
Phone: 0161 224 0700

#388
Marrakesh Shisha Bar
Category: Venues & Event Spaces
Area: Rusholme
Address: 119 Wilmslow Rd
Manchester M14 5AP
Phone: 0161 637 0424

#389
Sher Akbar
Category: Bar, Indian
Area: Chorlton
Address: 72-74 Manchester Road
Manchester M21 9PQ
Phone: 0161 862 0000

#390
The King's Arms
Category: Pub
Area: City Centre
Address: 11 Bloom Street
Salford M3 6AN
Phone: 0161 832 3605

#391
Duffy's Bar
Category: Dive Bar
Area: Chorlton
Address: 398 Barlow Moor Road
Manchester M21 8AD
Phone: 0872 107 7077

#392
The Huntington
Category: Pub
Area: Levenshulme
Address: Northmoor Road
Manchester M12 4HP
Phone: 0161 225 6400

#393
Strange Brew
Category: Pub
Area: Chorlton
Address: 370 Barlow Moor Road
Manchester M21 8AZ
Phone: 0161 862 9911

#394
Nouveau Mancurian
Male Escort Service
Category: Adult Entertainment
Area: Didsbury Village
Address: 792 Wilmslow Rd
Manchester M20 6UG
Phone: 07855 504838

#395
White Lion
Category: Pub, Sports Bar
Average price: Modest
Area: Castlefield
Address: 43 Liverpool Road
Manchester M3 4NQ
Phone: 0161 832 7373

#396
The Bridge
Category: Pub
Average price: Modest
Area: Spinningfields, City Centre
Address: 58 Bridge Street
Manchester M3 3BW
Phone: 0161 834 0242

#397
Cask
Category: Pub
Average price: Modest
Area: Castlefield
Address: 29 Liverpool Road
Manchester M3 4NQ
Phone: 0161 819 2527

#398
The Lowry
Category: Music Venues, Theatre
Average price: Expensive
Area: Salford Quays
Address: Pier 8 Salford M50 3AZ
Phone: 0161 876 2121

#399
Unicorn Hotel
Category: Pub
Area: Northern Quarter
Address: 26 Church Street
Manchester M4 1PW
Phone: 0161 879 9863

#400
Fantasy Bar
Category: Adult Entertainment
Area: Spinningfields
Address: 140 Deansgate
Manchester M3 2RP
Phone: 0161 835 1973

#401
Gainsborough House
Category: Bar
Area: Chinatown
Address: 109 Portland Street
Manchester M1 6DN
Phone: 0161 237 9990

#402
Lowry Hotel
Category: Hotel, Bar
Area: City Centre
Address: 50 Dearmans Place
Salford M3 5LH
Phone: 0161 827 4000

#403
Charlie's Night Club & Restaurant
Category: Club
Area: Oxford Road Corridor
Address: 1 Harter Street
Manchester M1 6HY
Phone: 0161 237 9898

#404
Kimberley Consultancy
Category: Club
Area: City Centre
Address: Back Bridge Street
Manchester M3 2PB
Phone: 0161 832 6975

#405
Mutz Nutz
Category: Club
Area: Oxford Road Corridor
Address: 105-107 Princess Street
Manchester M1 6DD
Phone: 0161 236 9266

#406
Baby Platinum
Category: Adult Entertainment
Area: Gay Village
Address: 109 Princess Street
Manchester M1 6JB
Phone: 0161 236 6126

#407
Cibar
Category: Pub
Area: Northern Quarter
Address: 28-34 High Street
Manchester M4 1QB
Phone: 0161 834 4828

#408
Presha
Category: Bar
Area: Northern Quarter
Address: 28-34 High Street
Manchester M4 1QB
Phone: 0161 834 1392

#409
Carlisle Staffing
Category: Bar
Area: City Centre
Address: 2 Old Bank Street
Manchester M2 7PF
Phone: 0161 835 3588

#410
The Lodge Bar
Category: Gay Bar, Cocktail Bar
Area: Gay Village
Address: Richmond Street The Village
Manchester M1 3HZ
Phone: 0161 237 9667

#411
Oscars
Category: Bar
Area: Gay Village
Address: 34 Canal Street
Manchester M1 3WD
Phone: 0161 237 9201

#412
Tiger Lounge
Category: Italian, Bar
Area: City Centre
Address: 5 Cooper Street
Manchester M2 2FW
Phone: 0161 236 6007

#413
Bar 38 Pub
Area: Gay Village
Address: 10 Canal Street
Manchester M1 3EZ
Phone: 0161 236 6005

#414
Industry
Category: Club
Area: Oxford Road Corridor
Address: 112-116 Princess Street
Manchester M1 7EN
Phone: 0161 273 5422

#415
The Sedgelynn
Category: Gastropub
Area: Chorlton
Address: 21A Manchester Road
Manchester M21 9PN
Phone: 0161 860 0141

#416
Sanctuary
Category: Bar
Area: Gay Village
Address: 46 Sackville Street
Manchester M1
Phone: 0161 237 5551

#417
Illusions Magic Bar
Category: Pub, Wine Bar
Area: City Centre
Address: 27 Withy Grove
Manchester M4 2BS
Phone: 0161 819 7791

#418
Pinnacle Intertional College
Category: University, Club
Area: Gay Village
Address: 10 Minshull Street
Manchester M1 3EF
Phone: 0161 236 5646

#419
The New Oxford
Category: Wine Bar, Pub
Address: 11 Bexley Square
Salford M3 6DB
Phone: 0161 832 7082

#420
Joe's Bar
Category: Wine Bar, Lounge
Area: Northern Quarter
Address: 4 Oldham Street
Manchester M1 1JQ
Phone: 0161 228 0517

#421
Hale Leisure
Category: Pub
Area: Oxford Road Corridor
Address: 106 Princess Street
Manchester M1 6NG
Phone: 0161 273 7543

#422
Goldsmith & Rybka
Category: Pub
Area: Northern Quarter
Address: 35-37 Thomas Street
Manchester M4 1NA
Phone: 0161 834 5650

#423
NQ Live
Category: Club, Music Venues
Area: Northern Quarter
Address: Tib Street
Manchester M4 1LN
Phone: 0161 834 8188

#424
The Engine House
Category: Theatre, Music Venues
Area: Oxford Road Corridor
Address: 3 Cambridge St
Manchester M1 5BY
Phone: 07874 152338

#425
D G P International
Category: Bar
Area: Oxford Road Corridor
Address: 54 Princess Street
Manchester M1 6HS
Phone: 0161 907 3500

#426
Babushka
Category: Bar
Area: City Centre
Address: Withy Grove
Manchester M4 2BS
Phone: 0161 832 1234

#427
Sweet P
Category: Pub
Area: Northern Quarter
Address: 46-50 Oldham Street
Manchester M4 1LE
Phone: 0161 228 1495

#428
North Nightclub
Category: Club
Area: Northern Quarter
Address: 34-43 Oldham Street
Manchester M1 1JG
Phone: 0161 839 1989

#429
Bravo Management
Category: Pub
Area: Northern Quarter
Address: 25 Swan Street
Manchester M4 5JZ
Phone: 0161 834 1786

#430
On Q Pool Club
Category: Snooker & Pool Hall
Area: Northern Quarter
Address: 7 Dale Street
Manchester M1 1JA
Phone: 0161 228 7808

#431
Tango's
Category: Cocktail Bar,
British, Champagne Bar
Area: City Centre
Address: 15 Chapel Walks
Manchester M2 1HN
Phone: 0161 819 1997

#432
Church Inn
Category: Pub
Area: Oxford Road Corridor
Address: 84 Cambridge Street
Manchester M15 6BP
Phone: 0161 227 9503

#433
Arch Wine Bar
Category: Wine Bar
Area: Oxford Road Corridor
Address: 20 Stretford Road
Manchester M15 6HE
Phone: 0161 227 7550

#434
Absolute Strippers Manchester
Category: Adult Entertainment
Area: Oxford Road Corridor
Address: Oxford Road
Manchester M1 6FU
Phone: 07956 22318

#435
Homes For You
Category: Pub
Area: Oxford Road Corridor
Address: Oxford Road
Manchester M1 7ED
Phone: 0161 236 0202

#436
King Inn
Category: Pub
Area: Northern Quarter
Address: 73 Oldham Street
Manchester M4 1LW
Phone: 0161 835 2548

#437
The Star and Garter
Category: Pub
Area: Piccadilly
Address: 18-20 Fairfield Street
Manchester M1 2QF
Phone: 0161 273 6726

#438
The Park Night Club
Category: Pub
Area: Oxford Road Corridor
Address: Grosvenor Street
Manchester M1 7HL
Phone: 0161 274 4442

#439
Barney Mcgrew's Public House
Category: Pub
Area: Oxford Road Corridor
Address: Oxford Road
Manchester M13 9RN
Phone: 0161 272 6806

#440
GX Bar
Category: Wine Bar
Area: Ancoats, Petersfield
Address: Great Ancoats Street
Manchester M60 4BT
Phone: 0161 236 0851

#441
Church Inn
Category: Pub
Area: Oxford Road Corridor
Address: 45-47 Ardwick Green North
Manchester M12 6FZ
Phone: 0161 273 5652

#442
Wheatsheaf Hotel
Category: Pub
Area: Ancoats, Petersfield
Address: 208 Oldham Road
Manchester M4 6BQ
Phone: 0161 205 4821

#443
Kimgary Fabrics
Category: Pub
Area: Ancoats, Petersfield
Address: Pollard Street
Manchester M4 7JB
Phone: 0161 273 7777

#444
Phoenix Karaoke
Category: Karaoke
Area: Oxford Road Corridor
Address: 62 Stockport Road
Manchester M12 6AL
Phone: 0161 273 7006

#445
Grafton Arms
Category: Pub
Area: Oxford Road Corridor
Address: 27 Grafton Street
Manchester M13 9WU
Phone: 0161 273 2303

#446
The Admiral
Category: Pub
Area: Ancoats, Petersfield
Address: Butler Street
Manchester M4 6JY
Phone: 0161 205 5896

#447
Gold Cup
Category: Pub
Area: Longsight
Address: 260 Stockport Road
Manchester M13 0RB
Phone: 0161 273 8887

#448
Clarence Inn
Category: Pub
Area: Rusholme
Address: 97 Wilmslow Road
Manchester M14 5SU
Phone: 0161 248 1911

#449
Maydale
Category: Pub
Area: Salford Quays
Address: Trafford Wharf Road
Manchester M17 1EX
Phone: 0161 872 6836

#450
Welcome Public House
Category: Pub
Area: Rusholme
Address: 26 Rusholme Grove
Manchester M14 5AR
Phone: 0161 224 4685

#451
Mason
Category: Pub
Area: Rusholme
Address: 257 Wilmslow Road
Manchester M14 5LN
Phone: 0161 257 0450

#452
Bay Horse Hotel
Category: Pub
Area: Longsight
Address: 548 Stockport Road
Manchester M12 4JJ
Phone: 0161 248 9855

#453
Springbank Public House
Category: Pub
Area: Levenshulme
Address: 579 Stockport Road
Manchester M13 0RG
Phone: 0161 225 8980

#454
Office
Category: Wine Bar
Area: Chorlton
Address: 537 Wilbraham Road
Manchester M21 0UE
Phone: 0161 860 6660

#455
Revise Cafe Bar
Category: Pub
Area: Chorlton
Address: 559 Wilbraham Road
Manchester M21 0AE
Phone: 0161 861 7626

#456
P Heathcote
Category: Pub
Area: Chorlton
Address: 478 Wilbraham Road
Manchester M21 9AS
Phone: 0161 881 9130

#457
Bar Baroque
Category: Music Venues
Area: Chorlton
Address: 478 Wilbraham Rd
Manchester M21 9AS
Phone: 0161 881 9130

#458
Vanessa's
Category: Adult Entertainment
Area: Chorlton
Address: 430a Barlow Moor Road
Manchester M21 8AD
Phone: 0161 861 7302

#459
Glass Public House
Category: Pub
Area: Fallowfield
Address: 258 Wilmslow Road
Manchester M14 6JR
Phone: 0161 257 0770

#460
Wetherspoon
Category: Pub
Area: Fallowfield
Address: 306 Wilmslow Road
Manchester M14 6NL
Phone: 0161 248 1740

#461
Garratt Hotel
Category: Pub
Area: Levenshulme
Address: Pink Bank Lane
Manchester M12 5RF
Phone: 0161 224 7530

#462
Hookahs Cafe
Category: Hookah Bar, Lounge
Area: Chorlton
Address: 320 Barlow Moor Road
Manchester M21
Phone: 0161 917 2713

#463
Tonic
Category: Pub
Area: Chorlton
Address: 48 Beech Road
Manchester M21 9EG
Phone: 0161 862 9934

#464
Old House At Home
Category: Pub
Area: Fallowfield
Address: 74-76 Braemar Road
Manchester M14 6PG
Phone: 0161 224 5557

#465
Pack Horse
Category: Pub
Area: Levenshulme
Address: 861 Stockport Road
Manchester M19 3PW
Phone: 0161 224 4355

#466
Church Inn
Category: Pub
Area: Levenshulme
Address: 874 Stockport Road
Manchester M19 3BP
Phone: 0161 221 0111

#467
Levenshulme Pub
Category: Pub
Area: Levenshulme
Address: 959 Stockport Road
Manchester M19 3NP
Phone: 0161 256 2255

#468
Clearissue Bar
Category: Wine Bar
Area: West Didsbury
Address: 2 Lapwing Lane
Manchester M20 2WS
Phone: 0161 448 1356

#469
Cotton Inn The Public House
Category: Pub
Area: Didsbury Village
Address: 2 Cotton Lane
Manchester M20 4UX
Phone: 0161 434 8545

#470
Cotton Tree Inn
The Public House
Category: Pub
Area: Didsbury Village
Address: 2-6 Cotton Hill
Manchester M20 4XR
Phone: 0161 448 2360

#471
The Sidings
Category: Pub
Area: Levenshulme
Address: Broom Lane
Manchester M19 2UB
Phone: 0161 257 2084

#472
The Muldeth Hotel
Category: Pub
Area: East Didsbury
Address: Kingsway
Manchester M19 1BB
Phone: 0161 224 6529

#473
The Barleycorn
Category: Pub
Area: Didsbury Village
Address: 120 Barlow Moor Road
Manchester M20 2PU
Phone: 0161 448 9941

#474
Clock Tower
Category: Pub
Area: Didsbury Village
Address: 700 Wilmslow Road
Manchester M20 2DN
Phone: 0161 445 1686

#475
Karma Sutra Girls
Category: Adult Entertainment
Area: Didsbury Village
Address: 743A Wilmslow Road
Manchester M20 2
Phone: 0161 434 0135

#476
Victoria Inn
Category: Pub
Area: Oldham
Address: 252 Grimshaw Lane
Manchester M24 2AL
Phone: 0161 643 3526

#477
Railway & Linnet
Category: Pub
Area: Oldham
Address: 369 Grimshaw Lane
Manchester M24 1GQ
Phone: 0161 655 3889

#478
Hare & Hounds
Category: Pub
Area: Oldham
Address: 228 Oldham Road
Manchester M24 2JZ
Phone: 0161 643 3100

#479
The Kenyon
Category: Pub
Area: Oldham
Address: 71 Kenyon Lane
Manchester M24 2QS
Phone: 0161 654 0898

#480
Royal Oak Hotel
Category: Pub
Area: Oldham
Address: 44 Boarshaw Road
Manchester M24 6AG
Phone: 0161 653 6142

#481
Old Cock Inn
Category: Pub
Area: Oldham
Address: 528 Oldham Road
Manchester M24 2EB
Phone: 0161 654 8333

#482
Gardners Arms
Category: Pub
Area: Oldham
Address: 266 Hollin Lane
Manchester M24 5LE
Phone: 0161 643 4761

#483
Papermakers Arms
Category: Pub
Area: Bury
Address: Church St East
Manchester M26 2PG
Phone: 0161 723 3415

#484
Old Tower Inn
Category: Pub
Area: Bury
Address: 6 Sandford Street
Manchester M26 2PT
Phone: 0161 723 4212

#485
The Masons Arms
Category: Pub
Area: Bolton
Address: 190 Sion Street
Manchester M26 3SB
Phone: 0161 725 9322

#486
Lord Nelson Hotel
Category: Pub
Area: Bolton
Address: Ringley Road
Manchester M26 1GT
Phone: 01204 579302

#487
The Black Bull
Category: Pub
Area: Oldham
Address: Rochdale Road
Manchester M24 2QA
Phone: 0161 643 6684

#488
Central Snooker Club
Category: Snooker & Pool Hall
Area: Bolton
Address: Abden Street
Manchester M26 3AT
Phone: 0161 723 1237

#489
Royal Oak
Category: Pub
Area: Bolton
Address: 28 Water Street
Manchester M26 4TW
Phone: 0161 723 3557

#490
Market Street Tavern
Category: Pub
Area: Bolton
Address: 131 Market Street
Manchester M26 1HF
Phone: 01204 572985

#491
Bridge Inn
Category: Pub
Area: Bury
Address: 409 Dumers Lane
Manchester M26 2QN
Phone: 0161 766 1370

#492
Horse Shoe
Category: Pub
Area: Bolton
Address: 395 Fold Road
Manchester M26 1NW
Phone: 01204 571714

#493
Hare & Hounds
Category: Pub
Area: Bolton
Address: 13 Market Street
Manchester M26 1GF
Phone: 01204 572974

#494
Beer Engine
Category: Pub
Area: Bolton
Address: 351 Bolton Road
Manchester M26 3QQ
Phone: 0161 723 3307

#495
Victoria Hotel
Category: Pub
Area: Bolton
Address: 119 Ainsworth Road
Manchester M26 4FD
Phone: 0161 724 4774

#496
Ship Inn
Category: Pub
Area: Oldham
Address: 693 Rochdale Road
Manchester M24 2RN
Phone: 0161 643 5871

#497
Wilton Arms
Category: Pub
Area: Bolton
Address: Coronation Road
Manchester M26 3LP
Phone: 0161 724 7068

#498
Railway Hotel
Category: Pub
Area: Bolton
Address: 427 Ainsworth Road
Manchester M26 4HN
Phone: 0161 723 1810

#499
Ainsworth Arms
Category: Pub
Area: Bolton
Address: 207 Bury Bolton Road
Manchester M26 4JY
Phone: 0161 764 1405

#500
**La Dolce Vita Restaurant
& Wine Bar**
Category: Italian, Wine Bar
Area: Stockport
Address: 27 Stockport Road
Manchester M12
Phone: 0161 449 0648

Manufactured by Amazon.com.au
Sydney, New South Wales, Australia